"The

Closing Lines of Over 3,000 Theatrically Released American Films

by

R. Donna Chesher

McFarland & Company, Inc., Publishers
Jefferson, North Carolina, and London

The present work is a reprint of the library bound edition of "The End": Closing Lines of Over 3,000 Theatrically Released American Films, *first published in 1992*. **McFarland Classics** *is an imprint of McFarland & Company, Inc., Publishers, Jefferson, North Carolina, who also published the original edition.*

Library of Congress Cataloguing-in-Publication Data

Chesher, R. Donna
　　The end : closing lines of over 3,000 theatrically released
　　American films / by R. Donna Chesher.
　　　　p.　　cm.
　　ISBN 0-7864-1107-4 (softcover : 50# alkaline paper) ∞
　　1. Motion picture plays—United States—History and criticism.
　　2. Closure (Rhetoric)　I. Title.
PN1995.C456　2001　　　791.43'75'0973—dc20　　　91-43699

British Library cataloguing data are available

On the cover: Joe E. Brown and Jack Lemmon in a shot from the final scene of the 1959 film *Some Like It Hot* (Photofest)

Manufactured in the United States of America

McFarland & Company, Inc., Publishers
　Box 611, Jefferson, North Carolina 28640
　　www.mcfarlandpub.com

to Jack Smith

Preface

As long as drama has existed, playwrights have acknowledged the importance of the ending as the point to which all the action leads. You must have been disappointed at some time in the ending of some play or movie, and knew that it wasn't right or didn't fit the events which led to it. This puts you in the company of great dramatic commentators of which Aristotle is perhaps the best known.

Early in the history of dramatic productions, Aristotle's *Poetics* established bases for judging theatrical performances that are in use today. Wonderfully succinctly, *Poetics* guides the dramatic composer and the dramatic viewer through all the elements of appealing dramatic production. His standards on plot development, structure, characters, images and thought, as valid today as they were in the 4th century B.C., all work together toward a final resolution, or "change," that takes the work forward to "The End."

To Aristotle, the end was not everything, but the culmination of every process preceding it. The fact that this great thinker from history attached such importance to dramatic endings should be reason in itself to study them.

When Aristotle speaks of "ending," he refers to a final scene and not a final line. If, indeed, the final scene is the one to which all the action leads, would it not be arguable that, to play this important dramatic role, the ending should summarize all that has preceded, if not by words, certainly by maintaining a theme or "flavor." I believe so. It also seems to me, that this very "flavor" should be preserved in the final spoken line, which is the ultimate ending. It is, therefore, the preservation of the theme that makes the closing line so important – one short statement that says so much. This is the reason that closing lines have been regarded as the most dramatic, powerful and revealing of any other lines, and that they are the most often remembered and quoted.

Novelists recognize the effect of closings as well as openings on their readers and strive for the most powerful beginning and ending paragraphs. What is film but cinematic novelization, and it follows that filmmakers also concern themselves with making powerful opening and closing statements. It is a source of disappointment to me that visual representations cannot be presented here to accompany the spoken words, for some statements are meaningful only with the scenes selected to make a complete and lasting impression. How can anyone forget the sight of Montgomery Clift in *The Heiress* pounding on the door and being ignored by Oliva De Havilland. Without that scene, the impact of the words is lost.

The words themselves can be powerful statements, and I have endeavored to include here not only those that do, but also the ones that fall short, with or without the visual scenes. I have chosen to concentrate on closing lines because I feel the summation effect very important to the understanding of the entire film.

As far as I have been able to determine, a compilation of this type has never before been attempted. I was, therefore, without guidelines or the experiences of others to draw upon in the formulation of this volume. The rules devised by me to follow in collecting closing lines seem to be fit for the task, but I would be most appreciated to receive comments, suggestions, and criticisms and other communication about my selections.

The closing line consists of the last spoken words of the film. This means all that is said by a single character, regardless of length. A scene change, or a pause of indeterminate length befitting the situation, represents a new line, even though the speaker has not changed. The pause and scene change situation are totally judgemental and are based on what seems appropriate for the content. However, a speech amplified by various cinematic devices, including rapid scene changes, is recorded in its entirety. Announcements and narration are considered dialogue for the purposes of this collection; they are, after all, the final spoken words. The roar of a crowd is not reported as a closing line unless a single voice stands out, or all voices speak in unison; the single stand-out voice is intended to be audible and therefore comprises the closing line. (Indeed, some scripts I have examined have called for a voice to be heard above the uproar.)

Recognizable song lyrics are not included, whether or not performed with musical accompaniment. Even though many scripts contain the song lyrics, they cannot be considered dialogue because (1) most are not written specifically for the movie in which performed, and (2) most songs, even those that are written for the movie, are performed outside that medium and do not require the setting of that film to be meaningful.

In the case of several voices speaking at once, I have decided to report the most powerful voice (an example, *The In-Laws*).

No films made in a language other than English are included here because I believe the closing line must be presented in the language in which spoken. Conversations spoken in languages other than English in English-language films are not considered to be closing lines, unless the phrases are readily recognizable for their English meanings. Short foreign phrases, though, are reported as closing lines when commonly understood by speakers of English.

No documentaries or animated films are included here. My collection also includes no made-for-television movies; I am limited to theatrical releases. Naturally, only intelligible lines can be reported. Unhappily, I was forced to discount totally unintelligible final statements and nonsense syllables. Partially intelligible closing lines were either (1) not included at all, or (2) recorded with my best effort at determining the spoken words, or (3) verified by the screenplay when the script was available. Insofar as possible, I have compared endings presented here with the original screenplays for the accuracy of the statements I recorded, as well as minor aspects, such as spelling of names. Scripts were available for me to review for about one-quarter of the films represented.

It would have been impossible to view all the films included here were television not available. Therein lies the distinct possibility that films have been shortened to fit an allotted time period, and the possibility that endings have been inaccurately recorded. For example, the television version of *Captain Horatio Hornblower* omitted the final line. Reediting for commercial television can alter an ending – as happened to *10*; the television ending went, "From now on we close the curtains." Sometimes reediting for other than commercial television produces a different ending. A second viewing of *Murder by Death* showed another closing line; I recorded the first one. These could be factors in what I perceive to be disparities between script and film closings. Of course, it is often impossible to see original releases. So, once again, I solicit information about inadvertent omissions due to incomplete films having been screened.

This work ended with films of 1990; but my collecting continues. I sincerely hope that you will enjoy using this compilation as much as I have enjoyed compiling it.

The End

Aaron Slick from Punkin' Crick
1952   Paramount
Hey, Merridew! ("Aaron Slick": Alan Young)

Abandon Ship
1956   Columbia
The story which you have just seen is a true one. In real life, Captain Alexander Holmes was brought to trial on a charge of murder. He was convicted and given the minimum sentence of six months because of the unusual circumstances surrounding the incident. If you had been a member of the jury, how would you have voted? Guilty or innocent? (Narrator)

Abbott and Costello in Hollywood
1945   MGM
Thank you. ("Abercrombie": Lou Costello)

Abbott and Costello Meet Frankenstein
1948   Universal
Allow me to introduce myself. I'm the Invisible Man. ("Voice of the Invisible Man": Vincent Price)

Abbott and Costello Meet the Killer, Boris Karloff
1948   Universal
This one I completely forgot about. ("Freddie Phillips": Lou Costello)

Abe Lincoln in Illinois
1940   RKO
Good-bye, Abe! (Spectator at speech)

The Abominable Dr. Phibes
1971   American International
Well, he'll be working on it, wherever he is. ("Dr. Longstreet": Terry-Thomas)

Above and Beyond
1952   MGM
Paul. Paul. ("Lucy Tibbets": Eleanor Parker)

Above Suspicion
1943   MGM
Well, how about some spaghetti? ("Richard Myles": Fred MacMurray)

Above the Law
1988   Warner Brothers
Gentlemen, whenever you have a group of individuals who are beyond any investigation, who can manipulate the press, judges, members of our Congress, you're always going to have in our government those who are above the law. ("Nico Toscani": Steven Seagal)

1

Abraham Lincoln

1930   United Artists
Get a doctor! Please get a doctor!
("Mary Todd Lincoln": Kay Hammond)

Absence of Malice

1981   Columbia
You, too. ("Megan Carter": Sally Field)

Absolution

1981   Trans World
It'll probably be more comfortable, and the sentence shorter. ("Arthur": Dai Bradley)

The Abyss

1989   20th Century–Fox
Hi, Mrs. Brigman. ("Bud Brigman": Ed Harris)

Accident

1967   Lippert
Good-bye. ("Anna": Jacqueline Sassard)

Accidental Tourist

1988   Warner Brothers
Uh, arretez, stop for that woman. ("Macon Leary": William Hurt)

The Accused

1988   Paramount
I don't know. I'd like to go home and I'd like to play with my dog. ("Sarah Tobias": Jodie Foster)

Ace in the Hole

1951   Paramount
How'd you like to make yourself a thousand dollars a day, Mr. Boot? I'm a thousand-dollar-a-day newspaper man. You can have me for nothing. ("Charles Tatum": Kirk Douglas)

Across the Pacific

1942   Warner Brothers
Right on time, eh, Doc. Any of your friends in Tokyo have trouble committing hara kiri, those boys will be glad to help them out. Right down there. Well, angel. ("Richard Lomas Leland": Humphrey Bogart)

Act One

1963   Warner Brothers
Bernie, don't forget your diploma! ("Mrs. Hart": Sylvie Strauss)

Action Jackson

1988   Lorimar
Can I have you any sooner? ("'Action' Jackson": Carl Weathers)

Action of the Tiger

1957   MGM
You know something, you might easily end up with one. ("Carson": Van Johnson)

Ada

1961   MGM
This is just the first step in a reform package that will take the government of this state back to the people. ("Joe Adams": Larry Gates)

Adam's Rib

1949   MGM
Which means hurray for that little difference. ("Adam Bonner": Spencer Tracy)

Adam's Woman

1970   Warner Brothers

If I hadn't you'd still be bloody well lying down there under that tree, twiddlin' your toes. ("Bess": Jan Merrow)

Adventure in Baltimore
1949 RKO
Sit down. Sit down. Bring up another chair. ("Dr. Sheldon": Robert Young)

Adventure of Sherlock Holmes' Smarter Brother
1975 20th Century–Fox
What the hell am I supposed to do now? ("Jenny Hill": Madeline Kahn)

The Adventures of Baron Munchausen
1989 Columbia
It wasn't just a story, was it? ("Sally": Sarah Polley)

The Adventures of Don Juan
1949 Warner Brothers
My dear friend, there's a little bit of Don Juan in every man, but since I am Don Juan, there must be more of it in me. ("Don Juan": Errol Flynn)

The Adventures of Ford Fairlane
1990 20th Century–Fox
Look at this, the sun, the sea. Unfucking-believable, eh? ("Ford Fairlane": Andrew Dice Clay)

The Adventures of Marco Polo
1938 United Artists
Oh, he's a very patient man. He can wait. ("Marco Polo": Gary Cooper)

The Adventures of Robin Hood
1938 Warner Brothers
May I obey all your commands with equal pleasure, sire. ("Sir Robin of Locklsey/Robin Hood": Errol Flynn)

Affair in Trinidad
1952 Columbia
Am I? ("Chris Emery": Rita Hayworth)

The Affairs of Cellini
1934 20th Century–Fox
Good night, m'lord, I, uh, oh, I was, I meant, I was, oh, good night. ("Alessandro, Duke of Florence": Frank Morgan)

Affairs of Dobie Gillis
1953 MGM
Yes, we promised you excitement and here they are, the most exciting band in the whole country, Happy Stella Kowalski and her Schottiche Five. ("Dobie Gillis": Bobby Van)

The African Queen
1951 United Artists
The way we're swimming, old girl. ("Charles Allnut": Humphrey Bogart)

After Hours
1985 Warner Brothers
Hey, what do you know, man? A stereo's a stereo. Art is forever. ("Neil": Cheech Marin)

After the Thin Man
1936 MGM
Why, Mrs. Charles. ("Nick Charles": William Powell)

Against All Flags
1952 Universal
Again. Again. ("Spitfire Stevens": Maureen O'Hara)

Against All Odds
1984   Columbia
I figure that's up to her. You're not gonna control us forever, believe me. ("Terry Brogan": Jeff Bridges)

Agatha
1978   Warner Brothers
Just before you leave, sir. Before you leave, now could you give us a statement? (A reporter)

Agnes of God
1985   Columbia
I don't know the meaning behind the song she sang. Perhaps it was a song of seduction, and the father was a field hand. Perhaps the song was some of a lullaby that she remembered from many years ago, and the father was hope and love and desire, the belief in miracles. I want to believe that she was blessed, and I do miss her, and I hope that she's left some little part of herself with me. That would be miracle enough, wouldn't it? ("Doctor Martha Livingston": Jane Fonda)

The Agony and the Ecstasy
1965   20th Century–Fox
To work, my son. ("Pope Julius II": Rex Harrison)

Air America
1990   Carolco
So sit back, relax, and, uh, we'll do what we do best. We fly. ("Gene Ryack": Mel Gibson)

Air Force
1943   Warner Brothers
We shall carry the attack against the enemy. We shall hit him and hit him again, wherever and whenever we can reach him, for we intend to bring this battle to him on his own home grounds. (Narrator)

Air Mail
1932   Universal
Sure. Sure. Well, I walked away from that one, didn't I? Hey, Mike, how do I look? ("Duke Talbot": Pat O'Brien)

Airplane
1980   Paramount
Municipal bonds, Ted. Talking double A rating. Best investment in America. ("Captain Rex Kramer": Robert Stack)

Airplane II: The Sequel
1982   Paramount
I don't know if this is a good time to ask, but would it be possible for me to get my briefcase back? ("The Bomber": Sonny Bono)

Airport
1970   Universal
Tell him to take care of it himself. ("Mel Bakersfield": Burt Lancaster)

Airport '77
1977   Universal
I love you. ("Eve Clayton": Brenda Vacarro)

Al Capone
1959   Allied Artists
He would never rise again. After seven years he was released, ill with an incurable disease. On January twenty-fifth, nineteen forty-seven, his mind half gone, Al Capone died. But the seeds of evil he planted still survive. And we must continue to fight

the remnants of the organization he built which still touches every one of us today. (Narrator)

Algiers
1938   United Artists
And so I have, my friend. ("Pepe le Moko": Charles Boyer)

Alias Nick Beal
1949 Paramount
I wouldn't ask. You won, that's the important thing. Forget him. Go home. ("The Rev. Thomas Garfield": George Macready)

Alice
1990   Orion
Yes, but she's a changed woman because you can't tell it's Gloria. ("Nina": Robin Bartlett)

Alice Adams
1935   RKO
I love you. ("Arthur Russell": Fred MacMurray)

Alice Doesn't Live Here Anymore
1974   Warner Brothers
Mom, I can't breathe. ("Tommy Hyatt": Alfred Lutter)

Alice's Adventures in Wonderland
1972   20th Century-Fox
It's getting late. ("Alice": Fiona Fullerton)

Alice's Restaurant
1969   United Artists
I wish we had him back. We'd have a real place, we'd all still been together. Not bugging each other. We'd all be

some kind of family. ("Ray": James Broderick)

Alien
1979   20th Century-Fox
Come on, cat. ("Ripley": Sigourney Weaver)

Alien from L.A.
1988   Cannon
Crazy. ("Wanda Saknussemm": Kathy Ireland)

Alien Nation
1988   20th Century-Fox
Well, my daughter's got a husband, I got a partner. You know, he really ain't half bad, except when he's got that rotten milk on his breath. ("Matthew Sykes": James Caan)

Aliens
1986   20th Century-Fox
Affirmative. ("Newt": Carrie Henn)

All About Eve
1950   20th Century-Fox
Sure, Miss Harrington. ("Phoebe": Barbara Bates)

All Hands on Deck
1961   20th Century-Fox
Sally. ("Lt. Donald": Pat Boone)

All Night Long
1981   Universal
Oh, George, you're so much more mature. ("Cheryl Gibbons": Barbra Streisand)

All of Me
1984   Universal
Try it with your own feet. ("Roger Cobb": Steve Martin)

All Quiet on the Western Front
1930 Universal
Yeah, Corporal Stanislas Katczinsky, three oh six. (A soldier)

All That Jazz
1979 20th Century-Fox
At least I won't have to lie to you anymore. ("Joe Gideon": Roy Scheider)

All the Brothers Were Valiant
1953 MGM
Lower away! ("Joel Shore": Robert Taylor)

All the King's Men
1949 Columbia
It could have been the whole world – Willie Stark. The whole world – Willie Stark. Why did he do it to me – Willie Stark. Why? ("Willie Stark": Broderick Crawford)

All the President's Men
1976 Warner Brothers
So help me God. (Richard Nixon)

All the Young Men
1960 Columbia
Same to you, Sergeant. ("Towler": Sidney Poitier)

All This, and Heaven Too
1940 Warner Brothers
Henriette, there are many kinds of love possible between a man and a woman. And peace, gentleness, and companionship are not the least of these. I promised you once that you would find a heaven on this earth. I'm going to keep that promise if it takes a lifetime of devotion. ("Henry Martyn Field": Jeffrey Lynn)

Allan Quatermain and the Lost City of Gold
1987 Cannon
Some other great adventure? ("Jesse Huston": Sharon Stone)

The Alligator People
1959 20th Century-Fox
Good night, Jane. ("Dr. Lorimer": Bruce Bennett)

All's Fair
1989 Moviestore
What a woman. ("Colonel": George Segal)

Altered States
1980 Warner Brothers
I love you, Emily. ("Eddie Jessup": William Hurt)

Always
1989 Universal
That's my girl. And that's my boy. ("Pete Sandich": Richard Dreyfuss)

Amadeus
1984 Orion
Mediocrities everywhere. I absolve you. I absolve you. I absolve you. I absolve you all. ("Antonio Salieri": F. Murray Abraham)

The Amazing Mrs. Holliday
1943 Universal
Well, what are you waiting for? What are you waiting for? ("Commodore": Harry Davenport)

Amazon Women on the Moon
1987 Universal

I know you have, but have you? Resist temptation or you may end up like Pete and Mary and Ken. ("Doctor": Paul Bartel)

Ambush
1949 MGM
Sooner or later Diablito had to be stopped. Ben was determined to do it. ("Ward Kinsman": Robert Taylor)

The Ambushers
1967 Columbia
Do you really like Perry Como that much? ("Matt Helm": Dean Martin)

American Dreamer
1984 Warner Brothers
End of chapter. ("Cathy Palmer": JoBeth Williams)

American Gothic
1988 Vidmark
My God, oh God, I want to talk to you, yes, I do. I want you to listen to me, listen. My family is dead, and we lived by your teachings. I beat it into them. I taught it to them, and what have you done? You did away with them. Well, I have news for you, I renounce you, God. I renounce you and I give my soul to Satan. ("Pa": Rod Steiger)

American Graffiti
1973 Universal
Good-bye. ("Laurie": Cindy Williams)

American Justice
1986 Movie Store
What do you want? ("Jake": Gerald McRaney)

The Americanization of Emily
1964 MGM
All right, fink. How do you want me to play it, modest and self-effacing? ("Lt. Commander Charles E. Madison": James Garner)

The Amsterdam Kill
1978 Columbia
Riley was so protective of this. Would you drive me back to your office? ("Quinlan": Robert Mitchum)

Anastasia
1956 20th Century–Fox
Say? Oh, I will say, "The play is over, go home." ("Empress": Helen Hayes)

Anatomy of a Murder
1959 Columbia
Yeah. ("Paul Biegler": James Stewart)

Anchors Aweigh
1945 MGM
In about five minutes, I will introduce to you a young singer discovered by the United States Navy. (Jose Iturbi, as himself)

And God Created Woman
1988 Vestron
Very true. ("Billy Moran": Vincent Spano)

And Justice for All
1979 Columbia
Hi, Arthur. Good to see ya. Nice day. ("Jay": Jeffrey Tambor)

The Andromeda Strain
1970 Universal
Precisely, Senator, what do we do? ("Jeremy Stone": Arthur Hill)

Andy Hardy Comes Home
1958 MGM
Jackson versus Ackerman. ("Andy": Mickey Rooney)

Andy Hardy Meets a Debutante
1940 MGM
Gosh, how one's women do mount up. ("Andy Hardy": Mickey Rooney)

Andy Hardy's Blonde Trouble
1944 MGM
I, uh, I hope you don't draw any wrong conclusions from that conversation. This, this girl, I, I'm not in love with her and she's not in love with me, but I think she's a very nice person and that's what she thinks of me. I'm good for her and she's good for me. This girl's past the silly stage of casual kissing and smooching. This girl, if she'd ever let a fella kiss her, it would be because at that particular moment in that particular place she'd want that particular fella to kiss her. And, oh, boy, I'm that fella. ("Andy": Mickey Rooney)

Andy Hardy's Double Life
1942 MGM
You know something, you're the most beautiful girl I ever saw in my life. Woo-woo. ("Andy": Mickey Rooney)

Angel and the Badman
1947 Republic
Hang it on the wall in my office, with a new rope. ("Wistful McClintock": Harry Carey)

Angel Face
1952 RKO
Watch it! ("Frank Jessup": Robert Mitchum)

Angel Heart
1987 Tri-Star
I know. In hell. ("Harold R. Angel": Mickey Rourke)

Angel in My Pocket
1969 Universal
I'll take it! ("Sam": Andy Griffith)

Angel on My Shoulder
1946 United Artists
You ought to know, brother. You ought to know. ("Eddie Kagle": Paul Muni)

Angels with Dirty Faces
1938 Warner Brothers
It's true, boys, every word of it. He died like they said. All right, fellows, let's go say a prayer for a boy who couldn't run as fast as I could. ("Jerry Connolly": Pat O'Brien)

Animal Crackers
1930 Paramount
Good, come on now, let's get out of here before, before they all wake up. Hurry up, come on, come on. Come on. ("Signor Emanuel Ravelli": Chico Marx)

Ann Vickers
1933 RKO
Well, son, I refuse to answer without advice of counsel. ("Barney Dolphin": Walter Huston)

Anna
1987 Vestron
Dear Noodle. I had a little accident last week and I was in a hospital for three days, but everything is fine now. Anna had a nervous breakdown, but it is a common thing with actors in

America. With the money I made from the film I'm going to take Anna and myself to Hawaii. Well, dear Noodle, blue ocean and a lot of flowers and palm trees. They don't have that in New York. Anna thinks she may get more work if she looks younger so I want to pay for her facelift. That's normal here too. I'm very sorry I couldn't attend Grandpa's funeral, but I was filming, and I couldn't possibly make it. I sent flowers through a special agency. Did you get them? I hope you did because they cost me a fortune. Please send me my childhood photos because a man wants to write a book about me. Boy, I love America. Yours, Krystyna. ("Krystyna": Paulina Porizkova)

Anna Christie
1930   MGM
Fog, fog all time. You can't tell where you was going. Only that old devil sea, she knows. ("Chris Christopherson": George F. Marion)

Anna Karenina
1935   MGM
Who knows? Who knows? ("Vronsky": Fredric March)

Anne of the Thousand Days
1969   Universal
Elizabeth shall be a greater queen than any king of yours. She shall rule a greater England than you could ever have built. My Elizabeth shall be queen and my life will have been well spent. ("Anne Bolyn": Genevieve Bujold)

Annie
1982   Columbia

To Annie with love. I love you, Daddy Warbucks. ("Annie": Aileen Quinn)

Annie Hall
1977   United Artists
After that it got pretty late. And we both hadda go, but it was great seeing Annie again, and I realized what a terrific person she was and how much fun it was just knowing her, and I, I, I thought of that old joke, you know, the, this, this guy goes to a psychiatrist and says, "Doc, my brother's crazy. He thinks he's a chicken." And, uh, the doctor says, "Well, why don't you turn him in?" And the guy says, "I would, but I need the eggs." Well, I guess that's pretty much now how I feel about relationships. You know, they're totally irrational and crazy and absurd, but, uh, I guess we keep goin' through it because most of us need the eggs. ("Alvy Singer": Woody Allen)

Annie Oakley
1935   RKO
Did I know Annie Oakley? ("Toby Walker": Preston Foster)

Another Country
1984   20th Century–Fox
I, I miss the cricket. ("Guy Bennett": Rupert Everett)

Another 48 Hours
1990   Paramount
Here, hold this for me. ("Jack Cates": Nick Nolte)

Another Woman
1988   Orion
I resumed work, it went well and I was undisturbed by extraneous dis-

tractions. The writing seemed to flow and I was full of energy. Once on a sunny morning I paused for a break and I thought I would look through Larry Lewis' novel which I'd never read. I was curious about the character Helenka which was rumored to have been based on me. I opened the book, leafed through, and sat down as my eye was caught by her name. "Helenka and I accidentally ran into one another one day while we were both buying tickets to a concert. I knew her because she was the lover of a man I knew quite well. Recently they had decided to marry. This was a catastrophe for me personally because from the first moment he had introduced me to her I was in love with her. I convinced her to have a drink with me. It was the only time I'd ever been alone with her since we met. She was lovely, and I spoke too much and too rapidly because I was embarrassed over my feelings for her, which I felt were painfully obvious. We walked around in Central Park and talked about lots of things. I told her about a book I was planning to write and about wanting to live out West. She spoke enthusiastically about her upcoming marriage, but I thought it was too enthusiastic, as if she were trying to convince herself rather than me. Soon it began to rain, we ducked into an underpass to avoid the cloudburst. I remember thinking how wonderful she was and how I wanted to tell her so many things because my feelings were swirling so. And I think she knew everything and that frightened her, and yet some instinct told me that if I kissed her she would respond. Her kiss was full of

desire and I knew I couldn't share that feeling with anyone else. And then a wall went up and just as quickly I was screened out. But it was too late because I now knew that she was capable of intense passion if she would one day just allow herself to feel." I closed the book and felt the strange mixture of wistfulness and hope. And I wondered if a memory is something you have or something you've lost. For the first time in a long time I felt at peace. ("Marion": Gena Rowlands)

Any Which Way You Can
1980   Warner Brothers
Onward. ("Philo Beddoe": Clint Eastwood)

Anzio
1968   Columbia
Well, we've seen the conquering hero. Let's go. ("Dick Ennis": Robert Mitchum)

Apache Uprising
1965   Paramount
Well, it's a start. ("Jim Walker": Rory Calhoun)

The Apartment
1960   United Artists
Shut up and deal. ("Fran Kubelik": Shirley MacLaine)

Apocalypse Now
1979   United Artists
The horror. The horror. ("Colonel Kurtz": Marlon Brando)

Appointment with Danger
1949   Paramount

I may join it then. ("Al Goddard": Alan Ladd)

Appointment with Death
1988 Cannon
Well, I think they'll be all right. ("Hercule Poirot": Peter Ustinov)

Arachnophobia
1990 Buena Vista
Let's do it. ("Molly Jennings": Harley Jane Kozak)

Arise, My Love
1940 Paramount
Augusta, I always said you were the best. ("Tom Martin": Ray Milland)

Arizona
1941 Columbia
Doggone it, Peter. If this is what it's like to be in love, I'm glad I'm only going to love but once. ("Phoebe Titus": Jean Arthur)

Arizona Heat
1988 Spectrum
Don't worry. He'll make it. ("Captain Samuels": Hugh Farrington)

Arizona Raiders
1965 Columbia
Good-bye. ("Martina": Gloria Talbott)

Armed and Dangerous
1986 Columbia
If I say you're gonna be a cop, you're gonna be a cop. ("Dooley": John Candy)

The Arnelo Affair
1946 MGM

Good night, Ricky. ("Anne Parkson": Frances Gifford)

Around the World Under the Sea
1966 MGM
Hold on, we're turning over. ("Dr. Doug Standish": Lloyd Bridges)

Arsenic and Old Lace
1944 Warner Brothers
I'm not a cab driver. I'm a coffee pot. (Taxi driver)

The Art of Love
1965 Universal
Oh, you, now why did you have me this way? ("Nikki": Elke Sommer)

Arthur
1981 Warner Brothers
Stop that! ("Linda Marolla": Liza Minelli)

Arthur 2: On the Rocks
1988 Warner Brothers
There you go. There you go. There you go. ("Linda Marolla Bach": Liza Minelli)

Artists and Models
1955 Paramount
Come on, we'll just make it. ("Eugene Fullstack": Jerry Lewis)

As You Desire Me
1931 MGM
I love you, I do. ("Zara": Greta Garbo)

The Asphalt Jungle
1950 MGM
Dix. Dix. Oh, God. Oh, my God. Dix. Dix. ("Doll Conovan": Jean Hagen)

Assassination
1986   Cannon
Nobody said anything about marriage. ("Jay Killian": Charles Bronson)

The Assisi Underground
1985   Cannon
Luigi, the town is once again ours. ("Padre Rufino": Ben Cross)

At Close Range
1986   Orion
He's my father. ("Brad, Jr.": Sean Penn)

At Long Last Love
1975   20th Century–Fox
I think she's more beautiful now than I've ever seen her. ("Michael Oliver Pritchard III": Burt Reynolds)

At Sword's Point
1951   RKO
Long live the king. (Swordsmen)

Attack
1956   United Artists
This is Lieutenant Harold Woodruff. ("Lt. Woodruff": William Smithers)

Audrey Rose
1977   United Artists
Dear Mr. Hoover. It is good to know that you are in India doing all the things you must for the peace of our daughter's soul. I include Bill in my thanks even though he still cannot accept the idea that while Ivy's body is gone, her soul continues to exist and will continue to exist through many lifetimes. There are moments when I too find it difficult to accept, yet I know in my heart it is true and that you are right, and that is what sustains me. In permitting you to take Ivy's ashes to India, I believe that Bill has taken the first step toward understanding that we are all immortal. Know that I add my prayers to yours for our daughter's soul to mend itself and find the peace and fufillment in heaven that it was denied in its earth life. And the day will come when her soul will feel free and able to seek a new rebirth, and that when it does she will find parents who are generous, understanding, and who will love her as we all love her. ("Janice Templeton": Marsha Mason)

Auntie Mame
1958   Warner Brothers
Oh, what times we're going to have, what vistas we're going to explore together. We'll spend a day at an ancient Hindu temple. The head monk there is a very good friend of Auntie Mame's, and perhaps he'll let you ring the temple bells that bring the monks to prayer. And there on the highest tower on a clear day you can see the Taj Majal and beyond that the beautiful. ("Auntie Mame": Rosalind Russell)

Author, Author!
1982   20th Century–Fox
Oh, that's so cold! ("Travalian": Al Pacino)

Avalon
1990   Tri-Star
No. He came to America in nineteen fourteen. He said it was the most

beautiful place he'd ever seen. ("Michael as an Adult": Tom Wood)

Avanti
1972   United Artists
Miss Piggott, you lose one pound, just one pound, and it's all over between us. Arrivaderci, Carlo. ("Wendell Armbruster": Jack Lemmon)

Awakenings
1990   Columbia
Let's begin. ("Dr. Malcolm Sayer": Robin Williams)

Away All Boats
1956   Universal
He started saving everybody when he came aboard. All of us are better than we ever thought we could be because of what he gave us. And we'll go home again because of him. ("Lieut. Dave MacDougall": George Nader)

The Awful Truth
1937   Columbia
Good night. ("Lucy Warriner": Irene Dunne)

The Babe Ruth Story
1948   Allied Artists
And so the Babe who had performed miraculous feats before millions of cheering fans made the greatest play of his life far from the din of the crowd. Unknown to the press, the public, the fans of America, even to the medical profession in general. The home run king who had drawn over fifty-five million people to the ballparks all over the land that night repaid every single fan for every single cheer by offering his life to help them and theirs. For the deeds he performed on the diamond, Babe Ruth has deservedly earned his place in baseball's hall of fame and endeared himself in the heart of every American for generations to come. His name will live as long as there is a ball, a bat, and a boy. ("Narrator": Knox Manning)

Babes in Arms
1939   MGM
Look at that kid, willya. ("Joe Moran": Charles Winninger)

Baby Boom
1987   MGM/UA
See? ("J. C. Wyatt": Diane Keaton)

The Bachelor and the Bobby Soxer
1947   RKO
Give up. Let's go. ("Dick": Cary Grant)

Bachelor Mother
1939 RKO
Of course. ("David Merlin": David Niven)

Bachelor Party
1984   20th Century-Fox
Hey, now, Brad. ("Rick Gasco": Tom Hanks)

Back Street
1941 Universal
Your son was just here. Walter, he was so nice to me. He might have been my son, our son. I wonder what would have happened if I had met you that Sunday at the boat. ("Ray Smith": Margaret Sullavan)

Back Street
1961 Universal
Miss Hatfield said we could, if it's all right with you. ("Caroline Saxon": Tammy Marihugh)

Back to School
1986 Orion
And so to all you graduates as you go out into the world, my advice to you is don't go. It's rough out there. Move back with your parents. Let them worry about it. ("Thornton Melon": Rodney Dangerfield)

Back to the Beach
1987 Paramount
Are we the corniest couple you've ever seen or what? ("Annette": Annette Funicello)

Back to the Future
1985 Universal
Roads? Where we're going we don't need roads. ("Doc Brown": Christopher Lloyd)

Back to the Future Part II
1989 Universal
Doc! Doc! Doc! ("Marty McFly": Michael J. Fox)

Back to the Future Part III
1990 Universal
No, already been there. ("Doctor Emmett Brown": Christopher Lloyd)

Backlash
1956 Universal
Whenever you're ready. ("Jim Slater": Richard Widmark)

Bad Company
1931 RKO
Oh yeah? I see. ("McBaine": Harry Carey, Sr.)

Bad Day at Black Rock
1955 MGM
Second time. ("John J. Macreedy": Spencer Tracy)

Bad Dreams
1988 20th Century–Fox
There's nothing there. There's nothing to be scared of, all right. You don't have to be afraid. You don't have to be afraid anymore. ("Dr. Alex Karmen": Bruce Abbott)

Bad for Each Other
1954 Columbia
This is it. And if you're looking for his nurse, she's ready to go to work. ("Joan Lasher": Dianne Foster)

The Bad News Bears in Breaking Training
1977 Paramount
All right. ("Mike Leak": William Devane)

The Bad Seed
1956 Warner Brothers
Oh, Kenneth, I love you. I love you. ("Christine": Nancy Kelly)

Badlands
1973 Warner Brothers
Think they'll take that into consideration? ("Kit": Martin Sheen)

Badman's Territory
1946 RKO
You're a little mite off key. ("Henryette Alcott": Ann Richards)

Bagdad Cafe
1988 Island
I'll talk it over with Brenda. ("Jasmin": Marianne Sagebrecht)

The Ballad of Josie
1967 Universal
Steaks are on over at my place, and you may never get back alive. ("Jason Meredith": Peter Graves)

Bananas
1971 United Artists
I think we should leave the happy couple on that note. It's hard to tell what may happen in the future. But they may live happily ever after. Again, they may not. Be sure of this, though, wherever the action is we will be there with "ABC's Wide World of Sports" to cover it. Now on behalf of Nancy and Fielding Mellish and all of the others who have made this possible, this is Howard Cosell thanking you for joining us and wishing you a most pleasant good night. (Howard Cosell, as himself)

Band of the Hand
1986 Tri-Star
Have a good night, officer. (Occupant of car)

The Band Wagon
1953 MGM
May we say something? ("Jeffrey Cordova": Jack Buchanan)

The Bandit of Sherwood Forest
1946 Columbia
I cannot disobey the king. ("Lady Catherine Maitland": Anita Louise)

Bandolero!
1968 20th Century–Fox
Perhaps not. ("Maria": Raquel Welch)

The Bank Dick
1940 Universal
Uh, say! ("Egbert Souse": W. C. Fields)

Barabbas
1962 Columbia
It is Barabbas. ("Barabbas": Anthony Quinn)

Barbarosa
1981 Universal
Barbarosa! (A spectator)

Barbary Coast
1935 United Artists
All right. What are you standing there for? Say good-bye? All right. That the way a gentleman does it? Come on. ("Louis Chamalis": Edward G. Robinson)

The Barefoot Contessa
1954 United Artists
Yeah, we'll get a good day's work done tomorrow. ("Harry Dawes": Humphrey Bogart)

Barefoot in the Park
1967 Paramount
Oh, good, they made up. ("Ethel Banks": Mildred Natwick)

Barfly
1987 Cannon
All right. Yeah. (Bar patron)

The Barkleys of Broadway
1949 MGM

Oh, that good old tempo. ("John Barkley": Fred Astaire)

The Barretts of Wimpole Street
1934 MGM
For as much as Robert and Elizabeth have consented together in holy wedlock, and have witnessed the same before God and this company, I pronounce that they be man and wife together. In the name of the father and of the son and of the holy ghost, amen. God the father, God the son, God the holy ghost, bless, preserve and keep that ye may so live together in this life that in the world to come ye may have life everlasting. Amen. ("Clergyman": Winter Hall)

The Barretts of Wimpole Street
1956 MGM
I love thee with breath, smiles, tears of all my life. And if God choose I shall but love thee better after death. ("Elizabeth": Jennifer Jones)

Barry Lyndon
1975 Warner Brothers
Utterly baffled and beaten, what was the lonely and broken-hearted man to do? He took the annuity and returned to Ireland with his mother to complete his recovery. Sometime later he traveled to the continent. His life there we have not the means of following accurately, but he appears to have resumed his former profession of a gambler, without his former success. He never saw Lady Lyndon again. ("Narrator": Michael Hordern)

Bataan
1943 MGM

Come on, ya. . . . ("Sgt. Bill Dane": Robert Taylor)

Bathing Beauty
1944 MGM
What am I doing? I can't swim. Help. ("Steve Elliott": Red Skelton)

Batman
1989 Warner Brothers
I'm not a bit surprised. ("Vicki Vale": Kim Basinger)

Batteries Not Included
1987 Universal
You're fired, kid. ("Lacey": Michael Greene)

Battle Circus
1952 MGM
Hi, Major. ("Lt. Ruth McCara": June Allyson)

The Battle of the Villa Fiorita
1964 Warner Brothers
Oh, help me, Debby, help me. ("Moira": Maureen O'Hara)

Battleground
1949 MGM
One, two, three, four, one, two—three, four. (Marching soldiers)

Beaches
1988 Buena Vista
Well, sure, we're friends, aren't we? ("CC [age 11]": Mayim Bialik)

The Bear
1989 Tri-Star
Good luck, little fella. ("Tom": Tcheky Karyo)

The Beast
1988   Columbia
I don't understand you. ("Kover-
chenko": Jason Patric)

Beast in the Cellar
1970   Cannon
There's something he didn't know,
something he'll never know now. He'll
never know that everything we did,
the whole thing, was all done for him.
("Joyce Ballantyne": Flora Robson)

The Beast of the City
1932   MGM
I, James Fitzpatrick, do solemnly
swear to uphold the constitution of
the United States, the constitution of
this state, and to discharge the duties
of the office of the chief of police according to the best of my ability. ("Jim
Fitzpatrick": Walter Huston)

The Beast with Five Fingers
1946   Warner Brothers
How do you like that? My own hand.
("Castanio": J. Carrol Naish)

The Beastmaster
1982   MGM/UA
You trained Tal well, and he will
make a fine king. ("Dar": Marc Singer)

Because You're Mine
1952   MGM
Now I'd like to sing "Because You're
Mine." And, Bridget, it's much better
as a duet. ("Renaldo Rossano": Mario
Lanza)

Becky Sharp
1935   RKO

My deepest gratitude, brother, for
virtue is its own reward. ("Becky
Sharp": Miriam Hopkins)

The Bedford Incident
1965   Columbia
Answer me, damn you! ("Ben Munce-
ford": Sidney Poitier)

Bedlam
1946   RKO
Are we lovers that you "thee" and
"thou" me? ("Hannay": Richard Fra-
ser)

Bedside
1934   Warner Brothers
Oh, Bob, you're marvelous. ("Caroline": Jean Muir)

Bedtime for Bonzo
1951   Universal
By golly, I'm the richest man in six
counties. ("Professor Peter Boyd":
Ronald Reagan)

Beer
1985   Orion
So long, suckers. ("Merle Draggett":
William Russ)

The Bees
1978   New World
They won't harm you, stay where you
are. Now listen. There are approx-
imately twenty trillion of these bees
in existence. And they're multiplying
at a rate of five million a day. From
now on they will dominate the earth
equally with mankind. Or without
mankind depending on whether or
not we accept their terms. I know you
will accept, there's no other way

to survive. ("John Norman": John Saxon)

Beetlejuice
1988   Warner Brothers
Oh, hey, wait a, hey, stop it, hey, you're messing up my hair. Come on, whoa, whoa, stop it. Whoa. Hey, this might be a good look for me. ("Betelgeuse": Michael Keaton)

Behave Yourself
1951   RKO
And why shouldn't he, in his own house? ("Mrs. Carter": Margalo Gillmore)

Behold a Pale Horse
1964   Columbia
Why did he come back? ("Captain Vinolas": Anthony Quinn)

Being There
1979   United Artists
Security, tranquility, a well-deserved rest. All the aims I have pursued will soon be realized. Life is a state of mind. ("President 'Bobby'": Jack Warden)

Belizaire the Cajun
1986   Norstar
Come along, my children. ("Belizaire": Armand Assante)

The Belle of New York
1952   MGM
Yes, they can, they're in love. ("Elsie Wilkins": Alice Pearce)

Belle of the Nineties
1934   Paramount
You're the best man, huh? That's

what you think. ("Ruby Carter": Mae West)

Belles on Their Toes
1952   20th Century–Fox
I wasn't asleep, dear. I was just thinking of someone who loved us all very much and saying thank you. ("Lillian Galbraith": Myrna Loy)

Bells
1981   New World
I'll call you. ("Nat Bridger": Richard Chamberlain)

Bells Are Ringing
1960   MGM
And so, ladies and gentlemen, you too, like this satisfied customer, can solve all your problems by subscribing to an answering service. (Narrator)

The Bells of St. Mary's
1945   RKO
Right. ("Father Chuck O'Malley": Bing Crosby)

Bells of San Angelo
1947   Republic
Enough for just the best story I ever wrote. I'm going to call it "The Bells of San Angelo." You'll never guess who it's about. ("Lee Madison": Dale Evans)

Beloved Infidel
1959   20th Century–Fox
Sheila, Sheila. I love you. I love you very much. I love you as you are. As you are. ("F. Scott Fitzgerald": Gregory Peck)

Ben-Hur
1959   MGM

Even then. And I felt His voice take the sword out of my hand. ("Judah Ben-Hur": Charlton Heston)

Bend of the River
1952 Universal
Hah, come on. ("Glyn McLyntock": Jimmy Stewart)

Berlin Express
1948 RKO
And other times I know why we keep trying. I know some day we make it. ("Dr. Bernhardt": Paul Lukas)

Bert Rigby, You're a Fool
1989 Warner Brothers
It's marvelous! (Spectator at performance)

The Best Little Whorehouse in Texas
1982 Universal
You all come back now, you hear. ("Mona Strangely": Dolly Parton)

The Best Years of Our Lives
1946 RKO
You know what it'll be, don't you, Peggy? It may take us years to get anywhere. We'll have no money, no decent place to live. We'll have to work, get kicked around. ("Fred Derry": Dana Andrews)

Betrayed
1988 MGM/UA
Come on. ("Gladys Simmons": Betsy Blair)

Betsy's Wedding
1990 Buena Vista
Oh, God, please, let them elope. ("Eddie Hopper": Alan Alda)

Between Two Worlds
1944 Warner Brothers
We're alive, Ann, alive. Oh, there is so much to do, we know that now. There is so much to live for. Ann, Ann, we're alive. ("Henry": Paul Henreid)

Beverly Hills Brats
1989 Taurus
Damn it, damn it, damn it, Grandma, you knew I wanted an airplane. ("Scooter": Peter Billingsley)

Beverly Hills Cop
1984 Paramount
Don't worry about it, just follow my lead. I know the perfect place, you guys will love it. Trust me. ("Alex Foley": Eddie Murphy)

Beverly Hills Cop II
1987 Paramount
Who's that black guy? ("Mr. Anderson": Richard Tienken)

Beyond the Forest
1949 Warner Brothers
Hello, hello, operator. I want to talk to the hospital in Ashwood. ("Jenny": Dona Drake)

Beyond the Limit
1983 Paramount
Don't cry. ("Charley Fortnum": Michael Caine)

Beyond the Poseidon Adventure
1979 Warner Brothers
I was going to kiss you anyway. ("Capt. Mike Turner": Michael Caine)

Big
1988 20th Century–Fox

OK, I'll call for you. ("Billy Kopeche": Jared Rushton)

The Big Bus
1976   Paramount
We did it, we did it! Ha-ha, baby, we did it! ("Dan Torrance": Joseph Bologna)

Big Business
1988   Buena Vista
Taxi. ("Bum": Leo Burmester)

The Big Circus
1959   Allied Artists
You know, neither did I. ("Hank Twirling": Victor Mature)

The Big Country
1958   United Artists
Here I come, Hannassey. ("Maj. Henry Terrill": Charles Bickford)

The Big Easy
1986   Columbia
Jesus Christ, it's gonna blow! Run! ("McSwain": Dennis Quaid)

The Big Fix
1978   Universal
Your version is too dirty. ("Moses Wine": Richard Dreyfuss)

The Big Hangover
1950   MGM
I do not belong here. I am standing here as proxy for another, a young man who. . . . ("David Maldon": Van Johnson)

The Big Heat
1953   Columbia
OK, sir. ("Hugo": Michael Granger)

The Big Lift
1950   20th Century–Fox
Well, I don't know. If they can take off when the birds won't even fly, I guess the blockade isn't much of a weapon. ("Hank": Paul Douglas)

Big Shots
1987   20th Century–Fox
Yeah. ("Obie": Ricky Busker)

The Big Sky
1952   RKO
There'll be time for that next year when I come back. You know, I didn't think you had the sense to do it. ("Deakins": Kirk Douglas)

The Big Sleep
1946   Warner Brothers
Nothing you can't fix. ("Vivian Sternwood": Lauren Bacall)

The Big Stampede
1932   Warner Brothers
Oh, no, there is the old saying, all is fair in love and war, but no slingshot. ("Sonora Joe": Luis Alberni)

The Big Store
1941   MGM
I'll see that you get a check in the morning, old man. Miss Phelps' residence. ("Wolf J. Flywheel": Groucho Marx)

Big Top Pee-wee
1988   Paramount
Ladies and gentlemen, the Cabrini Circus proudly presents, for the first time anywhere, Pee-wee Herman. ("Mace Montana": Kris Kristofferson)

The Big Trees
1952   Warner Brothers

Mrs. Fallon, please, couldn't I? Just one little one, huh? ("John Fallon": Kirk Douglas)

Big Trouble in Little China
1986   20th Century–Fox
Just listen to the old Pork Chop Express here now, and take this advice on a dark and stormy night when the lightning's crashing and the thunder's roaring and the rain's coming down in sheets thick as lead. Just remember what old Jack Burton does when the earth quakes and the poison arrows fall from the sky and the pillars of heaven shake. Yeah, Jack Burton just looks that old big storm right square in the eye and he says, "Give me your best shot, pal, I can take it." ("Jack Burton": Kurt Russell)

The Biggest Bundle of Them All
1967   MGM
Celli, you're a real cuckoo bird. ("Harry": Robert Wagner)

Bill and Ted's Excellent Adventure
1989   Orion
They do better. ("Rufus": George Carlin)

Billion Dollar Brain
1967   United Artists
How about two hundred pounds, sir? ("Harry Palmer": Michael Caine)

Biloxi Blues
1988   Universal
As I look back now, a lot of years later, I realize that my time in the Army was the happiest time of my life. God knows not because I like the Army, and there sure was nothing to like about a war. I liked it for the most selfish reason of all, because I was young. We all were, me and Epstein and Wykowski, Selridge, Carney, Hennesey, and even Sergeant Toomey. I didn't really like most of those guys then, but today I love every damn one of them. Life is weird, you know. ("Eugene": Matthew Broderick)

The Bingo Long Traveling All-Stars and Motor Kings
1976   Universal
Oh, Leon. You know something. It's you and me, Leon. We can't never lose. Never. ("Bingo [Pitcher]": Billy Dee Williams)

Bird
1988   Warner Brothers
He was thirty-four. ("Baroness Nica": Diane Salinger)

The Birds
1963   Universal
Oh, all right, bring them. ("Mitch Brenner": Rod Taylor)

Birds Do It
1966   Columbia
I do do it. ("Melvyn Byrd": Soupy Sales)

Birdy
1984   Tri-Star
Why? ("Birdy": Matthew Modine)

The Birth of the Blues
1941   Paramount
That ain't mine. That's gonna be everybody's blue music. ("Jeff Lambert": Bing Crosby)

The Bishop's Wife
1947   RKO
Tonight I want to tell you the story of an empty stocking. Once upon a midnight clear there was a child's cry. A blazing star hung over a stable and wise men come with birthday gifts. We haven't forgotten that night down through the centuries. We celebrate it with stars on Christmas trees, with the sound of bells, and with gifts. But especially with gifts. You give me a book, I give you a tie. Aunt Martha has always wanted an orange squeezer. And Uncle Henry could do with a new pipe. Oh, we forget nobody. And our poor child. All the stockings are stuffed. All that is, except one's, and we have even forgotten to hang up the stocking for the child born in a manger. It's his birthday we're celebrating. Don't let us ever forget that. Let us ask ourselves what he would wish for most, and then let each put in his share. Loving kindness, warm hearts, and a stretched out hand of tolerance. All the shining gifts make peace on earth. ("Henry Brougham": David Niven)

Bite the Bullet
1975   Columbia
People some people marry. ("Miss Jones": Candice Bergen)

Black Eagle
1988   VPD
As you say, Inspector. ("Ken Taal": Sho Kosugi)

The Black Hole
1979   Buena Vista
Let's pray you were the genius. ("Dr. Kate McCrea": Yvette Mimieux)

The Black Marble
1980   Avco
Natasha. ("Sgt. Valnikov": Robert Foxworth)

Black Rain
1989   Paramount
Nick-San! ("Masahiro Matsumoto": Ken Takakura)

The Black Stallion
1979   United Artists
Henry. ("Alec Ramsey": Kelly Reno)

The Black Stallion Returns
1983   MGM/UA
Maybe I'll be back. ("Alec Ramsey": Kelly Reno)

Blackbeard, the Pirate
1952   RKO
No, I don't want to see it. ("Edwina": Linda Darnell)

The Blackboard Jungle
1955   MGM
See you around. ("Richard Dadier": Glenn Ford)

Blade Runner
1982   Warner Brothers
Gaff had been there and let her live. Four years, he figured, he was wrong. Tyrell had told me Rachael was special, no termination date. I didn't know how long we'd have together. Who does? ("Deckard": Harrison Ford)

Blame It on Rio
1984   20th Century–Fox
It's hard to realize a whole year has gone by since then. Victor finally got

his divorce, and he and his wife turned around and married each other again. Victor said it was because she wanted to get the other half of everything he owned. With Karen and me it wasn't really a case of happily ever after. We were lucky to get any kind of ever after at all. I figure we're a few months away from happily. We'll make it. You only live once but it does help if you get to be young twice. ("Matthew Hollis": Michael Caine)

Blaze
1989   Buena Vista
Yes, ma'am, Miss Starr. ("Doc Ferriday": Garland Bunting)

Blazing Saddles
1974   Warner Brothers
Come on. ("Bart": Cleavon Little)

Blithe Spirit
1945   United Artists
Good-bye for the moment, my dears. I expect we're bound to meet again one day, but until we do I'm going to enjoy myself as I've never enjoyed myself before. ("Charles": Rex Harrison)

The Blob
1958   Paramount
Yeah, as long as the Arctic stays cold. ("Steve": Steve McQueen)

The Blob
1988   Tri-Star
And the lord will give me a sign. ("The Reverend Meeker": Del Close)

Blondie
1938   Columbia

Sometimes I think it's harder to raise a husband than a baby. ("Blondie": Penny Singleton)

Blondie Brings Up Baby
1939   Columbia
Blondie! ("Dagwood": Arthur Lake)

Blondie in the Dough
1947   Columbia
Good-bye. ("Blondie": Penny Singleton)

Blondie Meets the Boss
1939   Columbia
I wish they would make up their minds around here. ("Baby Dumpling": Larry Simms)

Blondie on a Budget
1940   Columbia
Oh, I give up. ("Mailman": Irving Bacon)

Blondie Plays Cupid
1940   Columbia
Those papers never get anything right. It's her tail. ("Baby Dumpling": Larry Simms)

Blondie's Big Deal
1949   Columbia
Darling, you made it. ("Blondie": Penny Singleton)

Blondie's Hero
1950   Columbia
Dagwood! ("Blondie": Penny Singleton)

Blondie's Reward
1948   Columbia
The first day you'll varnish the living

room. The second day you'll varnish our bedroom. The third day you'll varnish the children's room. And the fourth day you'll varnish the hallway. And the fifth day . . . ("Blondie": Penny Singleton)

Blood and Sand
1941   20th Century–Fox
Manolo's the greatest of the great! The first man of the world! ("Natalio Curro": Laird Cregar)

Blood of Heroes
1990   New Line
Walk, slowly. ("Sallow": Rutger Hauer)

Blood on the Moon
1948   RKO
Well, I guess Kris was right. This is a special occasion. Come on. ("John Lufton": Tom Tully)

Blood on the Sun
1945   United Artists
Sure, forgive your enemies, but first get even. ("Nick Condon": James Cagney)

Blood Simple
1983   Circle
Well, ma'am, if I see him, I'll sure give him the message. ("Private Detective Visser": M. Emmet Walsh)

Bloodfist
1989   Concorde
I thought you were. ("Kwong": Joe Mari Avellana)

Blow Out
1981   Filmways

It's a good scream. It's a good scream. ("Jack": John Travolta)

Blue City
1986   Paramount
But I'm a hungry man, Billy, you know that. Now come on, give up. You know I gotta have it all. ("Luther Reynolds": Paul Winfield)

Blue Hawaii
1961   Paramount
Um, here they come. ("Fred Gates": Roland Winters)

The Blue Iguana
1988   Paramount
Even after settling on fifty percent, Yano complained about the name for days. We couldn't agree so we left it as it was, the Blue Iguana. Funny thing is Yano was right about Diablo becoming the next big thing. Six months later they built a Club Med right next door. ("Dylan McDermott": Vince Holloway)

The Blue Lagoon
1980   Columbia
No, sir, they're asleep. (A sailor)

The Blue Max
1966   20th Century–Fox
We'll be late for lunch. ("Count von Klugermann": James Mason)

Blue Skies
1946   Paramount
I'll try. ("Johnny Adams": Bing Crosby)

Blue Skies Again
1983   Warner Brothers

Come on, Wallstreet, bring me home! ("Paula": Robyn Barto)

Blue Thunder
1983   Columbia
The five-million-dollar prototype was utterly destroyed when Officer Murphy, his gasoline supply exhausted, set the helicopter down in the tracks directly in front of a southbound freight train. That was the end of the special helicopter but not the end of this story. On the strength of a tape which Officer Murphy delivered to this reporter earlier today the mayor has reopened the investigation into the death of Councilwoman Diana McNeely, which might also be connected with the death of Officer Richard Lymangood of the Astro Division. Half a dozen members of the local police department and several government officials of both the State and the Justice Departments have been detained for questioning. Coming up, the weather and a sneak preview of a Japanese bullet train soon to be seen in the Southland, maybe. (Mario Machado, as himself)

The Bob Mathias Story
1954   Allied Artists
A clean sweep for the United States provides a precious nineteen points, putting the Americans ahead in the team scores. With this victory, Bob Mathias joins the sports immortals, the only man to win the Olympic decathlon twice. Honored in sports as a champion, he seeks further honor in accepting the responsibilities of his time and his generation. This is the kind of a boy a small town in America produced. (Narrator)

Body Chemistry
1990   Concorde
I love you. ("Claire Archer": Lisa Pescia)

Body Heat
1981 Warner Brothers
Yes. ("Matty Walker": Kathleen Turner)

Body Slam
1987   DEG
Put your belts on. You did it. You did it. (Spectator at wrestling match)

The Bonfire of the Vanities
1990   Warner Brothers
This is Sherman, who started with so much, lost everything, but he gained his soul. Whereas I, you see, who started with so little, gained everything. But what does it profit a man if he gains the whole world and loses? Ah, well, there are compensations. ("Peter Fallow": Bruce Willis)

Bonjour Tristesse
1957   Columbia
Good night, Raymond. ("Cecile": Jean Seberg)

Bonnie and Clyde
1967   Warner Brothers
Hey. ("Clyde Barrow": Warren Beatty)

Boom Town
1940   MGM
Kettleman Hills? Doesn't even sound like oil. ("Luther Alrich": Frank Morgan)

Boomerang
1947   20th Century-Fox

The case was never solved and within twenty-four hours, John Waldren was once again a free man. The case is still open on the police books of a Connecticut city. And it may interest you to know that there are those who still believe the accused man was guilty. It may interest you, too, to know that the man we have depicted for you as state's attorney Harvey was actually a Connecticut lawyer named Homer Cummings. He did not become governor of the state. He rose instead to one of the highest legal positions in the land, Attorney General of the United States. (Narrator)

The Boost
1988 Hemdale
Till I fall off the earth. ("Linda": Sean Young)

Boots Malone
1952 Columbia
Tell him I'll be there in a half an hour. Better make it six months. ("Boots Malone": William Holden)

Born Free
1965 Columbia
We saw her many times again, born free and living free. But to us, she was always the same, our friend Elsa. ("Joy Adamson": Virginia McKenna)

Born in East L.A.
1987 Universal
Go, Raiders. (One of the "What's Happening Boys")

Born on the Fourth of July
1989 Universal

Welcome home, Ronnie! (Attendee at speech)

Born to Dance
1936 MGM
I'll see ya in four years. ("Jenny Saks": Una Merkel)

Born Yesterday
1950 Columbia
Look it up. ("Billie Dawn": Judy Holliday)

Botany Bay
1952 Paramount
I won't. ("Hugh Tallant": Alan Ladd)

The Bottom of the Bottle
1956 20th Century–Fox
He's my brother. ("P.M.": Joseph Cotten)

Bound for Glory
1976 United Artists
I hate a song makes you think that you're not any good. I hate a song makes you think you're just born to lose, bound to lose, no good to nobody, no good for nothing. Because you're either too old or too young or too fat or too thin, you're too ugly or too dead to do that. Songs that run you down, songs that poke fun at you on account of your bad luck or your hard traveling. I am out to fight those kind of songs to my very last breath of air, to my last drop of blood. I'm out to sing songs that will prove to you that this is your world, and it has kicked you pretty hard and knocked you down for a dozen loops. No matter how hard it brung you down and rolled over you, no matter what color,

what size you are, how you're built. I am out to sing the songs that will make you take pride in yourself. ("Woody Guthrie": David Carradine)

The Bounty
1984   Orion
My lord. Thank you. ("Captain Bligh": Anthony Hopkins)

Boxcar Bertha
1972   American International
No, don't take him. Don't, take him. No. No. No. ("Bertha": Barbara Hershey)

Boy, Did I Get a Wrong Number
1966   United Artists
Yoo-hoo. If you're lookin' for another bubble girl, I'm ready. ("Lily": Phyllis Diller)

The Boy in Blue
1986   20th Century–Fox
You take the two on the left. ("Bill": David Naughton)

Boy's Night Out
1962   MGM
Isn't it amazing how much postgraduate work goes on in this town? ("Cathy": Kim Novak)

Boys Town
1938   MGM
There is no bad boy. ("Father Flanagan": Spencer Tracy)

Brain Damage
1988   Palisades
Brian! ("Mike": Gordon MacDonald)

Branded
1950   Paramount
Adios, amigo. ("Choya": Alan Ladd)

The Brasher Doubloon
1947   20th Century–Fox
I've got a feeling you're going to graduate with honors. ("Philip Marlowe": George Montgomery)

The Brass Bottle
1964   Universal
I'm looking forward to a long and happy association, my son. ("Fakrash": Burl Ives)

The Brass Legend
1956   United Artists
You'll be riding him soon. ("Wade Adams": Hugh O'Brian)

The Bravados
1958   20th Century–Fox
Thank you. And in your prayers, please. ("Jim Douglas": Gregory Peck)

Breakfast at Tiffany's
1961   Paramount
Cat! Cat! Oh, cat. ("Holly Golightly": Audrey Hepburn)

The Breakfast Club
1985   Universal
And a criminal. Does that answer your question? Sincerely yours, the Breakfast Club. ("Brian Johnson": Anthony Michael Hall)

Breakheart Pass
1975   United Artists
Your father's waiting for you out there. ("John Deakin": Charles Bronson)

Breaking Away
1979 20th Century–Fox
Bon jour, papa. ("Dave Stohler": Dennis Christopher)

Breaking In
1989 Goldwyn
You learn by doing, that's wisdom, Mike, that's beautiful. Beautiful. ("Mike's Prison Buddy": Jack Esformes)

Breakout
1975 Columbia
OK. ("Myrna": Sheree North)

Breathless
1983 Orion
Breathless. ("Jesse Lujack": Richard Gere)

Breezy
1973 Universal
A year. Just, just, just think of it, Frank, a whole year. ("Breezy": Kay Lenz)

The Bride Goes Wild
1948 MGM
Don't worry about a thing. Don't worry. ("'Pop'": Lloyd Corrigan)

The Bride of Frankenstein
1935 Universal
Oh, darling, darling. ("Henry Frankenstein": Colin Clive)

The Bridge on the River Kwai
1957 Columbia
Madness. Madness. ("Maj. Clipton": James Donald)

The Bridges at Toko-Ri
1954 Paramount
Launch jets. (Ship's crewmember)

Brigadoon
1954 MGM
You should not be too surprised. I told you if you love someone deeply enough anything is possible, even miracles. ("Mr. Lundie": Barry Jones)

Bright Leaf
1950 Warner Brothers
If we had it to do all over again, I wouldn't ask. Good-bye, Carpetbagger. If it means anything to you, the worst mistake I made was you. ("Brant Royle": Gary Cooper)

Bright Lights, Big City
1988 MGM/UA
It's six a.m. on the island of Manhattan. In the dawn's early light you can imagine the first ship from the Old World sailing slowly up the biggest river they had ever seen. That was almost how you felt the first time you saw the city from the window of a Greyhound. Like you were looking at a new world waiting to be discovered. And that's how it looks to you now. But you have to go slowly. You'll have to learn everything all over again. ("Jamie Conway": Michael J. Fox)

Bright Road
1953 MGM
I love you. ("C. T. Young": Philip Hepburn)

Bright Victory
1951 Universal
I want to be. Hey, come on inside, we'll get some seats. You know, Joe,

the most wonderful thing happened to me today – I gotta tell you about it. As a matter of fact, it was two things. ("Larry Nevins": Arthur Kennedy)

Brighton Beach Memoirs
1986 Universal
October the second, nineteen thirty-seven, an historic moment in the life of Eugene Morris Jerome. I have just seen the golden palace of the Himalayas. Puberty is over. Onwards and upwards. ("Eugene": Johnathan Silverman)

The Brighton Strangler
1945 RKO
Yes, darling, the play is ended. ("Dorothy": Rose Hobart)

British Intelligence
1940 Warner Brothers
I wish I were able to answer that question. We want to help humanity. We fight wars only because we crave peace so ardently. And we pray that each war will be the last. But always in the strange scheme of things some maniac with a lust for power arises and in one moment destroys the peace and tranquility we've created through the years. We hate war, we despise it. But when war comes we must and will fight on and on. ("James Yeats": Leonard Mudie)

Broadcast News
1987 20th Century–Fox
Great. ("Jane Craig": Holly Hunter)

Broadway to Hollywood
1933 MGM
Papa. ("Lulu Hackett": Alice Brady)

Broken Arrow
1950 20th Century–Fox
His words meant very little to me then, but as time passed I came to know that the death of Sonseeahray had put a seal upon the peace. And from that day on wherever I went, in the cities, among the Apaches, in the mountains, I always remembered, my wife was with me. ("Tom Jeffords": James Stewart)

Broken Lance
1954 20th Century–Fox
I know he would. ("Joe Devereaux": Robert Wagner)

Bronco Billy
1980 Warner Brothers
I've got a special message for you little partners out there. I want you to finish your oatmeal at breakfast and do as your mom and pa tell you because they know best. Don't ever tell a lie and say your prayers at night before you go to bed. And so as our friends south of the border say, adios, amigos. ("Bronco Billy": Clint Eastwood)

The Brothers Karamazov
1958 MGM
Oh, Father, how proud I am of you – how proud. ("Illusha Snegiryov": Miko Oscard)

The Brothers Rico
1957 Columbia
Oh, yeah. ("Eddie Rico": Richard Conte)

Brubaker
1980 20th Century–Fox

What the hell? ("Rory Poke": Albert Salmi)

Brute Force
1947   Universal
But they learn, they must. Nobody escapes. Nobody ever really escapes. ("Dr. Walters": Art Smith)

The Buccaneer
1937   Paramount
You are a funny one, eh. ("Jean Lafitte": Fredric March)

Buck and the Preacher
1971   Columbia
I run out. ("Preacher": Harry Belafonte)

Buck Benny Rides Again
1940   Paramount
Good-bye, Mr. Chips. ("Rochester": Eddie Anderson)

Buddy, Buddy
1981   MGM/UA
We don't have to be that neat. ("Trabucco": Walter Matthau)

The Buddy Holly Story
1978 Columbia
Come on. Remember, we'll see you next year. ("Buddy Holly": Gary Busey)

Buffalo Bill
1944   20th Century–Fox
And God bless you, too, Buffalo Bill. (Child in gallery)

Bulldog Drummond
1929   United Artists
My dear girl, why haven't you said that before? ("Bulldog Drummond": Ronald Colman)

Bulletproof
1987   CineTel
Well, uh, yeah, it's right behind me. ("Lt. Devon Shepard": Darlanne Fluegel)

Bundle of Joy
1956   RKO
Dan, those are the first true words that have passed your lips in the last twenty-four hours. ("J. B. Merlin": Adolphe Menjou)

Bunny Lake Is Missing
1965 Columbia
Sleep well. Both of you. Now that you exist. ("Newhouse": Laurence Olivier)

The 'Burbs
1989   Universal
God, I love this street. ("Ricky Butler": Corey Feldman)

Bus Stop
1956   20th Century–Fox
'Bye, everybody, 'bye, 'bye. ("Cherie": Marilyn Monroe)

Buster
1988   Tri-Star
Dear, we know what dreaming did. ("June Edwards": Julie Walters)

But Not for Me
1959   Paramount
Maybe you're right. ("Russ": Clark Gable)

Butch and Sundance:
The Early Days

1979 20th Century–Fox
Son of a bitch, we're gonna be famous. ("Sundance Kid": William Katt)

Butch Cassidy and the Sundance Kid
1969 20th Century–Fox
Oh, good. For a moment I thought we were in trouble. ("Butch Cassidy": Paul Newman)

Butterfield 8
1960 MGM
Emily, I'm going out looking for my pride alone and when I find it, if you're here, I'll come back, and we'll see if it still has any value to either of us. ("Weston Liggett": Laurence Harvey)

Bye Bye Birdie
1963 Columbia
'Bye now. ("Kim McAfee": Ann-Margret)

Cabaret
1972 Allied Artists
Where are your troubles now? Forgotten. I told you so. We have no troubles here. Here life is beautiful. The girls are beautiful. Even the orchestra is beautiful. ("Master of Ceremonies": Joel Grey)

Cabin in the Cotton
1932 Warner Brothers
Thank you, Mr. Neal. ("Marvin": Richard Barthelmess)

Cactus Flower
1969 Columbia
Sorry, miss, but Doctor Winston doesn't do that sort of work anymore. ("Toni Simmons": Goldie Hawn)

The Caddy
1953 Paramount
Yeah, Jer. ("Joe Anthony": Dean Martin)

Caddyshack
1980 Orion
Hey, everybody, we're all gonna get laid. ("Al Czervik": Rodney Danger-field)

Caddyshack II
1988 Warner Brothers
Todd, Todd. Oh, drat, I, I guess this means you won't be going to Bunny Schuyler's brunch. ("Harry": Jonathan Silverman)

Caesar and Cleopatra
1946 United Artists
Hail Caesar and farewell. (Roman soldiers)

Cafe Metropole
1937 20th Century–Fox
Get out your checkbook, Joe. Here we go again. ("Margaret Ridgeway": Helen Westley)

Caged
1950 Warner Brothers
Keep it active. She'll be back. ("Ruth Benton": Agnes Moorehead)

Calamity Jane
1953 Warner Brothers
Well, that's in case any more actresses roll in from Chicago. ("Calamity Jane": Doris Day)

California Suite
1978   Columbia
Oh, Sidney, let's get off. Tell them to let us off this bloody plane. ("Diana Barrie": Maggie Smith)

Call Me Bwana
1963   United Artists
You're wrong, he's adopted. ("Matt Merriwether": Bob Hope)

Call Northside 777
1948   20th Century–Fox
It's a good world outside. ("Frank Wiecek": Richard Conti)

Call of the Wild
1935   20th Century–Fox
I won it in a crap game. ("'Shorty' Hoolihan": Jack Oakie)

Callaway Went Thataway
1951   MGM
Callaway went thataway. ("Deborah Patterson": Dorothy McGuire)

Camille
1936   MGM
Marguerite, no. No, don't leave me. Marguerite, come back, come back. ("Armand": Robert Taylor)

The Camp on Blood Island
1958   Columbia
It's going to take even more courage for him to live with it. ("Dawes": Edward Underdown)

Cancel My Reservation
1972   Warner Brothers
Never mind, we'll walk. ("Dan Bartlett": Bob Hope)

The Candidate
1972   Warner Brothers
What do we do now? ("Bill McKay": Robert Redford)

Candleshoe
1977   Buena Vista
Perhaps she has. ("Lady St. Edmund": Helen Hayes)

Candy
1968   Cinerama
My God! It's Daddy! Dad! ("Candy": Ewa Aulin)

Cannery Row
1982   MGM/UA
The party didn't slow down till dawn. The crew of San Pedro tuna boat showed up about one and was routed. The police came by at two and stayed to join the party. Mack used their squad car to go get more wine. A woman called the police to complain about the noise and couldn't get anybody. The crew of the tuna boat came back about three and was welcomed with open arms. The police reported their own car stolen and found it later on the beach. Things were finally back to normal in Cannery Row. Once again the world was spinning in greased grooves. (Narrated by John Huston)

Can't Buy Me Love
1987   Buena Vista
Definitely. ("Cindy Mancini": Amanda Peterson)

The Canterville Ghost
1943   MGM
I shall be seven in May. ("Lady Jessica de Canterville": Margaret O'Brien)

Cape Fear
1962 Universal
No. No. That would be letting you off too easy, too fast. Your words, do you remember? I do. No. We're gonna take good care of you, gonna nurse you back to health. You're strong, Cady. You're gonna live a long life. In a cage. That's where you belong. That's where you're going. And this time for life. Bang your head against the walls. Count the years, the months, the hours. Until the day you rot. ("Sam Bowden": Gregory Peck)

Caprice
1967 20th Century-Fox
Do you promise to give up all women, exept me? ("Patricia Fowler": Doris Day)

Captain Blood
1936 Warner Brothers
Good morning, uncle. ("Dr. Peter Blood": Errol Flynn)

Captain Carey, U.S.A.
1950 Paramount
Oh, Giulia, Giulia, don't make it too long. ("Webster Carey": Alan Ladd)

Captain Horatio Hornblower
1951 Warner Brothers
Come now. Up. Up. ("Horatio Hornblower": Gregory Peck)

Captain Kidd
1945 United Artists
It shall be a wedding gift to you from the crown, for your loyalty and service to king and country. ("King William III": Miles Mander)

Captain Newman, M.D.
1963 Universal
Everybody sing! ("Cpl. Jackson Laibowitz": Tony Curtis)

Captains Courageous
1937 MGM
Phineas Sawyer. ("Priest": Jack LaRue)

The Captain's Paradise
1953 British Lion
Muchas gracias. ("Capt. Henry St. James": Alec Guinness)

Carbon Copy
1981 Avco Embassy
Hey, I almost forgot, uh, this picture of Mom. I think she'd like you to have it. ("Roger": Denzel Washington)

Career
1959 Paramount
Yes. Yes, it was worth it. ("Sam Lawson": Anthony Franciosa)

Carmen Jones
1954 20th Century-Fox
You tramp. You're no good. You never were. Two-timing me like it don't count for nothin'. Well, it does. You ain't never going to do that to no man again. ("Joe": Harry Belafonte)

Carnal Knowledge
1971 Avco Embassy
I don't mean weak kind the way so many men are. I mean the kindness that comes from enormous strength, from an inner power so strong that every act no matter what is more proof of that power. That's what all women resent. That's why they try

to cut you down. Because your knowledge of yourself and them is so right, so true that it exposes the lies which they, every scheming one of them, live by. It takes a true woman to understand that the purest form of love is to love a man who denies himself to her, a man who inspires worship because he has no need for any woman, because he has himself. And who is better, more beautiful, more powerful, more perfect. You're getting hard. More strong, more masculine, more extraordinary, more robust. It's rising, it's rising. More virile, more domineering, more irresistible. It's up. It's in the air. ("Louise": Rita Moreno)

Carnival Story
1954   RKO
Poor Groppo. ("Willie": Anne Baxter)

Carousel
1956   20th Century–Fox
I loved you, Julie. Know that. I loved you. ("Billy": Gordon MacRae)

The Carpetbaggers
1964   Paramount
And so ended the Jonas Cord legend, leaving its aspirations and its scars on those who lived under his creative genius, as well as his tyranny. (Narrator)

Casablanca
1942   Warner Brothers
Louis, I think this is the beginning of a beautiful friendship. ("Richard 'Rick' Blaine": Humphrey Bogart)

Casanova Brown
1944   RKO
Don't you worry. I'll, I'll teach you, Mama. ("Casanova Brown": Gary Cooper)

Casanova's Big Night
1954   Paramount
What's the matter with this theater, don't they sell popcorn? ("Pippo Popolino": Bob Hope)

The Case of the Black Cat
1936   Warner Brothers
No, but it's a very good idea. ("Perry Mason": Ricardo Cortez)

The Case of the Curious Bride
1935   Warner Brothers
You're so wonderful. If only you couldn't cook. ("Della Street": Claire Dodd)

Cash McCall
1960   Warner Brothers
I knew there was something I forgot. ("Cash McCall": James Garner)

Cass Timberlane
1947   MGM
Oh, darling. ("Virginia Marshland": Lana Turner)

Castaway
1986   United British
Right, let's work. ("Gerald Kingsland": Oliver Reed)

The Castaway Cowboy
1974   Buena Vista
Well, can't think of any reason why not. Throw your loop. ("Lincoln Costain": James Garner)

Castle in the Desert
1942   20th Century–Fox
Oh! Oh! Number Two son hot again. Water. Water. ("Charlie Chan": Sidney Toler)

Castle on the Hudson
1940   Warner Brothers
Yes. ("Warden Long": Pat O'Brien)

Casualties of War
1989   Columbia
It's over now, I think. . . . (Girl on bus)

The Cat and the Canary
1939   Paramount
Oh, that's funny, she says that's the eraser she use – huh – what? ("Wally Campbell": Bob Hope)

Cat Ballou
1965   Columbia
Yahoo! ("Clay Boone": Michael Callan)

Cat on a Hot Tin Roof
1958   MGM
Maggie, we're through with lies and liars in this house. Lock the door. ("Brick Pollitt": Paul Newman)

Catch 22
1970   Paramount
Jump! ("Chaplain Tappman": Anthony Perkins)

Catherine the Great
1934   United Artists
He always called me Little Catherine. ("Catherine II": Elisabeth Bergner)

Cattle King
1963   MGM

All right. We got a ranch to run. ("Sam Brassfield": Robert Taylor)

Cause for Alarm
1951   MGM
And then I knew what people meant when they said their heart was broken. All that was left of George and me and our marriage was that little pile of ashes. I knew that some way or somehow I had to begin to live again. But right then, all I could do was pray to lose that one day, that one terrifying day. ("Ellen Jones": Loretta Young)

Caveman
1981   United Artists
Atouk. ("Tala": Shelley Long)

Chain Lightning
1950   Warner Brothers
Well, there I was up sixty thousand feet. It was the quickest way to get down to you. ("Matt Brennan": Humphrey Bogart)

The Chairman
1969   20th Century–Fox
I'm here. ("Kay Hanna": Anne Heywood)

Challenge to Lassie
1949   MGM
She's well and comfortable and the lord promised. ("Sergeant Davie": Reginald Owen)

The Champ
1931   MGM
Oh, sonny, you'll be all right. ("Linda": Irene Rich)

The Champ
1979   MGM
T. J. ("Annie": Faye Dunaway)

Champion
1949   United Artists
He was a champion. He went out like a champion. He was a credit to the fight game to the very end. ("Connie Kelly": Arthur Kennedy)

Champions
1984   Embassy
Bob! Bob! ("Jo Beswick": Jan Francis)

Chances Are
1989   Tri-Star
Dearly beloved, we have come together in the presence of God to witness and bless. . . . ("Second Minister": Dennis Mancini)

Chapter Two
1979   Columbia
Not that Walter's features were awesome by any means. He had the sort of powder-puff eyes that. . . . ("George Schneider": James Caan)

Charade
1963   Universal
Well, before you start them, may I have the stamps? ("Peter Joshua": Cary Grant)

Chariots of Fire
1981   20th Century–Fox
He ran them off their feet. ("Aubrey Montague": Nicholas Farrell)

Charley and the Angel
1974   Buena Vista
Oh, uh, I was just waving good-bye to summer, Rupe. I'll bet this is one we'll never forget. ("Charley Appleby": Fred MacMurray)

Charley's Aunt
1930   Columbia
Oh! Oh! I hate you! I hate you! I hate you! ("Ela Delahay": Flora Le Breton)

Charlie Chan at the Circus
1936   20th Century–Fox
Maybe more later. ("Charlie Chan": Warner Oland)

Charlie Chan in the Secret Service
1944   Monogram
From my last employer? Are you kidding? ("Birmingham Brown": Manton Moreland)

Charlie Chan's Murder Cruise
1940   20th Century–Fox
You said it, Pop. ("Jimmy Chan": Sen Yung)

Charlie Chan's Secret
1936   20th Century–Fox
If family continue to increase, may consider generous offer. ("Charlie Chan": Warner Oland)

Charly
1968   Cinerama
Good night. ("Charly Gordon": Cliff Robertson)

The Chase
1966   Columbia
My son died at five o'clock. ("Val Rogers": E. G. Marshall)

Chato's Land
1972   United Artists

We shouldn't take the risk. ("Gavin Malechie": Roddy McMillan)

Cheaper by the Dozen
1950   20th Century–Fox
Yes, Dad, Galbraith and Company will go on. Mother and your even dozen will see to that. Mother will go to Europe and you'll be proud of the way she delivers those speeches for you. And she'll go right on following in your footsteps to become the foremost woman industrial engineer in the world. And by nineteen forty-eight America's woman of the year. But wherever you are, Dad, somehow I'm sure you know that, and never doubted it for a moment. ("Ernestine": Barbara Bates)

Cherry 2000
1988   Orion
Pretty. ("Cherry": Pamela Gidley)

The Cheyenne Social Club
1970   National General
I'm telling you, just leave me alone, Harley, that's all. You can wear a man down to nothing. ("John O'Hanlan": James Stewart)

Children of a Lesser God
1986   Paramount
I don't want to be without you either. Do you think that we could find a place where we can meet, not in silence and not in sound? ("James Leeds": William Hurt)

The Children's Hour
1961   United Artists
Good-bye, Martha. I'll miss you with all my heart. ("Karen Wright": Audrey Hepburn)

Child's Play
1988   MGM/UA
Andy, come on, we're going to go to the hospital with Mike. Let's go. ("Karen Barclay": Catherine Hicks)

China Girl
1943   20th Century–Fox
Well, we got that one, China Girl. ("Johnny Williams": George Montgomery)

China Seas
1935   MGM
Perhaps not, Mr. Kingston, but whatever it is he has, he gets things done. ("Sir Guy Wilmerding": C. Aubrey Smith)

The China Syndrome
1979   Columbia
The Sharp Carousel. It turns the food so you don't have to. (Voice in commercial)

Chinatown
1974   Paramount
All right, come on, clear the area. On the sidewalk. On the sidewalk. Get off the street. Get off the street. ("Escobar": Perry Lopez)

The Chinese Ring
1947   Monogram
However, man who ride on merry-go-round all the time sooner or later must catch brass ring. ("Charlie Chan": Roland Winters)

Chisum
1970   Warner Brothers
Not in this house. ("Sallie Chisum": Pamela McMyler)

The Chocolate War
1988 MCEG
I don't know what you're always complaining about. ("Obie": Doug Hutchison)

A Chorus Line
1985 Embassy
You know, you can get arrested for wearing those colors. ("Zack": Michael Douglas)

The Chosen
1978 American International
Exactly on my thirty-third birthday. ("Angel": Simon Ward)

Christine
1983 Columbia
God, I hate rock and roll. ("Leigh Cabot": Alexandra Paul)

A Christmas Carol
1938 MGM
God bless us, every one. ("Tiny Tim": Terry Kilburn)

Cimarron
1961 MGM
Yancey. ("Sabra Cravet": Maria Schell)

Cinderella Liberty
1973 20th Century–Fox
Get outa here. ("John Baggs, Jr.": James Caan)

Circle of Iron
1979 Avco Embassy
Everything. ("Cord": Jeff Cooper)

Cisco Pike
1971 Columbia

It's a set-up. I know a set-up when I see one. ("Officer Leo Holland": Gene Hackman)

The Citadel
1938 MGM
I do, sir. I am supposed to have done something infamous by assisting Stillman, an unregistered man and probably the best man in the world on this type of case. I ask you, gentlemen, is it infamous for a doctor to be directly instrumental in saving a human life? Gentlemen, it's high time we started putting our house in order. We're everlastingly saying we'll do things and we don't. Doctors have to live but they have a responsibility to mankind, too. If we go on trying to make out that everything's all right inside the profession and everything's wrong outside, it'll be the death of scientific progress. I only ask you to remember the words of our own Hippocratic oath, "Into whatsoever houses I shall enter I will work for the benefit of the sick, holding aloof from all wrong and corruption." How many of us remember that? How many of us practice that? I have made mistakes, mistakes I bitterly regret, but Stillman isn't one of them. And if by what has been called my infamous conduct, I have done anything to benefit humanity, I am more than proud, gentlemen, I am profoundly grateful. Thank you, sir, for letting me speak. ("Dr. Andrew Manson": Robert Donat)

Citizen Kane
1941 RKO
Throw that junk. ("Raymond, Head Butler": Paul Stewart)

City Heat
1984 Warner Brothers
You'll always be Shorty to me. ("Lieutenant Speer": Clint Eastwood)

City of Shadows
1955 Republic
Big Tim has taught you a lot of things, but this you have to do yourself. ("Big Tim Channing": Victor McLaglen)

The Clan of the Cave Bear
1985 Warner Brothers
She had spoken out for Creb because she loved him. The sign had come. Finally she understood the vision. Durc was of the clan and one day he would be their leader. She must find her own people, she must walk alone. Everything she had lived through had prepared her for this journey and she was not afraid. For the first time Ayla felt the strength of her own spirit. ("Narrator": Salome Jens)

Clara's Heart
1988 Warner Brothers
Whether you see me the next time, or whether you ever see me again, you must know, David, that no matter where I am, for as long as I live, that I will carry you right here in my heart always. ("Clara Mayfield": Whoopi Goldberg)

Clarence, the Cross-Eyed Lion
1965 MGM
This is absolutely the end. ("Dr. Marsh Tracy": Marshall Thompson)

Clash by Night
1952 RKO
Go take your child home. ("Jerry D'Amato": Paul Douglas)

Clash of the Titans
1981 MGM/UA
Perseus and Andromeda will be happy together, have fine sons, rule wisely. And to perpetuate the story of his courage, I command that from henceforth he will be set among the stars and constellations. He, Perseus, the lovely Andromeda, the noble Pegasus, and even the vain Cassiopeia. Let the stars be named after them forever. As long as men shall walk the earth and search the night sky in wonder, they will remember the courage of Perseus forever. Even if we, the gods, are abandoned or forgotten, the stars will never fade, never. They will burn till the end of time. ("Zeus": Laurence Olivier)

Class of 1984
1982 Columbia
It's over, baby. It's all over now. ("Andy Norris": Perry King)

Clean and Sober
1988 Warner Brothers
So here we go, and thank you. And thanks for my chip. And thanks for not smoking. ("Daryl Poynter": Michael Keaton)

Cleopatra
1934 Paramount
Little Iras, Charmion, look well for love, look well. And not finding it, give nothing. But if left with Cleopatra's fortune, give all. Now go. ("Cleopatra": Claudette Colbert)

Clive of India
1934 20th Century–Fox

I beg of you, my lord, to convey my humble thanks to his majesty. ("Robert Clive": Ronald Colman)

Cloak and Dagger
1984   Universal
I don't need him anymore, I've got you, Dad. ("Davey Osborne": Henry Thomas)

The Clock
1945   MGM
See you soon. ("Alice Mayberry": Judy Garland)

A Clockwork Orange
1971   Warner Brothers
I was cured all right. ("Alex": Malcolm McDowell)

Close Encounters of the Third Kind
1977   Columbia
Good-bye. ("Barry Guiler": Cary Guffey)

The Clown
1952   MGM
He's dead. Dodo's dead. ("Dick Delwyn": Tim Considine)

Club Paradise
1986   Warner Brothers
What are you doing? What are you talking about? ("Barry": Rick Moranis)

Clue
1985   Paramount
They all did it. But if you want to know who killed Mr. Boddy, I did. In the hall with the revolver. OK, Chief, take them away. I'm going to go home and sleep with my wife. ("Mr. Green": Michael McKean)

Cluny Brown
1946   20th Century–Fox
Oh, Mr. Belinski! I don't think I'll have much time for plumbing. ("Cluny Brown": Jennifer Jones)

Cobra
1986   Warner Brothers
Catchy name, isn't it? ("Marion Cobretti": Sylvester Stallone)

Cocktail
1988   Buena Vista
Bar is open! ("Brian Flanagan": Tom Cruise)

The Cocoanuts
1929   Paramount
Hooray! (Spectators on balcony)

Cocoon
1985   20th Century–Fox
There can never be an accounting in human terms for the tragedy at sea which has taken the lives of these men and women in what should have been the beautiful and peaceful sunset of their lives. Do not fear. Your loved ones are in safekeeping. They have moved on to a higher expression of life, not life as we know it, but in the spirit everlasting. Our loved ones are in good hands for now and forever more. Join with me now in a moment of silent prayer. ("The Reverend": Harold Bergman)

Cocoon: The Return
1988   20th Century–Fox
A captain? ("Sara": Courteney Cox)

Code of Silence
1985 Orion
Yeah. ("Eddie Cusack": Chuck Norris)

Cold Feet
1989 Avenue
Well, that's the way the story should
end, but it doesn't. The hardest thing
for me to accept about all this is that
some people never change. The first
time we visited Monte in jail he
started raving about how our horse
was full of emeralds. I had to smile
and remember my father's warnings
about Monte, only he could come up
with such a story. I told him I got to
the slaughterhouse too late. But to
make him feel better of course I'd
send him the money we got paid for
the meat. As for our new extended
family, Rosemary's getting pretty
handy with the horses and I'm gain-
ing weight from not worrying. Laura
wakes in the middle of the night and
starts laughing for no reason. There's
nothing like a woman's laughter to
tell you you've done the right thing.
("Buck": Bill Pullman)

Cold Steel
1987 CineTel
I hate sushi. ("Kathy Connors":
Sharon Stone)

Cold Turkey
1970 United Artists
Mercury Missile Plant. (Crowd on
street)

Colonel Blimp
1945 United Artists
Sir? ("Johnny Cannon": Deborah
Kerr)

The Color of Money
1986 20th Century-Fox
Hey, I'm back. ("'Fast' Eddie Felson":
Paul Newman)

The Color Purple
1985 Warner Brothers
This is my sister. ("Sadie": Oprah
Winfrey)

Colorado Territory
1949 Warner Brothers
A happy couple who passed this way.
("Brother Tomas": Frank Puglia)

Colors
1988 Orion
There were these two, uh, bulls, standing on top of a mountain, and, uh uh,
looking down at a bunch of cows. And
then, uh, the older one says to the
younger one, no, the younger one, the
younger one says, "Hey, Pop, what
say we run down and fuck one of them
cows?" And, uh, and then the older
one says, "No, son, let's walk down
and fuck 'em all." ("Danny McGavin":
Sean Penn)

The Colossus of New York
1958 Paramount
Well, you were right, Carrington.
Without a soul there's nothing but
monstrousness. I only wish that
heaven and Jeremy could forgive me
for what I did. ("Dr. William Spens-
ser": Otto Kruger)

Comanche Station
1960 Columbia
Hello, sweetheart. ("Mr. Lowe": Dyke
Johnson)

Come Fill the Cup
1951   Warner Brothers
Don't you see, Mr. Ives, I am home.
("Lew Marsh": James Cagney)

Come Fly with Me
1962   MGM
First thing, mind you, if we get married I'll go to the president of the airline. If that man doesn't make you a captain, I'll give him such a blast. ("Carol Brewster": Pamela Tiffin)

Come Live with Me
1941   MGM
Hi ya, sucker. ("Bill Smith": James Stewart)

Come on Danger
1933   RKO
Well, good-b-b-b, good-b-b-b, uh, adios. ("Rusty": Roscoe Ates)

Come to the Stable
1949   20th Century–Fox
Oh, it will. And it will please God so much. ("Sister Margaret": Loretta Young)

Comes a Horseman
1978   United Artists
Cut the rope on my hands. ("Ella": Jane Fonda)

The Comic
1969   Columbia
Morning low clouds and light, hazy sunshine by mid-afternoon. The high today ought to be about eighty degrees, low tonight around sixty. The APCD predicts light smog in the basin. And now, you early bird fans, here's that treat I promised you the other day, a Billy Bright comedy. This one was made about, uh, well, way, way back in nineteen twenty-six, which is, uh, that's about three years before I was born. It's called "Forget-Me-Not." According to my notes this was Billy Bright's first full-length comedy. It featured Mary Gibson, and if I'm not mistaken Mary Gibson was Mrs. Billy Bright. Well, here now is the first act of your early bird feature, Billy Bright in "Forget-Me-Not" with Mary Gibson. (Television announcer)

Coming Home
1978   United Artists
And now I'm here to tell ya that I have killed for my country or whatever. And I don't feel good about it. Because there's not enough reason, man. But to feel a person die in your hands or to see your best buddy get blown away. I'm here to tell you, it's a lousy thing, man. I don't see any reason for it. There's a lot I did over there that I find hard to live with. And I don't want to see people like you, man, coming back and having to face the rest of your life with that kind of stuff. It's as simple as that. I don't feel sorry for myself. I'm a lot smarter now than when I went. And I'm just telling you there's a choice to be made here. ("Luke Martin": Jon Voight)

Coming to America
1988   Paramount
Nah. ("Lisa McDowell": Shari Headley)

Command Decision
1949   MGM
I already thought of that. ("Brigadier

General Clifton L. Garnet": Brian Donlevy)

Commando
1985 20th Century-Fox
No chance. ("Matrix": Arnold Schwarzenegger)

The Competition
1980 Columbia
Now, listen here, little one. It took nature about a million years to develop Grant's Gazelle. You've got about a century to wait before evolution produces the man you have in mind. So in the meantime, get out there and dance with what there is. ("Greta Vandemann": Lee Remick)

Compulsion
1959 20th Century-Fox
Are you sure, Judd? In those years to come you might find yourself asking if it wasn't the hand of God dropped those glasses and if he didn't, who did? ("Jonathan Wilk": Orson Welles)

Comrade X
1940 MGM
Uh-huh. The counter-revolution. ("Vanya": Felix Bressart)

Conan the Barbarian
1982 Universal
My child. You have come to me, my son. For who now is your father if he is not me, who gave you the will to live. I am the wellspring from which you flow. When I am gone, you will have never been. What will your world be without me, my son. My son. ("Thulsa Doom": James Earl Jones)

A Connecticut Yankee in King Arthur's Court
1949 Paramount
I'm glad you asked me. Won't you sit down. This may take a little time. ("Hank Martin": Bing Crosby)

The Conquerer
1955 RKO
So be it, my brother. ("Temujin": John Wayne)

The Conquerers
1932 RKO
We're both proud of him, aren't we, Carol? ("Roger Standish": Richard Dix)

Conrack
1974 20th Century-Fox
It hurts very bad to leave you. My prayer for ya is that the river is good to you in the crossing. ("Pat Conroy": Jon Voight)

Conspirator
1949 MGM
You know I will, Hugh, you know I will. ("Melinda Greyton": Elizabeth Taylor)

Consuming Passions
1988 Goldwyn
Yes, a bridal assortment, yes. ("Ian Littleton": Tyler Butterworth)

Continental Divide
1981 Universal
And I love us both. ("Souchak": John Belushi)

Cookie
1989 Warner Brothers

Eternal rest grant to him, oh, lord, and let perpetual light shine upon him. May he rest in peace. Amen. (Priest at funeral)

Cool Hand Luke
1967   Warner Brothers
That's right, you know, that, that, that Luke smile of his. He had it on his face right to the very end. Hell, if they didn't know it 'fore, they could tell right then that they weren't ever gonna beat him. That old Luke smile. Old Luke, he was some boy. Cool Hand Luke, hell, he's a natural-born world-shaker. ("Dragline": George Kennedy)

Cop
1988   Atlantic
Well, there's some good news and there's some bad news. The good news is you're right, I'm a cop, and I've gotta take you in. The bad news is I've been suspended and I don't give a fuck. ("Lloyd Hopkins": James Woods)

Cop-Out
1967   Cinerama
Those are the final words of, uh, *Crime and Punishment.* ("John Sawyer": James Mason)

Coroner Creek
1948   Columbia
I'm glad. ("Kate Hardison": Marguerite Chapman)

The Cotton Club
1984   Orion
Here's to a happy ending, Vera Cicero. ("Dixie Dwyer": Richard Gere)

The Couch Trip
1988   Orion
Becker, there are worse things than being crazy. ("John Burns": Dan Aykroyd)

Counterattack
1945   Columbia
No, no, no. I'm all right, Doc. I could walk out, and I could stay awake for weeks, for months. ("Alexei Kulkov": Paul Muni)

A Countess from Hong Kong
1967   Universal
See, you can't get rid of me. May I have this dance? ("Ogden Mears": Marlon Brando)

The Country Girl
1954   Paramount
Thanks, Larry. ("Bernie Dodd": William Holden)

Courage of Lassie
1946   MGM
Oh, Bill. ("Kathie Merrick": Elizabeth Taylor)

Courageous Dr. Christian
1940   RKO
There isn't even any smoke. ("Dr. Paul Christian": Jean Hersholt)

Court Martial
1955   British Lion
All right, I'll lodge my appeal. ("Maj. Carrington, V.C.": David Niven)

The Courtney Affair
1947   British Lion
Very nice. ("Sir Edward Courtney": Michael Wilding)

The Courtship of Eddie's Father
1962   MGM
Hello. ("Elizabeth Marten": Shirley Jones)

Cousins
1989   Paramount
What are you doing? What are you doing? Come on. ("Mitch Kozinski": Keith Coogan)

Cover Girl
1944   Columbia
Thank you, darling. Oh, oh, oh, thank you. ("Rusty Parker/Maribelle Hicks": Rita Hayworth)

Cowboy
1957   Columbia
Frank. ("Tom Reece": Glenn Ford)

The Cowboy and the Lady
1938   United Artists
Get! Get out! There's work to be done! Get! You think this is a hang out? Oh! Stretch Willoughby, that's my kitchen. ("Elly": Mabel Todd)

Crash Dive
1943   20th Century–Fox
I think so, sir. The PT boats are swell. They do a grand job, and they'll play their part in winning the war. But not without the submarines. They've got their job to do in all the seven seas, and, boy, how they're doing it. And the carriers that bring the planes that drop the bombs that sink the enemy ships. And the cruisers that protect the airplane carriers. And the battleships, the dreadnaughts and super dreadnaughts, the big shots of the fleet. They're in there punching too. They're all in there doing their job, working together. I found that out, sir. It isn't one branch of the service, it's all branches. And it isn't all ships, it's men. The men behind the guns of the PT boats and the submarines and the Coast Guard ships and the mine layers and the tenders and the tankers and the troop ships. The men that take them out, who fight their way over and land them there. That's the Navy. The United States Navy. ("Lt. Ward Stewart": Tyrone Power)

Crazy Moon
1987   Miramax
I love you too. ("Brooks": Kiefer Sutherland)

Creator
1985   Universal
I'm going to be a father! ("Harry": Peter O'Toole)

Creature from the Black Lagoon
1954   Universal
No. ("David Reed": Richard Carlson)

The Creeping Flesh
1972   Columbia
Help me. Help me. Please help me. ("Immanuel Hildern": Peter Cushing)

Creepshow
1982   United Film Distribution
Ready for another shot, Doc? ("Billy": Joe King)

Creepshow 2
1987   New World
Venus flytraps, giant venus flytraps. They eat meat. (Animated character)

Crime School
1938   Warner Brothers
Yeah, you, no, I'm gonna be the best man. You can be second best. You be a nothing. ("Frankie Warren": Billy Halop)

Crimes and Misdemeanors
1989   Orion
We are all faced throughout our lives with agonizing decisions, moral choices. Some are on a grand scale, most of these choices are on lesser points. But we define ourselves by the choices we have made. We are in fact the sum total of our choices. Events unfold so unpredictably, so unfairly. Human happiness does not seem to have been included in the design of creation. It is only we, with our capacity to love, that give meaning to the indifferent universe. And yet most human beings seem to have the ability to keep trying and even to find joy from simple things, like their family, their work and from the hope that future generations might understand more. ("Professor Louis Levy": Martin Bergmann)

Crimes of the Heart
1986   DEG
Oh, how I do love birthday cake. ("Lenny Magrath": Diane Keaton)

Criminal Lawyer
1951   Columbia
I've waited five years. Now he can't wait five minutes. ("Maggie Powell": Jane Wyatt)

The Crimson Kimono
1959   Columbia

Thank you, dear boy, but I prefer something made by man to something made by an oyster. ("Mac": Anna Lee)

The Crimson Pirate
1952   Warner Brothers
Hold it, Professor! We've won! Get rid of that stuff! ("Vallo": Burt Lancaster)

Cripple Creek
1952   Columbia
Well, if we ever need one, we got a job. ("Larry Galland": Jerome Courtland)

Crisis
1950   MGM
Same old cry, down through the ages. Save me, doctor. Save me, anybody. ("Dr. Eugene Norland Ferguson": Cary Grant)

Criss Cross
1949   Universal
Anna. ("Steve Thompson": Burt Lancaster)

Critic's Choice
1963   Warner Brothers
Angie! ("Parker Ballantine": Bob Hope)

Crocodile Dundee
1986   Paramount
Oh, well, look out. ("Mick 'Crocodile' Dundee": Paul Hogan)

Crocodile Dundee II
1988   Paramount
I am home. ("Sue Charlton": Linda Kozlowski)

Cross Country Romance
1940 RKO
Four rabbits? ("Larry": Gene Raymond)

Cross Creek
1983 Universal
I had become a part of Cross Creek. I was more than a writer. I was a wife, a friend, a part of the earth. Who owns Cross Creek? The earth may be borrowed, not bought, may be used, not owned. It gives itself in response to love and tenderness, offers its seasonal flowering and fruiting. Cross Creek belongs to the wind and the rain, to the suns and seasons, to the cosmic secrecy of seed, and beyond all to time. ("Marjorie Kinnan Rawlings": Mary Steenburgen)

Cross My Heart
1987 Universal
Then come in. Come in. ("Kathy": Annette O'Toole)

The Cross of Lorraine
1944 MGM
Then we'll join General Cartier and fight. ("Victor": Gene Kelly)

Crossfire
1947 RKO
Sure. ("Leroy": William Phipps)

Crossing Delancey
1988 Warner Brothers
Take my arm, Sam. It's OK, you can touch me. A hundred and twenty pounds of pure gold, that's me. Come, children, come, let's put the Bubbie to bed. ("Bubbie Kantor": Reizl Bozyk)

Crossroads
1942 MGM
Remember? But darling, how can I? I have amnesia. ("David Talbot": William Powell)

Crosswinds
1951 Paramount
There goes the world, Mrs. Singleton. ("Steve Singleton": John Payne)

The Crusades
1935 Paramount
Oh, merciful God! ("Richard": Henry Wilcoxon)

Crusoe
1988 Island
I'd like to get some information about the cannibal's habits. I had thought, alongside the cannibal exhibit, you could lecture about your experiences on the island. ("Dr. Martin": Michael Higgins)

Cry-Baby
1990 Universal
Help me! ("Mrs. Vernon-Williams": Polly Bergen)

Cry for Happy
1961 Columbia
Look at this. Fellas, will you please try and.... Hey, take it easy now, come on, fellas. Will you please give me a hand here and be a little more quiet. Here we go. ("Andy Cyphers": Glenn Ford)

Cry Havoc
1943 MGM
Ready. ("Pat": Ann Sothern)

A Cry in the Dark
1988   Warner Brothers
Uh, I don't think a lot of people realize how important innocence is to innocent people. ("Michael Chamberlain": Sam Neill)

Cry of the Werewolf
1944   Columbia
You can tell your grandchildren about it, Ed. You can say, "I saw it with my own eyes." ("Lieutenant Barry Lane": Barton MacLane)

Cry Terror
1958   MGM
Don't go down there, there's a train due. You're gonna get killed. (Woman at subway station)

Crystal Heart
1987   New World
This is a song written for me by a friend of mine. Even though he's not, um, here tonight, I'd like to say thank you. ("Alley Daniels": Tawny Kitaen)

Cujo
1983   Warner Brothers
Donna? Donna? Donna! ("Vic Trenton": Daniel Hugh-Kelly)

Curly Top
1935   20th Century–Fox
Mary, do you mind if Uncle Edward could come now and read me the funnies? Oh, my word. ("Elizabeth Blair": Shirley Temple)

The Curse
1987   Trans World
Are you OK? ("Carl Willis": John Schneider)

The Curse of the Cat People
1944   RKO
I see her, too, darling. ("Kent Smith": Oliver Reed)

Curse of the Demon
1958   Columbia
You're right. Maybe it's better not to know. ("John Holden": Dana Andrews)

Curse of the Mummy's Tomb
1964   Columbia
Right, throw her the rope, Inspector, I'll go down. ("John Bray": Ronald Howard)

Cutting Class
1989   Gower Street
Shouldn't you be in school? You're not cutting class, I hope. ("William Carson, III": Martin Mull)

Cyborg
1989   Cannon
It's strange, but I feel he's the real cure for this world. ("Pearl Prophet": Dayle Haddon)

Cyborg 2087
1967   Feature Film Corporation of America
Those were the days. I should have been around eighty years ago. Now take Matt Dillon. There was a lawman who was alive in a time when things really happened. Nothing ever happens around here. Just a quiet, peaceful, little town. ("Sheriff": Wendell Corey)

D-Day, the Sixth of June
1956   20th Century–Fox

Thank you, doctor. ("Valerie": Dana Wynter)

D.O.A.
1988 Buena Vista
Just somebody's homework, that was all. ("Dexter Cornell": Dennis Quaid)

Dad
1989 Universal
Yeah, me too. ("Billy Tremont": Ethan Hawke)

Dakota
1988 Miramax
Sometimes a man has to go back to go forward. We watched him ride out that day chasing the great American race and a lonely driver named Charles Dakota. We had no doubts that he'd finish the course and win. ("Walt Lechner": Eli Cummins)

Damn the Defiant
1962 Columbia
Thank you, Mr. Crawford. ("Captain Crawford": Alec Guinness)

Damn Yankees
1958 Warner Brothers
Listen to me, you wife-loving louse. You belong to me. You sold me your soul. You can't run out on me like this. Ya thief. Ya crook. You robbed me, that's what you did. You robbed me. You robbed me. ("Applegate": Ray Walston)

Dancers
1987 Cannon
This is not funny, it's crazy. I even went to the church looking for you. I was sure you were dead. Where the hell were you? ("Anton": Mikhail Baryshnikov)

Dances with Wolves
1990 Orion
Sergeant! Over here! Now! (A soldier)

Dangerous
1935 Warner Brothers
Darling. Darling. Oh, darling. Oh, darling. ("Joyce Heath": Bette Davis)

Dangerous Curves
1988 Lightning
Oh, come here. ("Blake Courtland": Valerie Breiman)

Dangerous Liaisons
1988 Warner Brothers
Boo! (Opera audience)

Dangerous Mission
1954 RKO
Now there's an idea. ("Joe Parker": William Bendix)

Dangerously Close
1986 Cannon
Yeah, OK. ("Donny": J. Eddie Peck)

Dante's Inferno
1935 20th Century–Fox
Darling, that, that's all I ever wanted. ("Betty McWade": Claire Trevor)

Dark City
1950 Paramount
We've got other plans. ("Danny Haley": Charlton Heston)

Dark Command
1940 Republic

Shakespeare, huh? Why, he must have come from Texas. We been saying that down there for years. ("Bob Seton": John Wayne)

The Dark Past
1948   Columbia
All some of them need is a break. A little understanding and guidance, maybe we can salvage some of this waste. ("Dr. Andrew Collins": Lee J. Cobb)

Darling
1965   Embassy
I have a family now. That gives me all I could possibly want. ("Diana Scott": Julie Christie)

Date with an Angel
1987   DEG
Do you like it? Look at that. I got a leave of absence for good behavior. I guess he thought we could make some good music together. Jim, I'm starving. Do you feel well enough to take me out for some french fries? ("Angel": Emmanuelle Beart)

A Date with Judy
1948   MGM
I forgive you for everything. ("Judy Foster": Jane Powell)

David and Bathsheba
1951   20th Century–Fox
No man can ever hope to know the real nature of God, but he has given us a glimpse of his face. ("Nathan": Raymond Massey)

David and Lisa
1962   Continental

Take my hand. Lisa, take my hand. ("David": Keir Dullea)

A Day at the Races
1937   MGM
Emily, I have a little confession to make. I really am a horse doctor. But marry me and I'll never look at another horse. ("Dr. Hugo Z. Hackenbush": Groucho Marx)

A Day of Fury
1956   Universal
Where? ("Jagade": Dale Robertson)

Day of the Animals
1977   Film Ventures International
It's over. ("Terry Marsh": Lynda Day George)

The Day of the Dolphin
1973   Avco Embassy
Pa! (A dolphin)

The Day of the Locust
1975   Paramount
Tod, please! ("Faye Greener": Karen Black)

The Day the Earth Caught Fire
1961   Universal
And if there's a future for man, insensitive as he is, proud and defiant in his pursuit of power, let him resolve to live it lovingly, for he knows well how to do so. Then he may say once more, truly the light is sweet and what a pleasant thing it is for the eyes to see the sun. ("Peter Stenning": Edward Judd)

The Day the Earth Stood Still
1951 20th Century–Fox

Gort veracto. ("Klaatu": Michael Rennie)

Days of Heaven
1978   Paramount
This girl, she didn't know where she was going or what she was going to do. She didn't have no money on her. Maybe she'd meet up with a character. I was hoping things would work out for her. She was a good friend of mine. ("Linda": Linda Manz)

Days of Thunder
1990   Paramount
Walk, hell. I'll race you there. Let's go. ("Harry Hoggs": Robert Duvall)

Days of Wine and Roses
1962   Warner Brothers
Good night, honey. ("Joe": Jack Lemmon)

Dead Bang
1989   Warner Brothers
And there's more out there than death and taxes, a hell of a lot more. All you gotta do is give it half the chance. ("Chief Dixon": Tim Reid)

Dead Calm
1989   Warner Brothers
You know what I'd love for lunch? Fresh asparagus, then um pasta, angel hair pasta with heaps of basil, garlic, olive oil, and um, ah, apple pie, yeah. Uh, John, have you got the towel? ("Rae Engram": Nicole Kidman)

Dead End
1937   United Artists
That's right. That's it. ("T.B.": Gabriel Dell)

Dead Heat
1988   New World
This could be the end of a beautiful friendship. ("Roger": Treat Williams)

Dead Poets Society
1989   Buena Vista
Thank you, boys, thank you. ("John Keating": Robin Williams)

The Dead Pool
1988   Warner Brothers
Inspector, what happened here? Is this another hit attempt by Janero? Does it have anything to do with the Dead Pool case? ("Reporter at Pier": Martin Ganapoler)

Dead Ringer
1964   Warner Brothers
I'm Margaret De Lorca, Sergeant. As you said, Edie would never have hurt a fly. ("Margaret/Edith": Bette Davis)

Dead Ringers
1988   20th Century–Fox
Hello. Hello. Who is this? ("Claire Niveau": Genevieve Bujold)

Deadline at Dawn
1946   RKO
Home. ("June Goff": Susan Hayward)

The Deadly Affair
1966   Columbia
I have to tell you. ("Charles Dobbs": James Mason)

Deadly Blessing
1981   United Artists
The beast that thou sawest was and is not and shall ascend out of the bottomless pit and go into perdition, and

they that dwell on the earth shall wonder. ("Narrator": Percy Rodrigues)

Deadly Friend
1986   Warner Brothers
Baby. ("Samantha": Kristy Swanson)

Deadly Illusion
1987   CineTel
I never did like two-faced women. It's amazing how greed and growing old make people act strange. At least those are two things I'll never have to worry about. By the way, what the hell was in those green bottles? ("Hamberger": Billy Dee Williams)

Deal of the Century
1983   Warner Brothers
We make a really good team. I think I'll ask her to marry me tonight. Together, I don't see how we can miss. ("Eddie Muntz": Chevy Chase)

Dear Murderer
1947   Universal
Till death us do part. ("Vivien Warren": Greta Gynt)

Death Before Dishonor
1986   New World
Let's take him home, Gunny. ("Col. Halloran": Brian Keith)

Death on the Nile
1978   Paramount
The great ambition of women is to inspire love. ("Hercule Poirot": Peter Ustinov)

Death Takes a Holiday
1934   Paramount
Then there is love which casts out fear, and I have found it. And love is greater than illusion, and as strong as death. ("Prince Sirki [Shadow]": Fredric March)

Death Wish
1974   Paramount
Excuse me. ("Paul Kersey": Charles Bronson)

Death Wish 2
1981   Columbia
What else would I be doing? ("Paul Kersey": Charles Bronson)

Deathrow Gameshow
1987   Crown International
We've been asked to show you the gripping power of the new Acme chew-em-up tree shredder. ("Chuck Toedan": John McCafferty)

Decameron Nights
1952   RKO
Let me go. ("Fiametta": Joan Fontaine)

The Deep
1977   Columbia
David, here! ("Romer Treece": Robert Shaw)

Deep in My Heart
1954   MGM
This is the wonderful thing about music, it is never quite new and never quite the same. And just when you love it best, you think that you have heard it before. And who knows, maybe you have, deep in your heart. But here is a new one, at least I think so. You boys won't find parts for this

on your stands, so when you think you've got it, just join in. Do you know something else. I have never dedicated a song before, but tonight I feel like it. So this song is for my wife and of my wife and to my wife. Every word and every note is written in her image. And that is why we call it. . . . ("Sigmund Romberg": Jose Ferrer)

Deepstar Six
1989   Tri-Star
Thank you. ("McBride": Greg Evigan)

The Delicate Delinquent
1956   Paramount
Well, gentlemen, I suppose you're wondering why I've asked you here. Well, uh, let's put it this way. Your problems are um my problems. Artie, tell me something about yourself. What are you and what do you want to be? ("Sidney Pythias": Jerry Lewis)

Delightfully Dangerous
1945   United Artists
I think so. ("Josephine Williams": Constance Moore)

Demetrius and the Gladiator
1954   20th Century–Fox
Demetrius, my husband and I wish you good fortune. ("Messalina": Susan Hayward)

Demon Seed
1977   MGM
I'm alive. (The child)

The Denver and the Rio Grande
1952   Paramount
It's all right, forget it. We've still got a railroad to build. ("Jim Vesser": Edmond O'Brien)

Desert Bloom
1985   Columbia
Good morning, survivors, this is radio Keno, Las Vegas. Well, the A-bomb went off and we're all still here, folks. It's forty-seven degrees and six a.m. (Voice on radio)

The Desert Rats
1953   20th Century–Fox
So after two hundred and forty-two days ended the siege of Tobruk. Not the biggest action of the war and far from the last but one in which a sweating, dirty, hopelessly outnumbered garrison by its stubborn courage won for itself an unforgettable place in the world's history of battles. (Narrator)

The Desert Song
1953   Warner Brothers
You're sweet, Paul, I like you very much, but there'll never be anyone else. ("Margot Birabeau": Kathryn Grayson)

Desert Trail
1935   Monogram
Get outa here. I want this thing to be legal. ("John Scott": John Wayne)

Desire
1936   Paramount
Yes, sir. Gentlemen, if you please. ("Tom Bradley": Gary Cooper)

Desiree
1954   20th Century–Fox
Desiree. Our engagement. It wasn't only the dowry. Go along now before I repent. ("Napoleon Bonaparte": Marlon Brando)

The Desperados
1968   Columbia
David! ("Parson Josiah Galt": Jack Palance)

Destination Moon
1950   Universal
We're going home. ("Dr. Charles Cargraves": Warner Anderson)

Destination Tokyo
1943   Warner Brothers
To the United States Navy, our thanks for making this picture possible. To the gallant officers and men of the silent service, to our submarines now on war patrol in hostile waters, good luck and good hunting. ("Narrator": Lou Marcelle)

Destroyer
1943   Columbia
Come on, Dad, swagger. ("Mary Boleslavski": Marguerite Chapman)

Destry Rides Again
1939   Universal
I had a friend once down in Amarillo. ("Tom Destry": James Stewart)

Detour
1945   Producers Releasing Corp.
I keep trying to forget what happened and wonder what my life might have been if that car of Haskell's hadn't stopped. But one thing I don't have to wonder about, I know. Someday a car will stop to pick me up that I never thumbed. Yes, fate or some mysterious force can put the finger on you or me for no good reason at all. ("Al Roberts": Tom Neal)

The Devil and the Deep
1932   Paramount
Hey, taxi! ("Lt. Sempter": Gary Cooper)

The Devil to Pay
1930   United Artists
I won't. ("Dorothy Hope": Loretta Young)

Devil's Island
1939   Warner Brothers
Come along, darling. Good-bye. ("Dr. Charles Gaudet": Boris Karloff)

Dial M for Murder
1954   Warner Brothers
I suppose you're still on duty, Inspector? ("Tony Wendice": Ray Milland)

Diamond Head
1962   Columbia
Get some new stuff in here. None of this second-hand junk. After all, he is half a Howland. ("Richard Howland": Charlton Heston)

Diamonds Are Forever
1971   United Artists
James, how the hell do we get those diamonds down again? ("Tiffany Case": Jill St. John)

The Diary of Anne Frank
1959   20th Century–Fox
In spite of everything, I still believe that people are really good at heart. ("Anne Frank": Millie Perkins)

Dick Tracy
1990   Buena Vista
You know something, Tracy, I kind of like that dame. ("Kid": Charlie Korsmo)

Die Hard
1988 20th Century–Fox
If this is their idea of Christmas, I gotta be here for New Year's. ("Argyle": De'voreaux White)

A Different Story
1978 Avco
You son of a bitch, Albert. You son of a bitch. ("Stella": Meg Foster)

Dillinger
1945 Monogram
Articles. One nickel-plated watch. A wallet, seven dollars and twenty cents. (FBI Agent)

Dinner at Eight
1933 MGM
Oh, my dear, that's something you need never worry about. Say, I want to sit next to Oliver. Oliver, where are you now? ("Carlotta Vance": Marie Dressler)

Dinosaurus!
1960 Universal
I shouldn't be at all surprised. On a peaceful, quiet island like this, I don't suppose they've anything better to do. (Ship passenger)

Dirty Dancing
1987 Vestron
You looked wonderful out there. ("Jake Houseman": Jerry Orbach)

Dirty Dingus Magee
1970 MGM
Dingus! You dirty no-good-son of a . . . ! Dingus! ("Hoke": George Kennedy)

The Dirty Dozen
1967 MGM
Boy, oh, boy, oh, boy. Killing generals could get to be a habit with me. ("Joseph Wladislaw": Charles Bronson)

Dirty Harry
1971 Warner Brothers
I know what you're thinking, punk. You're thinking, "Did he fire six shots or only five?" You know, to tell you the truth I've forgotten myself in all this excitement. But being this is a forty-four magnum, the most powerful handgun in the world and will blow your head clean off, you gotta ask yourself a question, "Do I feel lucky?" Well, do ya, punk? ("Harry Callahan": Clint Eastwood)

Dirty Rotten Scoundrels
1988 Orion
Fellas, last year I made three million dollars, but your fifty thousand was the most fun. Are you ready? Then let's go get them. ("Janet Colgate": Glenne Headly)

Disorderlies
1987 Warner Brothers
OK, Buffy, hit it. ("Albert Dennison": Ralph Bellamy)

Disraeli
1929 Warner Brothers
Yeah. ("Disraeli": George Arliss)

Distant Thunder
1988 Paramount
Maybe you're right! Maybe everyone around you does die! ("Jack Lambert": Ralph Macchio)

Dive Bomber
1941 Warner Brothers

Thanks. Thanks, I would like to. ("Lieutenant Doug Lee": Errol Flynn)

The Divided Heart
1954   Republic
Ya, ya. ("Sonja": Yvonne Mitchell)

Divorce American Style
1967   Columbia
Will you do me a favor? Just tell me one thing, one thing. ("Richard Harmon": Dick Van Dyke)

The Divorcee
1930   MGM
I like that right arm. How about putting it around me. ("Jerry": Norma Shearer)

Do Not Disturb
1965   20th Century–Fox
Janet! It's me! ("Mike Harper": Rod Taylor)

Do the Right Thing
1989   Universal
Hey, Mook, it's the Mook man. I see you walkin' down the block. Go on home to your kids. Now the news and weather. Our mayor has commissioned a blue-ribbon panel and I quote, to get to the bottom of last night's disturbance. The city of New York will not let property be destroyed by anyone end quote. His honor plans to visit our block today. Maybe he should hook up with our own Da Mayor, buy him a beer. Your love daddy says register to vote. The election is coming up. There's no end in sight from this heat wave so today the cash money word is chill. That's right C-H-I-L-L. When you hear "chill" call in at 5-5-5-L-O-V-E,

and you'll win cash money, honey. This is Mister Senor Love Daddy coming at you from what's last on your dial but first in your hearts, and that's the quintessential truth, Ruth. The next record goes out to Radio Raheem. We love you, brother. ("Mister Senor Love Daddy": Sam Jackson)

The Doctor and the Devils
1985   Brooksfilm
My name is a ghost to frightened children. Did I set myself up as a god over death, did I set myself up over pity? Oh, my God, I knew what I was doing. ("Dr. Thomas Rock": Timothy Dalton)

Doctor at Sea
1956   Republic
There's a telegram. ("Simon Sparrow": Dirk Bogarde)

Doctor in Clover
1966   Rank
Matron, how would you suggest we get my pulse rate down? Shall we talk about it? ("Dr. Gaston Grimsdyke": Leslie Phillips)

Doctor in Distress
1963   Rank
Well, as a matter of fact, I'm waiting for you to drive me up to London, because by a fabulous coincidence I've got the evening off. ("Simon Sparrow": Dirk Bogarde)

Dr. Jeckyll and Mr. Hyde
1931   Paramount
Dr. Jeckyll. ("Poole": Edgar Norton)

Dr. Jeckyll and Mr. Hyde
1941 MGM
The lord is my shepherd, I shall not want. He maketh me to lie down in green pastures. He leadeth me beside the still waters. He restoreth my soul. He leadeth me in the path of righteousness for his name's sake. Yea, though I walk through the valley of the shadow of death. ("Dr. Harry Jeckyll/Mr. Hyde": Spencer Tracy)

Dr. Kildare's Wedding Day
1941 MGM
No, but she said if it was any good you'd find some way to chisel in on it. ("Dr. James Kildare": Lew Ayres)

Dr. Strangelove or, How I Learned to Stop Worrying and Love the Bomb
1963 Columbia
Sir, I have a plan. Mein Feuhrer, I can walk! ("Dr. Strangelove": Peter Sellers)

Doctor Zhivago
1965 MGM
Then it's a gift. ("Yevgraf": Alec Guinness)

A Dog of Flanders
1959 20th Century–Fox
Petrasche. ("Nello": David Ladd)

Dollars
1971 Columbia
I figured they'd never kill you, at least not until after they found the money. ("Dawn Divine": Goldie Hawn)

A Doll's House
1973 Paramount
Oh, Torvald, I don't believe in miracles anymore. We would have to change so much. ("Nora": Jane Fonda)

Dominick and Eugene
1988 Orion
Oh, well. ("Dominick Luciano": Tom Hulce)

The Domino Principle
1977 Associated General Films
When they wreck everything you've got you'll see there's no way you can win. You end up saying to yourself, what am I fighting for? That's what they count on. They figure sooner or later you'll give up. But if you're gonna do that, you might as well be dead. I can't give up. I never learned how. ("Tucker": Gene Hackman)

The Don Is Dead
1973 Universal
We got a deal, Don Antonio. ("Don Aggimio Bernardo": J. Duke Russo)

Don't Drink the Water
1969 Avco Embassy
Unload. ("Walter Hollander": Jackie Gleason)

Don't Knock the Rock
1956 Columbia
Well, then, let's get on with the show. Ladies and gentlemen, some rock and roll terpsichory. One, two, three, four. ("Arnie Haines": Alan Dale)

Don't Look Now
1973 Paramount
Laura! ("John Baxter": Donald Sutherland)

Double Dynamite
1951 RKO
Mr. Keck, arrivaderci. ("Johnny Dalton": Frank Sinatra)

Double Indemnity
1944 Paramount
I love you, too. ("Walter": Fred MacMurray)

A Double Life
1947 Universal
Brita. Brita. ("Anthony John": Ronald Colman)

The Dove
1974 Paramount
Patti! I love you, Patti! ("Robin Lee Graham": Joseph Bottoms)

Downtown
1990 20th Century–Fox
May I see your license and registration please? ("Alex Kearney": Anthony Edwards)

Dracula
1931 Universal
Not yet, ah, presently. Come, John. ("Van Helsing": Edward Van Sloan)

Dracula's Widow
1988 DEG
It's over now. It's all over. ("Raymond": Lenny Von Dohlen)

Dragnet
1954 Warner Brothers
No, sir, we hardly knew him. ("Sgt. Joe Friday": Jack Webb)

Dragnet
1987 Universal

Wait a minute, Connie Swail? Don't you mean the virgin Connie Swail? ("Pep Streebek": Tom Hanks)

Dragon Seed
1944 MGM
So it came about that while Ling Tan left the land behind him, he did not leave hope. For he carried it with him in Jade's child, that child so truly the seed of the dragon. ("Narrator": Lionel Barrymore)

Dragonwyck
1946 20th Century–Fox
Would next week be too soon? ("Dr. Jeff Turner": Glenn Langan)

Dream a Little Dream
1989 Vestron
You, too, Bobby. ("Coleman Ettinger": Jason Robards)

Dreamscape
1984 20th Century–Fox
Thank you. Have a good trip. ("Train conductor": Ben Kronen)

Dressed to Kill
1946 Universal
Oh, thank you, Inspector. I don't think I could have done it entirely without Mr. Holmes' help, you know. ("Dr. Watson": Nigel Bruce)

The Drifter
1988 Concorde
No! ("Julia": Kim Delaney)

Driving Miss Daisy
1989 Warner Brothers

Here, open some more. ("Hoke Colburn": Morgan Freeman)

Drugstore Cowboy
1989 Avenue
I was still alive. Hope they could keep me alive. ("Bob": Matt Dillon)

Drums Along the Mohawk
1939 20th Century-Fox
Well, I reckon we'd better be gettin' back to work. There's gonna be a heap to do from now on. ("Gilbert Martin": Henry Fonda)

Duchess of Idaho
1950 MGM
Paying attention? Oh, yes, I am. ("Dick Layn": Van Johnson)

Duck Soup
1933 Paramount
Victory is ours. ("Mrs. Teasdale": Margaret Dumont)

Dudes
1987 Vista
Whoa, whoa, whoa, whoa. ("Grant": Jon Cryer)

Duel at Diablo
1966 United Artists
General. ("Toller": Sidney Poitier)

Duel in the Sun
1946 Selznick
Just hold me. Hold me once more. ("Pearl Chavez": Jennifer Jones)

Duet for One
1986 Cannon
She's coming. ("Dr. Louis Feldman": Max Von Sydow)

The Duke of West Point
1938 United Artists
That's the beginning of Volume Two of the Personal History of Steve Early at West Point. It will make such nice reading on those long winter nights. ("Steven Early": Louis Hayward)

Dutch Treat
1987 Cannon
That's my mama. Mama! ("Elmo": Robbie Sella)

Dynamite
1929 MGM
I was wrong about that feller. He was a great guy. ("Hagon Derk": Charles Bickford)

Dynamite Pass
1950 RKO
I liked him a lot, but that doesn't mean I loved him. ("Mary": Lynne Roberts)

E. T. The Extra-Terrestrial
1982 Universal
I'll be right here. (Voice of E.T.)

Each Dawn I Die
1939 Warner Brothers
Frank. ("Joyce Conover": Jane Bryan)

The Eagle and the Hawk
1949 Paramount
He was a patriot. Are there any greater? ("Todd Croyden": John Payne

The Earl of Chicago
1939 MGM
It's a breeze, me lord, it's a breeze. ("Munsey": Edmund Gwenn)

East of Eden
1955 Warner Brothers
He said, don't get anybody else. He said, you stay with me. You take care of me. ("Cal Trask": James Dean)

East of Sudan
1964 Columbia
No, sir, I'm sorry, sir. I, I don't imagine you would, sir. ("Private Richard Baker": Anthony Quayle)

East of the River
1940 Warner Brothers
Let's get out of here. ("Cy Turner": Douglas Fowley)

East Side, West Side
1949 MGM
Yes, Jessie will be there for dinner on Thursday night as usual. But alone. ("Brandon Bourne": James Mason)

Easter Parade
1948 MGM
Here, let's look. Oh, very nice. ("Hannah Brown": Judy Garland)

Easy Living
1937 Paramount
Johnny, this is where we came in. ("Mary Smith": Jean Arthur)

Easy Money
1983 Orion
My mother-in-law. For years I wouldn't kiss her face. I ended up kissing her ass. ("Monty": Rodney Dangerfield)

Easy Rider
1969 Columbia
I'm gonna get 'em. We're ready now. ("Billy": Dennis Hopper)

Eddie and the Cruisers
1983 Embassy
Eddie! Eddie! Eddie! Eddie! Eddie! Eddie! Eddie! Eddie! Eddie! Eddie! Eddie! Eddie! Eddie! Eddie! (Spectators at performance)

Eddie and the Cruisers II: Eddie Lives
1989 Scotti Brothers
And me, I'm Eddie Wilson. ("Eddie Wilson/Joe Westz": Michael Pare)

The Eddy Duchin Story
1955 Columbia
You're getting awfully good, son. It's hard to tell where I leave off and you begin. ("Eddy Duchin": Tyrone Power)

Edge of the City
1957 MGM
Hey, Charlie! (Spectator at railroad yard fight)

Edison the Man
1940 MGM
Mr. Toastmaster, Mr. Toastmaster, ladies and gentlemen. To be told by the outstanding men and women of your time that you have contributed a great deal to human betterment is pleasant, very pleasant. I'd hardly be human if my heart didn't fill from such a magnificent compliment. But somehow I have not yet achieved a success I want. Earlier this evening I talked with two schoolchildren. Tomorrow the world will be theirs. It's a troubled world, full of doubt and uncertainty. You say we men of science have been helping it. Are those children and their children going to

approve of what we've done, or are they going to discover too late that science was trusted so much that it has turned into a monster whose final triumph is man's own destruction. Some of us are beginning to feel that danger, but it can be avoided. I once had two dynamos. They needed regulating. It was a problem of balance and adjustment. And I feel that the confusion in the world today presents much the same problem. The dynamo of man's God-given ingenuity is running away with the dynamo of his equally God-given humanity. I am too old now to do much more than to say put those dynamos in balance. Make them work in harmony as the great designer intended they should. It can be done. What man's mind can conceive, man's character can control. Man must learn that and then we needn't be afraid of tomorrow. And man will go forward toward more light. ("Thomas A. Edison": Spencer Tracy)

Edward, My Son
1949   MGM
Well, ladies and gentlemen, something went wrong, just a little wrong. But it wasn't Larry who did it, mind you, or the bank inspectors, it took the whole British empire. They did send me to prison, prison, mind you, for burning down a furniture store back in nineteen twenty-four. But that's all behind me now and I can get on with the search for my grandson. He'd be ten now, ten years old. Well, that's the story, ladies and gentlemen, what I did and why I did it. What's your answer? If you had been me, what would you have done? Well,

I guess that's all, ladies and gentlemen. Look after yourselves, because the way things are in the world today, if you don't nobody else will. Good night. ("Arnold Boult": Spencer Tracy)

The Effect of Gamma Rays on Man-in-the-Moon Marigolds
1972   20th Century–Fox
No, Mama, I don't hate the world. ("Matilda": Nell Potts)

The Egg and I
1947   Universal
See what I mean? I could write a book. ("Betty MacDonald": Claudette Colbert)

Eight Men Out
1988   Orion
He was one of the guys that threw the series back in nineteen. One of them bums from Chicago, kid. One of the Black Sox. (Spectator at baseball game)

Eighteen Again
1988   New World
About Harry Truman. Be my pleasure, David. ("Jack Watson": George Burns)

Eighteen and Anxious
1957   Republic
Danny, take me home. ("Judy": Mary Webster)

Electra Glide in Blue
1973   United Artists
Hey! Hey! ("John Wintergreen": Robert Blake)

Electric Dreams
1984   MGM/UA
You're on K-A-Y. ("D.J.": Frazer Smith)

Eleni
1985   Warner Brothers
My dear family, I am sending you this tape instead of a letter. I'll be coming home soon. The hunt for my mother's killer is over. I did not inherit the necessary hate to end a human life. I am still mystified by the kind of love my mother felt for me and my sisters. The question of being worth it or not is no longer applicable. I accept it is as something she gave me. I accept her love as my inheritance. I miss you and I love you. I miss and love my children. I only hope, and I hope with all my heart, that the kind of love I've discovered is not reserved for mothers alone. I want to feel it too. I've a need to feel it, to share the inheritance my mother left me with you my children. I know that they are ours. I know I may be a little late in returning home to claim them, but I hope you can understand my need to say those words. My children. ("Nick Gage": John Malkovich)

Elephant Boy
1937   United Artists
All together, to Toomai of the elephants. ("Machua Appa": Allan Jeayes)

The Elephant Man
1980   Paramount
Nothing will die. ("Merrick's Mother": Phoebe Nicholls)

Elephant Walk
1954   Paramount
I'm not. Let them have their elephant walk. Ruth, we'll build a new place, a home somewhere else. ("John Wiley": Peter Finch)

The Emerald Forest
1985   Embassy
You've got to evacuate the men. ("Bill Markham": Powers Boothe)

Emma
1932   MGM
Oh, that's nothing. That isn't the first time that's happened to me, Ronnie. ("Emma Thatcher": Marie Dressler)

Empire of the Sun
1987   Warner Brothers
Jimmy? Jimmy? Jimmy. Jimmy. ("Jim's Mother": Emily Richard)

The Empire Strikes Back
1980   20th Century–Fox
Ow! ("Luke Skywalker": Mark Hamill)

Employees Entrance
1933   Warner Brothers
Oh, honey, I love you, more than ever. We're gonna start all over again. It's been done before. Oh, honey. ("Martin West": Wallace Ford)

The Enchanted Cottage
1945   RKO
Oliver, we've never written our names. Somehow I think they'd want us to. ("Laura": Dorothy McGuire)

The End
1978   United Artists
God, God, fifty percent, God, remember what I said, fifty percent. I'll give

you eighty, God, I'll give you eighty percent! Gross, eighty percent gross. ("Wendell Sonny Lawson": Burt Reynolds)

Enemies, a Love Story
1989   20th Century–Fox
Masha, Masha, Masha, Masha, Masha. ("Tamara": Anjelica Huston)

The Enemy Below
1957   20th Century–Fox
I think you will. ("Von Stolberg": Curt Jergens)

An Enemy of the People
1978   Warner Brothers
Nails. ("Dr. Thomas Stockmann": Steve McQueen)

The Enforcer
1976   Warner Brothers
Maxwell, Bobby Maxwell. This is Captain McKay speaking. We have your money. The plane is waiting for you at the airport. We have acceded to all your demands so release the mayor. The pilot of this helicopter will fly you and your men to safety. ("Capt. McKay": Bradford Dillman)

England Made Me
1972   Atlantic
Doesn't it? Good-bye, Erich. ("Kate Farrant": Hildegard Neil)

The Entertainer
1960   Continental
Take the front curtains up. (A stagehand)

Escape from New York
1981   Avco Embassy

Good evening. Although I shall not be present at this historic summit meeting, I present this in the hope that our great nations may learn to live in peace. ("The President": Donald Pleasence)

Escape Me Never
1947   Warner Brothers
But I don't want a better man, Sebastian. I just want you. ("Gemma Smith": Ida Lupino)

Escape to Witch Mountain
1974   Buena Vista
Well, they're home now. ("Jason": Eddie Albert)

Eternally Yours
1939   United Artists
Darling, look. ("Tony Halstead": David Niven)

Every Girl Should Be Married
1948   RKO
I, uh, trust I'm not late. I, uh, came to discuss the wedding plans. Now, if you're planning on a large wedding, you may have use of the church. Or if you prefer. . . . ("Clergyman": Selmer Jackson)

Every Which Way But Loose
1978   Warner Brothers
All right, you ready? Let me get you focused. Now smile, big smile. ("Clerk at D.M.V.": George Chandler)

Everybody Wins
1990   Orion
You're leaving early. How about a drink? ("Charlie Haggerty": Frank Converse)

Everybody's All-American
1988   Warner Brothers
Let's go home, precious. ("Babs":
Jessica Lange)

Everything You Always Wanted to Know About Sex (But Were Afraid to Ask)
1972   United Artists
Fatigue reading four and a half.
Looks good! We're going for seconds.
Attention, gonads, we're going for a
record. ("Operator": Tony Randall)

The Evil That Men Do
1984   Tri-Star
Bring me my sister this instant!
("Molloch": Joseph Maher)

Evil Under the Sun
1982   Universal
How many classes are there? ("Hercule Poirot": Peter Ustinov)

The Ex-Mrs. Bradford
1936   MGM
I do, and may heaven have mercy on
my soul. ("Dr. Lawrence Bradford":
William Powell)

Excalibur
1981   Warner Brothers
Arthur! Arthur! ("Perceval": Paul
Geoffrey)

Executive Suite
1954   MGM
We did. ("Erica Martin": Nina Foch)

The Exorcist
1973   Warner Brothers
I thought you'd like to keep this.
("Chris MacNeil": Ellen Burstyn)

The Experts
1989   Paramount
We're here. All right, everybody, let's
get off. ("Travis": John Travolta)

Exposed
1983   MGM/UA
Oh! Daniel! Oh! Oh! ("Elizabeth
Carlson": Nastassia Kinski)

Eye of the Needle
1981   United Artists
Stop, please! ("Lucy": Kate Nelligan)

Eye of the Tiger
1986   Scotti Brothers
It's good seeing you. ("Devereaux":
Yaphet Kotto)

Eyes of Laura Mars
1978   Columbia
I'm Laura Mars. ("Laura Mars": Faye
Dunaway)

F/X
1985   Orion
I don't know, Leo, it's hard for me to
do anything else. ("Rollie Tyler":
Bryan Brown)

The Fabulous Baker Boys
1989   20th Century–Fox
Intuition. ("Jack Baker": Jeff Bridges)

The Face Behind the Mask
1941   Columbia
I hope you'll find this, Mr. O'Hara. I
am Janos. You remember the fire at
the Excelsior Palace? You were kind
to me and I never forgot. Those you
find here were unkind and I did not
forget them either. Janos Szabo. P.S.

Here is the five dollars I owe you. ("Janos Szabo": Peter Lorre)

A Face in the Crowd
1957   Warner Brothers
Marcia, come back! Don't leave me! Don't leave me! Don't leave me! Marcia, don't leave! Come back! Come back! Come back! ("Lonesome Rhodes": Andy Griffith)

The Face of Fu Manchu
1965   Warner Brothers
The world shall hear from me again. ("Fu Manchu": Christopher Lee)

The Falcon in Hollywood
1944   RKO
Sorry. ("Lt. Higgins": Frank Jenks)

The Falcon Out West
1944   RKO
Forward my mail to Havana. ("Falcon": Tom Conway)

The Falcon Takes Over
1942   RKO
Yeah, only this time he hit the jackpot. ("Goldie Locke": Allen Jenkins)

The Fall of the Roman Empire
1964   Paramount
This was the beginning of the fall of the Roman Empire. A great civilization is not conquered from without until it has destroyed itself from within. (Narrator)

The Fallen Idol
1948   British Lion
Felipe. Felipe, your mother. ("Ambassador": Gerard Heinz)

Falling in Love Again
1980   International Picture Show
Maybe sports equipment and we'll have music piped in. And, darling, we'll build that dream house I always promised you, Sue. And the kids are going to help us build it. We'll do it! We're going to do it all! Everything we always dreamed of. We shouldn't have to go to sleep to dream. It's life. We can live a dream. ("Harry Lewis": Elliott Gould)

Fame
1980   MGM/UA
OK, honey, you're finished. Stand over there. Come on, keep the line moving. Come on, come on, next. (School worker)

Family Business
1989   Tri-Star
I think I heard it once before. ("Adam McMullen": Matthew Broderick)

Family Plot
1976   Universal
Operator, can I have the police? ("George Lumley": Bruce Dern)

The Family Secret
1951   Columbia
It makes a lot of sense. ("Lee Pearson": Jody Lawrence)

Fancy Pants
1950   Paramount
A kiss like that could kill a guy. ("Humphrey": Bob Hope)

Fandango
1985   Warner Brothers
Have a nice life. ("Dorman": Chuck Bush)

The Fantasist
1987   Blue Dolphin
Man overboard. ("Patricia Teeling":
Moira Harris)

Fantastic Voyage
1966   20th Century-Fox
Open that door, please. ("Col. Donald
Reid": Arthur O'Connell)

The Far Country
1954   Universal
I know, we eat, we sleep, we rest, and
soon we be all better again. ("Jeff":
James Stewart)

The Far Horizons
1955   Paramount
There is much we both can do for our
people. Many things we have learned
from each other we can teach to
them, patience, kindness and the
wisdom to know the truth. You would
not have let me say these things to
you, but in your heart you will know
they are true. You will be sad as I am
sad, and you will think of me as I will
think of you many times in the years
to come, when you see a river of white
water dancing in the sun or clouds
hanging high above the mountains.
But soon the memories will grow dim
as memories should and there will be
others to take their place. May they
be happy ones for you, my love, as
happy as those we shared together,
all the days of your life. ("Sacajawea":
Donna Reed)

Farewell My Lovely
1975   Avco Embassy
I had two grand inside my breast
pocket that needed a home, and I

knew just the place. ("Philip Marlowe": Robert Mitchun)

The Farmer Takes a Wife
1935   20th Century-Fox
Oh, Molly. ("Dan Harrow": Henry
Fonda)

The Farmer's Daughter
1947   RKO
I'm not quite sure of the protocol in a
case like this, but. ("Glenn Morley":
Joseph Cotten)

The Fast Lady
1962   Rank
If I may say so, you're one of the
loveliest girls I've ever met. I don't
know why it is, but I've always been
mad about–. ("Freddy Fox": Leslie
Phillips)

Fat City
1972   Columbia
OK. ("Ernie": Jeff Bridges)

Fat Man and Little Boy
1989   Paramount
Kathleen, my love, you asked me a
question once, was it instinct to save
a life or to take it. I don't know, my
darling. All I do know is that if we are
free to choose, I hope to God we
choose life over death. Not because I
believe the implacable universe cares
a damn, but because as I look at you,
my darling, I realize how glorious,
how magical, life can be. ("Michael
Merriman": John Cusack)

Fatal Attraction
1987   Paramount
Dan! ("Beth Gallagher": Anne
Archer)

Fatal Beauty
1987 MGM/UA
You're gonna be fine. ("Det. Rita Rizzoli": Whoopi Goldberg)

Father Goose
1964 Universal
Oh, I wonder if they serve coconut milk on submarines. ("Walter Eckland": Cary Grant)

Father of the Bride
1950 MGM
Nothing's really changed, has it. You know what they say: my son's my son till he gets him a wife, but my daughter's my daughter all of her life. All of our life. ("Stanley T. Banks": Spencer Tracy)

Father Takes a Wife
1941 RKO
Oh, no, no, you don't. There are too many people in the room already. I'll handle this. This time the bases are empty and Aunt Julie's up at bat. I may strike out before we get to the elevator but don't wait up for me, folks. ("Aunt Julie": Helen Broderick)

Father's Little Dividend
1951 MGM
Stanley Banks, my grandchild. My first grandchild. ("Stanley Banks": Spencer Tracy)

Fathom
1967 20th Century–Fox
Pedro's. Seven-thirty. And don't be late. ("Peter Merriweather": Tony Franciosa)

Fatso
1980 20th Century–Fox
Oh, yes. ("Lydia": Candice Azzara)

Fear
1989 CineTel
Let's go. Let's go. ("Don Haden": Cliff De Young)

Fedora
1978 United Artists
Six weeks later the woman who called herself the Countess Sobryanski died peacefully on the island of Corfu. The news rated one short paragraph in the local paper. The electric blanket I had sent her came back undelivered. ("Barry Detweiler": William Holden)

Feds
1988 Warner Brothers
Oh behalf of Janice and myself, I'd like to take this moment to thank all the instructors that voted for us. And I hope the people of the United States of America will be able to sleep better knowing that women like us have guns. ("Elizabeth DeWitt": Rebecca de Mornay)

Female on the Beach
1955 Universal
Oh, please forgive me, please. ("Lynn Markham": Joan Crawford)

Ferris Bueller's Day Off
1986 Paramount
Yup, I said it before and I'll say it again. Life moves pretty fast. You don't stop and look around once in a while, you could miss it. ("Ferris Bueller": Matthew Broderick)

Fever Pitch
1985 MGM/UA

You wanna bet? ("Taggart": Ryan O'Neal)

Fiddler on the Roof
1971   United Artists
All right, children, let's go. ("Tevye": Chaim Topol)

The Field
1990   Avenue
Go back and leave him alone! Leave him alone! Leave him alone, go back! Go back! Damn you, go back! ("'Bill' McCabe": Richard Harris)

Field of Dreams
1989   Universal
I'd like that. ("John Kinsella": Dwier Brown)

The Fiendish Plot of Dr. Fu Manchu
1980   Warner Brothers
Wiped out. Poor, demented fools. Ha, you've really done it this time, Fu. ("Naylor Smith": Peter Sellers)

Fifth Avenue Girl
1939   RKO
Why don't you mind your own business? ("Mary Grey": Ginger Rogers)

52 Pick-Up
1986   Cannon
So long, sport. ("Harry Mitchell": Roy Scheider)

The Fighting Seabees
1944   Republic
I'm doing a very bad job of saying I love you, Commander. ("Constance Chesley": Susan Hayward)

The Final Option
1983   MGM/UA
Of course we do, all the time in the world. ("Sir Richard": Paul Freeman)

Finders Keepers
1984   Warner Brothers
Not to worry. This side is mine. ("Century": Louis Gossett, Jr.)

Fingers at the Window
1942   MGM
And, baby, the way I feel, I hope you live forever. ("Oliver Duffy": Lew Ayres)

Finian's Rainbow
1968   Warner Brothers
Oh, well, you see, it's always somewhere, over there. ("Sharon McLonergan": Petula Clark)

Fire Down Below
1957   Columbia
Like the man says, some days win, some days you lose. Drinks are on me. ("Tony": Jack Lemmon)

Fire over England
1937   United Artists
Do give thee most humble and hearty thanks. ("Queen Elizabeth": Flora Robson)

Firepower
1979   Associated Film Dist.
It's a pleasure. ("Adela Tasca": Sophia Loren)

Firestarter
1984   Universal
I'm doing it, Daddy. I love you. ("Charlie McGee": Drew Barrymore)

The First Deadly Sin
1980 Filmways
The little old lady reached out, patted the earth. "Always remember, Honey Bunch, people who grow flowers in beautiful colors are all very special people. Not only do they find pleasures every day but they also plant the seeds of tomorrow for others to enjoy." And then Honey Bunch ran to tell her mommy and her daddy what a lucky little girl she was and that this had been the happiest adventure of her life. ("Edward Delaney": Frank Sinatra)

First Men in the Moon
1964 Columbia
He did have such a terrible cold. ("Arnold Bedford": Edward Judd)

First Monday in October
1981 Paramount
Damned right we do. ("Dan Snow": Walter Matthau)

The First Power
1990 Orion
See ya around, buddy boy. ("Patrick Channing": Jeff Kober)

The First Time
1952 Columbia
This is the most important street in the world to me because this is the street where my parents live. This is my mother, this is my father, and this is my big brother, Tim, who saw it all that first year, the year my parents grew up even more than he did, the year they changed from just a husband and a wife to a father and a mother. (A child)

The First Traveling Saleslady
1956 RKO
But just imagine. ("Rose Gillray": Ginger Rogers)

A Fish Called Wanda
1988 MGM/UA
Asshole! ("Otto": Kevin Kline)

Five
1951 Columbia
I want to help you. ("Roseanne": Susan Douglas)

5 Card Stud
1968 Paramount
If you're not made of iron, I'll see you in Denver. You sure didn't feel like iron. ("Van Morgan": Dean Martin)

Five Days from Home
1979 Universal
It's me. It's your daddy. And I brought you a puppy for Christmas. ("Thomas M. Pryor": George Peppard)

Five Easy Pieces
1970 Columbia
That's OK. I'll be fine. Fine. I'll be fine. ("Robert": Jack Nicholson)

Five Fingers
1952 20th Century-Fox
Anna. Poor Anna. ("Cicero": James Mason)

The Five Pennies
1959 Paramount
Give me my horn, Tony. ("Loring 'Red' Nichols": Danny Kaye)

The 5,000 Fingers of Dr. T.
1953 Columbia

Sporty boy. Hiya, Sport. ("Bart": Tommy Rettig)

The Flame of New Orleans
1941   Universal
Where can she be? ("Giraud": Roland Young)

Flaming Star
1960   20th Century–Fox
Pacer! Hey, Pacer! Pacer! ("Clint Burton": Steve Forrest)

The Flamingo Kid
1984   20th Century–Fox
Oh, no. Oh, no. ("Jeffrey Willis": Matt Dillon)

Flamingo Road
1949   Warner Brothers
Dan Reynolds, I told you one of these days you'd make me cry. ("Lane Bellamy": Joan Crawford)

Flashback
1990   Paramount
Hell, kid, I'm too old to grow up. ("Huey Walker": Dennis Hopper)

Flashdance
1983   Paramount
Can I start again? ("Alex Owens": Jennifer Beals)

Flashpoint
1985   Tri-Star
I'll tell 'em. ("Sheriff Wells": Rip Torn)

Flatliners
1990   Columbia
Hey, thank you. ("Nelson": Kiefer Sutherland)

Fletch
1985   Universal
When it came to basketball, Gail was a loss. But we had our own version of one on one, and she thought I was the bravest man in the world, which, of course, I am. By the way, I charged the entire vacation to Mr. Underhill's American Express card. Want the number? ("Fletch": Chevy Chase)

The Flight of the Phoenix
1965   20th Century–Fox
Metres, Mr. Towns. Metres. ("Heinrich Dorfmann": Hardy Kruger)

The Flim-Flam Man
1967   20th Century–Fox
Get in. ("Sheriff Slade": Harry Morgan)

Flipper
1963   MGM
I think it was written for us today to share with the dolphins, not to kill them. ("Porter Ricks": Chuck Connors)

Flower Drum Song
1961   Universal
Mother. ("Linda Low": Nancy Kwan)

Flowers in the Attic
1987   New World
We finally got our revenge, we managed to make it on our own. I got a job to help put Chris through medical school. Little Carrie grew up but she was never truly healthy. I even started dancing again. We left the past behind, all except the memories, my mother, grandmother, and the attic. I sometimes wonder if grand-

mother is still alive, still presiding over Foxworth Hall, still awaiting my return. ("Cathy": Kristy Swanson)

Flowing Gold
1940 Warner Brothers
You bet we will. Excuse me. ("Johnny Blake": John Garfield)

The Fly
1986 20th Century–Fox
No, no, I can't. No, I can't. No, no, no, no. ("Veronica Quaife": Geena Davis)

The Fly II
1989 20th Century–Fox
I'm all right. ("Martin Brundle": Eric Stoltz)

Flying Down to Rio
1933 RKO
Gosh, that gal don't care who she gets thrown out of what. ("Fred Ayres": Fred Astaire)

The Flying Fontaines
1959 Columbia
Hey, come here. Where you goin'? ("Rick Rias": Michael Callan)

Flying Fortress
1942 Warner Brothers
We shall bomb Germany by day, as well as by night, in ever-increasing measure, casting upon them month by month a heavier discharge of bombs and making the German people taste and gulp each month a sharper dose of the miseries they have showered upon mankind. Once underway, our attack will be relent-

less. We will smash Cologne, Essen, Emden, Bremerhaven, Kiel, Danzig, building with increasing fury towards the day when we shall visit upon Berlin itself the complete destruction to which our preliminary raids have been but a prelude, that great day when we will strike with devastation and unconquerable strength at the detested enemy of all the free peoples of the earth. (Narrator)

Flying Leathernecks
1951 RKO
For the future record, all orders are right away. ("Capt. Carl Griffin": Robert Ryan)

Flying Tigers
1942 Republic
Swell. ("Brooke Elliott": Anna Lee)

Footlight Serenade
1942 20th Century–Fox
Glad to see you. ("Slap": Phil Silvers)

For Keeps
1988 Tri-Star
I love you, Stan. ("Darcy Elliot": Molly Ringwald)

For Pete's Sake
1974 Columbia
How'd you like to buy some hot cows? Hello? Hello? ("Henry": Barbra Streisand)

For the First Time
1959 MGM
The world is full of Alessandros and Angelos. They are your public. You owe them something – your voice. ("Christa": Johanna von Koczian)

For the Love of Mary
1948   Universal
Oh, hello, Mr. President, this is Mary Peppertree. I wanted you to know that everything is perfect. Just perfect. ("Mary Peppertree": Deanna Durbin)

Forced Vengeance
1982   MGM/UA
Hong Kong, a borrowed place that lives on borrowed time. The British rent it now, but in seventeen years the lease runs out, and the People's Republic is the landlord. But this is a city of survivors, and whatever happens, Hong Kong will always be the place. ("Josh Randall": Chuck Norris)

Forever Darling
1956   MGM
No, I dunt. ("Susan Vega": Lucille Ball)

Fort Apache
1948   RKO
Forward by fours – Ho! ("Captain Kirby York": John Wayne)

The Fortune
1975   Columbia
Oh, no. I would never believe that in a million years. ("Freddie": Stockard Channing)

Fortunes of Captain Blood
1950   Columbia
All hands stand by to make sail. ("Tom Mannering": Lumsden Hare)

40 Carats
1973   Columbia
Now she tells me. ("Billy Boylan": Gene Kelly)

40 Guns to Apache Pass
1967   Columbia
Go ahead, Captain. ("Colonel Reed": Byron Morrow)

40 Pounds of Trouble
1962   Universal
Good-bye, Uncle Bernie. ("Penny Piper": Claire Wilcox)

42nd Street
1933   Warner Brothers
Some guys get all the breaks. ("Julian Marsh": Warner Baxter)

The Four Horsemen of the Apocalypse
1961   MGM
My God, Julio. Have you done this? ("Heinrich Von Hartrott": Karl Boehm)

The Four Seasons
1981   Universal
Would you listen to me? ("Jack Burroughs": Alan Alda)

The Fourth Protocol
1987   Rank
Home! ("John Preston": Michael Caine)

The Fox
1967   Warner Brothers
Will I? ("Ellen March": Anne Heywood)

Foxes
1980   United Artists
Back in the heavy stone days when we used to stay up and talk a lot, Annie and me, we were talking about dying, how it feels and all. I said I'd never

get buried, couldn't stand them shoveling dirt in my face. Like I know I'd be dead, but I still might have this strong compulsion to breathe, OK? But Annie, she said she wanted to be buried right in the ground under a pear tree, really, not in a box or anything. She said she wanted the roots going right through her, and each year they'd come along, take a pear and go, "Hey, Annie's tasting good this year, huh?" ("Jeanie": Jodie Foster)

Foxfire
1955   Universal
Come with me. ("Jonathan Dartland": Jeff Chandler)

Francis
1950   Universal
Here we go again. ("Voice of Francis the Talking Mule": Chill Wills)

Francis Covers the Big Town
1953   Universal
Oh, don't be impatient, sugar. ("Voice of Francis the Talking Mule": Chill Wills)

Francis of Assisi
1961   20th Century–Fox
Once you thought you were called to build churches of mortar and stone, but you were building chapels in the hearts of millions of men and women everywhere. ("Sister Claire": Dolores Hart)

Frankenstein
1931   Universal
Indeed, sir, we hope so, sir. (Maids)

Frantic
1988   Warner Brothers
I love you, baby. I love you. ("Dr. Richard Walker": Harrison Ford)

Freeway
1988   New World
Frederick's of Hollywood. Dr. David Lazarus. You're on the air. ("Dr. David Lazarus": Richard Belzer)

The French Lieutenant's Woman
1981   United Artists
Sarah! ("Charles/Mike": Jeremy Irons)

Frenzy
1972   Universal
Mr. Rusk, you're not wearing your tie. ("Chief Inspector Oxford": Alec McCowen)

Fresh Horses
1988   Weintraub
Thank you. ("Jewel": Molly Ringwald)

The Freshman
1990   Tri-Star
Make it easy for you. ("Carmine Sabatini": Marlon Brando)

Friends
1971   Paramount
Good-bye. ("Paul Harrison": Sean Bury)

Fright Night
1985   Columbia
No. ("Charley Brewster": William Ragsdale)

Fright Night – Part 2
1989   Tri-Star
Making babies. ("Alex": Traci Lin)

The Frisco Kid
1979   Warner Brothers
Music, maestro, please. ("Samuel Bender": Jack Somack)

Frogs
1972   American International
Hello? You can't be dead. It rang! Hello? Oh. ("Jason Crockett": Ray Milland)

From Here to Eternity
1953   Columbia
Robert E. Lee Prewitt. Isn't that a silly old name? ("Alma Lorene": Donna Reed)

From the Hip
1987   DEG
Yeah, I know. I'm a hell of a guy. ("Robin Weathers": Judd Nelson)

From the Mixed-up Files of Mrs. Basil E. Frankweiler
1973   Cinema 5
Quite right, Saxonburg, quite right. ("Mrs. Frankweiler": Ingrid Bergman)

From This Day Forward
1946   RKO
There aren't any. We don't need them anymore. ("Susan": Joan Fontaine)

The Front
1976   Columbia
Fellows, I don't recognize the right of this committee to ask me these kind of questions. And, furthermore, you can all go fuck yourselves. ("Howard Prince": Woody Allen)

The Front Page
1931   United Artists
That's right. I want you to send a wire to chief of police there. Tell him to stop that train and arrest Hildy Johnson. Bring him back here. Wire him a full description. The son of a [bitch] stole my watch. ("Walter Burns": Adolphe Menjou)

The Front Page
1974   Universal
Yeah. The son of a bitch stole my watch. ("Walter Burns": Walter Matthau)

Frontier Hellcat
1966   Columbia
Ride on. ("Old Surehand": Stewart Granger)

Full Fathom Five
1990   Concorde
I sure do hope I see you again. ("Mackenzie": Michael Moriarty)

Full Metal Jacket
1987   Warner Brothers
My thoughts drift back to erect-nipple wet dreams, about Mary Jane Rottencrotch, and the great homecoming fuck fantasy. I'm so happy that I am alive, in one piece, and short. I'm in a world of shit, yes, but I am alive, and I am not afraid. ("Pvt. Joker": Matthew Modine)

Fun with Dick and Jane
1976   Columbia

Jane. Jane. ("Richard Harper": George Segal)

Funeral in Berlin
1967   Paramount
No, thank you, sir. I'll walk. ("Harry Palmer": Michael Caine)

Funny Farm
1988   Warner Brothers
What? ("Andy Farmer": Chevy Chase)

Funny Girl
1968   Columbia
Good-bye, Nick. ("Fanny Brice": Barbra Streisand)

Funny Lady
1975   Columbia
I need you. ("Billy Rose": James Caan)

The Further Adventures of Tennessee Buck
1988   Trans World Entertainment
Well, let's get the hell out of here. ("Buck Malone": David Keith)

Fury
1936   MGM
Joe. ("Katherine Grant": Sylvia Sidney)

The Fury
1978   20th Century–Fox
You go to hell. ("Gillian Bellaver": Amy Irving)

Fury at Gunsight Pass
1956   Columbia
Come along. ("Doc Phillips": Morris Ankrum)

G Men
1935   Warner Brothers
It's gonna be nice having a nurse in the family. ("Brick Davis": James Cagney)

G.I. Blues
1960   Paramount
Did you ever? ("Tulsa McCauley": Elvis Presley)

Gaby—A True Story
1987   Tri-Star
Gaby and I continued living in the family house. We adopted a newborn baby girl and Gaby named her Alma Florencia. I take care of her up-bringing and Gaby sees to her education. Gaby's writing two new books and it makes her laugh to see Almita crawling around the room. To most people we must seem like a strange family, but that doesn't matter. The house is full of life again. ("Florencia Morales": Norma Aleandro)

Gallipoli
1981   Paramount
Gangway! ("Frank Dunne": Mel Gibson)

Gandhi
1982   Columbia
When I despair, I remember that all through history the way of truth and love has always won. There have been tyrants and murderers and for a time they can seem invincible, but in the end they always fall. Think of it. Always. ("Mahatma Gandhi": Ben Kingsley)

Gaslight
1944   MGM

Well! ("Miss Thwaites": Dame May Whitty)

The Gate
1987   New Century
You're my best buddies. ("Glen": Stephen Dorff)

Gay Divorcee
1934   RKO
Scusi! Scusi! I'm also very good at parties. ("Rodolfo Tonetti": Erik Rhodes)

The Gay Lady
1949   General Films
Yes, Digby. ("Trottie True": Jean Kent)

The General Died at Dawn
1936   Paramount
He was a talented man, but very, very corrupt. ("Mr. Wu": Dudley Digges)

General Spanky
1936   MGM
To never tell no one where the secret cave is at. ("Yankee General": Ralph Morgan)

Generation
1969   Avco Embassy
Just what we need, another trouble-maker. ("Jim Bolton": David Janssen)

Geronimo
1962   United Artists
We're going down. ("Geronimo": Chuck Connors)

The Getaway
1941   MGM

You'll never get rid of me, Terry. ("Jeff Crane": Robert Sterling)

Getting Straight
1970   Columbia
I don't like him. I don't belong there. ("Jan": Candice Bergen)

Ghost
1990   Paramount
'Bye. ("Molly Jensen": Demi Moore)

The Ghost and Mrs. Muir
1947   20th Century–Fox
Martha? ("Mrs. Muir": Gene Tierney)

The Ghost Breakers
1940   Paramount
You would? ("Larry Lawrence": Bob Hope)

Ghost Fever
1987   Miramax
Us dead people sure know how to live. ("Buford": Sherman Hemsley)

Ghostbusters
1984   Columbia
I love this town! ("Winston Zedd-more": Ernie Hudson)

Ghostbusters II
1989   Columbia
No, I believe it's one of the Fettucinis. ("Dr. Peter Venkman": Bill Murray)

Giant
1956   Warner Brothers
You want to know something, Leslie. If I live to be ninety, I'm never going to figure you out. ("Jordan Benedict": Rock Hudson)

Gidget
1959 Columbia
Oh, just wait. Wait till the girls get a load of this. Honest to goodness, it's the absolute ultimate. ("Gidget": Sandra Dee)

Gidget Goes to Rome
1962 Columbia
God bless you, one and all. ("Aunt Albertina": Jessup Royce Landis)

The Gig
1986 The Gig Company
B flat. ("Marty Flynn": Wayne Rogers)

Gigi
1958 MGM
Thank heaven. ("Mme. Alvarez": Hermione Gingold)

Gilda
1946 Columbia
Johnny, let's go. Let's go home. ("Gilda": Rita Hayworth)

The Gilded Lily
1935 Paramount
You old mug. Take off your shoes and kiss me. ("Marilyn David": Claudette Colbert)

Girl Happy
1965 MGM
I'm paying you to watch her, ain't I? So why don't you get to work? ("Big Frank": Harold J. Stone)

The Girl Hunters
1963 Colorama
So long, baby. ("Mike Hammer": Mickey Spillane)

Girl in the Picture
1986 Rank
Uh, I'll just be a second. You can take your prints out of the fixer now. I think they've been in long enough. ("Ken": David McKay)

The Girl Most Likely
1958 Universal
Wait, Pete! ("Dodie": Jane Powell)

A Girl Named Tamiko
1962 Paramount
Tamiko. ("Ivan Kalin": Laurence Harvey)

The Girl of the Golden West
1938 MGM
And tell her not to try to thank me for it. It's, uh, it's bad luck. ("Jack Rance": Walter Pidgeon)

Girlfriends
1978 Warner Brothers
I think it's Martin. ("Anne Munroe": Anita Skinner)

The Girls of Pleasure Island
1953 Paramount
Jimmy. Jimmy. Jimmy. ("Hester Halyard": Audrey Dalton)

The Glass Key
1935 Paramount
I suppose you think I'm nuts. No, the other one. But if you figure on getting married with my rock, you're nuts. ("Paul Madvig": Brian Donlevy)

The Glass Menagerie
1950 Warner Brothers
And that is how I remember them, my mother and my sister. Good-bye. ("Tom Wingfield": Arthur Kennedy)

The Glass Menagerie
1987   Cineplex
And so, good-bye. ("Tom": John Malkovich)

The Glass Slipper
1954   MGM
And so the prophecy came true, and Ella went to live in the palace. As for the fairy godmother, and she was the fairy godmother, she went back where she came from. And everybody lived happily ever after. ("Narrator": Walter Pidgeon)

Gleaming the Cube
1989   20th Century–Fox
Gotcha. ("Al Lucero": Steve Bauer)

The Glenn Miller Story
1953   Universal
As some of you might know, Major Glenn Miller is not with us today. But in his absence we shall do this program exactly as he had planned it. Our first number, therefore, will be a new arrangement which Major Miller himself made especially for this performance. This tune should be a familiar one. Especially to the members of Major Miller's family across the ocean who are listening. ("Don Haynes": Charles Drake)

Gloria
1980   Columbia
Aren't you going to kiss your grandmother? ("Gloria Swenson": Gena Rowlands)

Glory
1989   Tri-Star
Come on! Come on! ("John Rawlins": Morgan Freeman)

The Go-Between
1970   Columbia
Our love was a beautiful thing, wasn't it? Tell him he can feel proud to be descended from our union, a child of so much happiness and beauty. Tell him. ("Marian Maudsley": Julie Christie)

Go Naked in the World
1960   MGM
She knew I'd always come back, Pop. ("Nick Stratton": Anthony Franciosa)

Go West
1940   MGM
We owe you boys an honor. It shall be your honor to drive the golden spike. ("Railroad President": George Lessey)

The Goddess
1958   Columbia
Of course. ("John Tower": Steve Hill)

The Godfather
1972   Paramount
Don Corleone. (Visitor)

The Godfather, Part II
1974   Paramount
Surprise! (Family members)

The Godfather, Part III
1990   Paramount
No! ("Kay Adams": Diane Keaton)

God's Little Acre
1958   United Artists
Come on, mule. ("Griselda": Tina Louise)

The Gods Must Be Crazy
1984   20th Century–Fox

Xi was beginning to think he would never find the end of the earth. And one day, suddenly, there it was. ("Narrator": Paddy O'Byrne)

The Gods Must Be Crazy II
1988   Columbia
Now can you do it right? ("Dr. Ann Taylor": Lena Farugia)

Goin' Coconuts
1978   Osmond
Yeah. ("Marie": Marie Osmond)

Goin' South
1978   Paramount
Why, sure you will, honey pie. You got used to me, didn't you? Anyways, first let's get used to being rich. ("Henry Moon": Jack Nicholson)

Going Home
1971   MGM
Well, what the hell do you think happens, kid? You get to be twenty. ("Harry K. Graham": Robert Mitchum)

Going in Style
1979   Warner Brothers
And besides, no tinhorn joint like this could ever hold me. ("Joe": George Burns)

Going Undercover
1988   Miramax
Your hat. ("Marigold de la Hunt": Lea Thompson)

Gold Diggers of 1935
1935   Warner Brothers
Well, if I'm going to start fainting in my old age, I may as well have a doc-tor in the family. Think of all the money I could save on medical bills. ("Mrs. Mathilda Prentiss": Alice Brady)

Gold Is Where You Find It
1938   Warner Brothers
That's the future of California, not gold. And it'll be our future, too, Jared. Isn't that something to live and work for? ("Serena Ferris": Olivia De Havilland)

Golden Boy
1939   Columbia
Papa, I've come home. ("Joe Bonaparte": William Holden)

The Golden Seal
1983   New Realm
Good-bye. ("Eric": Torquil Campbell)

The Golden Voyage of Sinbad
1973   Columbia
But tie up your camel. ("Sinbad": John Phillip Law/"Vizier": Douglas Wilmer)

Goldengirl
1979   Avco Embassy
Lose? Well, lose is a four-letter word, and I don't use those. ("Goldengirl": Susan Anton)

Goldfinger
1964   United Artists
Oh, no, you don't. This is no time to be rescued. ("James Bond": Sean Connery)

Gone with the Wind
1939   MGM
Tara. Home. I'll go home. And I'll

think of some way to get him back. After all, tomorrow is another day. ("Scarlett O'Hara": Vivien Leigh)

The Good Earth
1937 MGM
O-lan, you are the earth. ("Wang Lung": Paul Muni)

Good Fellas
1990 Warner Brothers
And that's the hardest part. Today everything is different. There's no action. I have to wait around like everyone else. Can't even get decent food. Right after I got here I ordered some spaghetti with marinara sauce and I got egg noodles and catsup. I'm an average nobody. Get to live the rest of my life like a schnook. ("Henry Hill": Ray Liotta)

The Good Guys and the Bad Guys
1969 Warner Brothers
Damn you, Flagg, listen to me! ("McKay": George Kennedy)

The Good Humor Man
1950 Columbia
My good humor man. ("Margie Bellew": Lola Albright)

Good Morning, Vietnam
1987 Buena Vista
Good-bye, Vietnam. That's right. I'm history. I'm out of here. I got the lucky ticket home, baby. Rollin', rollin', rollin', keep them wagons rollin', rawhide. Yeah, that's right, the final Adrian Kronauer broadcast, and this one is brought to you by our friends at the Pentagon. Remember the people who brought you Korea, that's right, the U. S. Army. If it's being done correctly, here or abroad, it's probably not being done by the Army. I heard that. Ha-ha, you're here, good to see you. I'm here to make sure you don't say anything controversial. Speaking of things controversial, is it true that there is a marijuana problem here in Vietnam? No, it's not a problem, everybody has it. I don't know, Adrian. Leo, Leo. Adrian, take care of yourself. I just want you to know one thing, if you're going to be dressing in civilian clothes don't forget pumps. Thank you, Leo, thanks for these. Oh, these are special. They're ruby slippers, Adrian. Put these on and say there's no place like home, there's no place like home, and you can be there. Ha, ha, ha, I hope, I hope we all could. ("Adrian Kronauer": Robin Williams)

The Good Mother
1988 Buena Vista
I see Molly every second weekend and during school vacations and we try to make the most of our time together. Sometimes I'm all right, but other times the pain of the loss is terrible. And then I, I think of something that Gram said to me when my losing Molly seemed unthinkable, something that could never come to pass. She said, "Everybody knows you're a good mother, Anna." ("Anna": Diane Keaton)

Good Neighbor Sam
1964 Columbia
Um hm, yes, things are back to normal. ("Sam Bissell": Jack Lemmon)

Good News
1947 MGM
They sure are blue. ("Tommy Marlowe": Peter Lawford)

Good Sam
1948 RKO
Glowing. ("Lee Clayton": Ann Sheridan)

The Good Wife
1987 Atlantic
Who else have I got to give it to? ("Sonny Hills": Bryan Brown)

Goodbye, Columbus
1969 Paramount
You don't understand anything. All you've ever done is accuse me of things and criticize me of things, analyze me, telling me why don't I have this fixed, why don't I have that fixed, as if it were my fault that I couldn't have them fixed. ("Brenda Patimkin": Ali MacGraw)

The Goodbye Girl
1977 Warner Brothers
Never mind that, you're rusting my guitar. ("Elliott Garfield": Richard Dreyfuss)

Goodbye, Mr. Chips
1939 MGM
Good-bye, Mr. Chips. Good-bye. ("Peter Colley, III": Terry Kilburn)

Goodbye, Mr. Chips
1969 MGM
Here. (A student)

The Gorgeous Hussy
1936 MGM

Good-bye, John Randolph. ("Peggy O'Neal Eaton": Joan Crawford)

The Gorgon
1964 Columbia
She's free now, Paul. She's free. ("Meister": Christopher Lee)

Gorillas in the Mist
1988 Universal
Instead you've got an album full of gorillas, who wouldn't be alive if it weren't for you. ("Rose Carr": Julie Harris)

Gorky Park
1983 Orion
One day, Akasha, one day. ("Irina Asanova": Joanna Pacula)

The Graduate
1967 Embassy
Not for me! ("Elaine Robinson": Katharine Ross)

Grand Hotel
1932 MGM
Grand Hotel. (Chauffeur)

The Grapes of Wrath
1940 20th Century–Fox
I know. That's what makes us tough. Rich fellas come up an' they die, an' their kids ain't no good, an' they die out. But we keep a-comin'. We're the people that live. They can't wipe us out, they can't lick us. We'll go on forever, Pa, 'cause we're the people. ("Ma Joad": Jane Darwell)

The Grass Is Greener
1960 Universal
Oh, I sprained my wrist. (Victor Rhyall": Cary Grant)

Gray Lady Down
1978 Universal
Thanks. ("Captain Paul Blanchard": Charlton Heston)

Grease
1978 Paramount
What do you mean, how do I know? ("Danny": John Travolta)

Grease 2
1982 Paramount
Certainedest. Yeah, I like that. I'd love to kiss you again. ("Michael Carrington": Maxwell Caulfield)

The Great Caruso
1950 MGM
Bravo! (Audience member)

Great Day in the Morning
1955 RKO
We've lost him. No use wasting any more time around here. ("Stephen Kirby": Alex Nicol)

The Great Dictator
1940 United Artists
Listen. ("Hannah": Paulette Goddard)

Great Expectations
1946 Universal
Oh, Pip! ("Estella": Valerie Hobson)

The Great Gabbo
1929 World-Wide
Well, don't you call me no dummy. Or you'll get a chance to do that single you've been talking so much about. ("A dummy": Otto Gabbo)

The Great Gatsby
1974 Paramount
I thought of Gatsby's wonder when he first picked out the green light at the end of Daisy's dock. He had come a long way to this lawn and his dream must have seemed so close that he could hardly fail to grasp it. He did not know that it was already behind him. ("Narrator/Nick Carroway": Sam Waterston)

The Great Imposter
1961 Universal
Gentlemen. ("Ferdinand Waldo Demara, Jr.": Tony Curtis)

The Great Lie
1941 Warner Brothers
If you're going to look like that, people will think I beat you. If you don't stop, I will. ("Pete": George Brent)

The Great Outdoors
1988 Universal
Get the hell in the car, we've got to beat Uncle Roman home. Move it, move it, move it, everybody. Let's go. ("Chet Ripley": John Candy)

The Great Race
1965 Warner Brothers
Relax. This time I'm going to win it my way. Push the button, Max. ("Prof. Fate": Jack Lemmon)

The Great Waltz
1972 MGM
Don't leave me, Jetty, I love you. ("Johann Strauss, Jr.": Horst Bucholz)

The Great White Hope
1970 20th Century–Fox
No, you're new here like I is, huh?

Come on, chillun, let 'em pass by. ("Jack Jefferson": James Earl Jones)

The Great Ziegfeld
1936   MGM
I've got to have more steps. I need more steps. I've got to get higher, higher. ("Florenz Ziegfeld": William Powell)

The Greatest Story Ever Told
1965   United Artists
And, lo, I am with you always, even unto the end of the world. ("Jesus": Max von Sydow)

The Greek Tycoon
1978   Universal
Here. Have another piece of herring. Good luck. It's what we need. ("Theo Tomasis": Anthony Quinn)

Green Card
1990   Buena Vista
So do I. ("Bronte": Andie MacDowell)

Green Fire
1954   MGM
Hey! If you don't mind, it's raining! ("Vic Leonard": Paul Douglas)

Green Ice
1981   ITC
No, I guess I'll never learn. ("Wiley": Ryan O'Neal)

Green Mansions
1959   MGM
If you look in this place tomorrow, and it's gone, you musn't be sad, because you know it still exists, not very far away. ("Rima's voice": Audrey Hepburn)

Gremlins
1984   Warner Brothers
Well, that's the story. So if your air conditioner goes on the fritz or your washing machine blows up or your video recorder conks out, before you call the repairman, turn on all the lights, check all the closets and cupboards, look under all the beds. Because you never can tell, there just might be a gremlin in your house. (Narrator)

Gremlins 2: The New Batch
1990   Warner Brothers
That's very generous, sir. A half-day off once the building is operational. Thank you, sir. ("Forster": Robert Picardo)

Greystoke: The Legend of Tarzan, Lord of the Apes
1984   Warner Brothers
As I watched him disappear into the green of the forest, I knew that this parting had broken both their hearts. John had implored Jane to go with him, but we knew that this was an impossible course for their love. How could she survive? But I hope for their sake that the world will turn in their favor, and one day, somehow, they will find each other again. ("Captaine Phillippe D'Arnot": Ian Holm)

The Grifters
1990   Miramax
No! No! No! No! No! No! ("Lilly Dillon": Anjelica Huston)

Grounds for Marriage
1950   MGM
You said it. This always cures every-

thing. ("Dr. Lincoln I. Bartlett": Van Johnson)

Guadalcanal Diary
1943   20th Century–Fox
OK, we'll be there waiting for you. ("Taxi Potts": William Bendix)

Guardian of the Wilderness
1977   Sunn
On June thirtieth, eighteen sixty-four, President Lincoln signed the historic bill providing for protection of twenty thousand acres in the California mountains. It was the first step ever taken toward preserving our country's great wilderness, and it brought about the formation of America's national park system. The doctor had told Galen he would die at the age of forty-two, but he lived on to be ninety-six years old. He always wanted to do something special, and I knew he wouldn't give up until he did. To me he became an example of what a man can really accomplish if he believes in himself. It was through Galen's hard work and far-sighted efforts that the land he loved and fought for would remain forever exactly as it was when he first saw it, for all future generations to enjoy. Oh, he named this magnificent valley for the bear that was his lifelong friend and protector, Yosemite. (Narrator)

Guess Who's Coming to Dinner
1967   Columbia
Well, Tillie, when the hell are we going to get some dinner? ("Matt Drayton": Spencer Tracy)

A Guide for the Married Man
1967   20th Century–Fox

I'll break that camera over your head if you don't. . . . ("Ed Stander": Robert Morse)

Gun Glory
1957   MGM
Oh, Jo, you better stay. We've got a boy to raise and a whole new church to build. ("Tom Early": Stewart Granger)

The Gun That Won the West
1955   Columbia
Yeah, I did once. ("Jim Bridger": Dennis Morgan)

Gunfight at the O.K. Corral
1957   Paramount
What's the name of this game? ("John H. 'Doc' Holliday": Kirk Douglas)

The Gunfighter
1950   20th Century–Fox
Come on in, Peggy. ("Sheriff Mark Strett": Millard Mitchell)

Gunfire at Indian Gap
1958   Republic
I wanted to. I think of you all the time. When you stood up to Pike, I. It's finished, Juan. I've never been so happy. ("Cheel": Vera Hruba Ralston)

Gung Ho!
1943   Universal
Gung ho! (Marines of Carlson's Raiders)

Gung Ho
1986 Paramount
Let's rock. ("Hunt Stevenson": Michael Keaton

Gunpoint
1966 Universal
It's not too late. ("Uvalde": Joan Staley)

Guns at Batasi
1964 20th Century–Fox
That will be all, lad. ("Regimental Sergeant Major Lauderdale": Richard Attenborough)

Guns for San Sebastian
1967 MGM
This time only, only God knows. ("Leon Alastray": Anthony Quinn)

The Guns of Navarone
1961 Columbia
To tell you the truth, neither did I. ("Capt. Mallory": Gregory Peck)

Guys and Dolls
1955 MGM
Yay! (Wedding attendee on street)

Gypsy
1962 Warner Brothers
Only it was you and me wearing exactly the same gown. It was an ad for Minsky. And the headline said, "Madame Rose, and her daughter Gypsy." ("Rose": Rosalind Russell)

Gypsy Girl
1966 Continental
Yes, that's it. ("Vicar Philip Moss": Geoffrey Bayldon)

The Gypsy Moths
1969 MGM
And me. ("V. John Brandon": William Windom)

Hair
1979 United Artists
My God! ("Claude": John Savage)

Hairspray
1988 New Line
Let's dance! ("Tracy Turnblad": Ricki Lake)

Half Moon Street
1986 20th Century–Fox
You're incorrigible, Dr. Slaughter. ("Lord Bulbeck": Michael Caine)

The Half-Naked Truth
1932 RKO
Hurry up and get it over with, baby. I, uh, I got a big surprise for you. ("Harry Bates": Lee Tracy)

Hallelujah
1929 MGM
I sure is glad to be back home. ("Zeke": Daniel L. Haynes)

Halls of Montezuma
1950 20th Century–Fox
Come on, men, give 'em hell! ("Lt. Anderson": Richard Widmark)

Hammett
1982 Warner Brothers
Never is like a story. ("Hammett": Frederic Forrest)

Hang 'Em High
1967 United Artists
Cooper, Charlie Blackfoot was seen in the town of Ridgeway. I got two unfilled warrants here. Blackfoot and Maddow. The law still wants them. ("Judge Adam Fenton": Pat Hingle)

Hangman's Knot
1952   Columbia
Don't worry about us, Molly. This Indian token is our passage home. ("Major Stewart": Randolph Scott)

Hangover Square
1944   20th Century–Fox
It's better this way, sir. ("Dr. Allan Middleton": George Sanders)

Hannah and Her Sisters
1985   Orion
I'm pregnant. ("Lee": Barbara Hershey)

Hanna's War
1988   Cannon
You know so well why words aren't necessary. With love forever. Your daughter Hanna. ("Hanna Senesh": Maruschka Detmers)

Hanover Street
1979   Columbia
I love you, Maggie. Think of me when you drink tea. ("David Halloran": Harrison Ford)

The Happy Hooker
1975   Cannon
She likes you. (Boy in street)

The Happy Hooker Goes Hollywood
1980   Cannon
Good-bye, Xaviera. (Army Archerd as himself)

Happy Land
1943   20th Century–Fox
Good. ("Lew Marsh": Don Ameche)

Happy New Year
1987   Columbia
So that night we were all on the plane to Rio. Carolyn opened an antique store. Me, I'm in the export business now, beef and wallets. And Nick tells me Harry Winston is gonna open a place down here in May. Some people just never learn. ("Charlie": Charles Durning)

The Happy Years
1950   MGM
Not a bit. ("John Humperdink Stover": Dean Stockwell)

A Hard Day's Night
1964   United Artists
Get rid of those pictures. ("Paul": Paul McCartney)

Hard, Fast and Beautiful
1951   RKO
You won't forget, will you? ("Milly Farley": Claire Trevor)

The Hard Man
1957   Columbia
No, Larry, I'll never forget it. ("Steve Burden": Guy Madison)

Hard Times
1975   Columbia
Yeah. ("Speed": James Coburn)

Hard to Hold
1984   Universal
I love you. ("Diana Lawson": Janet Eilber)

The Harder They Fall
1956   Columbia
A man that gives away twenty-six

thousand dollars you can't talk to. I want to tell you one more thing. I wouldn't give twenty-six cents for your future. ("Nick Benko": Rod Steiger)

Hardly Working
1981 20th Century–Fox
Hi, lady. You know, Millie, I'm sure we're doing the right thing, but since we only work days at the college, I could moonlight and pick up some extra bucks. I can't decide what to do. It's a toss-up. It'll either be brain surgery or trying for that opening at the nuclear plant. ("Bo Hooper": Jerry Lewis)

The Hardys Ride High
1939 MGM
Well, that's more like it. ("Andy Hardy": Mickey Rooney)

Harlem Nights
1989 Paramount
Sweet as sugar. ("Sugar Ray": Richard Pryor)

Harriet Craig
1950 Columbia
I see. Well, good night, Mrs. Craig. ("Mrs. Frazier": Fiona O'Shiel)

Harry and the Hendersons
1987 Universal
I don't know. There's always Loch Ness. ("Jacques Lafleur": David Suchet)

Harry and Tonto
1974 20th Century–Fox
Kitty, kitty, kitty, kitty, kitty. Kitty, kitty, kitty, kitty, kitty, kitty. Kitty, kitty, kitty, kitty. All right, all right, what's your name, kiddo, huh? ("Harry Coombs": Art Carney)

Harry and Walter Go to New York
1976 Columbia
Well, uh, pick it up a little, a little more tempo. Harry, I don't know. . . . ("Walter Hill": Elliott Gould)

Harum Scarum
1965 MGM
Be a nice king and don't exile him to the U.S.A. ("Johnny Tyrone": Elvis Presley)

Harvey
1950 Universal
Well, thank you, Harvey. I prefer you, too. ("Elwood P. Dowd": James Stewart)

The Harvey Girls
1946 MGM
Good-bye. ("Susan Bradley": Judy Garland)

The Hasty Heart
1949 Warner Brothers
Tommy. ("Sister Margaret": Patricia Neal)

A Hatful of Rain
1957 20th Century–Fox
It's my husband, my husband. Would you hurry, please? ("Celia Pope": Eva Marie Saint)

Haunted Honeymoon
1986 Orion
Before you all settle back into the cozy comfort of a happy ending, let

me ask you one question. Are you so sure that our story has ended, hm? Until next time, this is your host wishing you pleasant dreams. ("The Host": Bill Bailey)

Havana
1990   Universal
I do this sometimes, drive down from Miami. It isn't that I expect her, the ferry doesn't run anymore. But it happens sometimes. I see a boat offshore and something goes faster in me, hope I guess. What the hell, Fidel Castro was on the Jack Paar show so anything can happen. I even read the newspapers now, not just looking for the point spread or the odds or the morning line. Human interest, that's what I read. A dozen lines about what happened on a street corner in Indianapolis, or identical twins meet after thirty years, smoke the same brand of cigarettes and both married to somebody named Shirley, like that. Somebody came out of Havana, told me Baby Hernandez was the big winner that night, lives in Jersey now. And I got a postcard from Joe Volpi, postmarked Santo Domingo, so I guess he's still doing it, running things for Meyer. It's a new decade, things are different. We got our own kind of revolution going. I'm doing OK these days, I'm way ahead, but it's not the same. I sit with my back to the wall, watch the entrance. You never know who's gonna walk in. Somebody blown off course. This is hurricane country. ("Jack Weil": Robert Redford)

Hawaii
1966   United Artists

Do you remember? ("Abner Hale": Max Von Sydow)

Heart Beat
1979   Warner Brothers
Ned thought that life was destroyed by compromises, that was his weakness. Jack thought it was made by them, and that was his. I decided that compromises are like dental appointments. You're damned if you make them and you're damned if you don't. ("Carolyn Cassady": Sissy Spacek)

The Heart Is a Lonely Hunter
1968   Warner Brothers
Mr. Singer, can you hear me? I just wanted you to know, Mr. Singer, that I loved you. Loved you. ("Mick Kelly": Sondra Locke)

Heart of Dixie
1989   Orion
You pull out all the stops, Maggie. You go get 'em. ("Hoyt": Treat Williams)

Heartbeat
1946   RKO
Oh, I am, darling. ("Arlette": Ginger Rogers)

Heartbreak Hotel
1988   Buena Vista
Hey, Elvis. You're still the king. ("Johnny Wolfe": Charlie Schlatter)

Hearts of the West
1975   MGM
The slightest smile broke across the kid's face as the barking revolvers became nothing but a memory. Secure

in the knowledge of his friendship with the old trapper and the girl, he sped along, he'd done his job. ("Lewis Tater": Jeff Bridges)

Heathers
1989 New World
Yeah, so would I. ("Veronica Sawyer": Winona Ryder)

Heaven Can Wait
1943 20th Century-Fox
No, up. ("His Excellency": Laird Cregar)

Heaven Can Wait
1978 Paramount
Yes. I'd love to have a cup of coffee with you. ("Betty Logan": Julie Christie)

The Heavenly Kid
1985 Orion
Someone very special. ("Lenny": Jason Gedrick)

Heidi
1937 20th Century-Fox
And please make every little boy and girl in the world as happy as I am. Amen. ("Heidi": Shirley Temple)

The Heiress
1949 Paramount
Catherine! Catherine! Catherine! Catherine! Catherine! Catherine! Catherine! Catherine! ("Morris Townsend": Montgomery Clift)

Hell High
1989 MGM
I'm talking to you. You, wake up. Are you deaf? I said eyes to me. There's

going to be trouble if you don't turn your head in this direction. I said eyes to me. ("Substitute teacher": Janet Atwood)

Hell in the Pacific
1969 Cinerama
You better watch how you talk to me. ("American Soldier": Lee Marvin)

Hell to Eternity
1960 Allied Artists
Yeah. His name is Kioshi. ("Guy Gabaldon": Jeffrey Hunter)

Heller in Pink Tights
1960 Paramount
Also you're much stronger than he is. You could have hurt him. ("Angela Rossini": Sophia Loren)

Hello, Dolly
1969 20th Century-Fox
Wonderful woman. ("Horace Vandergelder": Walter Matthau)

Hells Angels on Wheels
1967 U.S. Films
Buddy! ("Shill": Sabrina Scharf)

Help!
1965 United Artists
Ah, so. Hah! He who wears the ring. ("Ahme": Eleanor Bron)

Hemingway's Adventures of a Young Man
1962 20th Century-Fox
So for the last time you look at the lake beside the house where you were born. For tomorrow you will try again. But this time you're not running away. You're moving towards

something, far away. That's the difference. Whatever you have to do men have always done. If they have done it, then you could do it too. ("Nick Adams": Richard Beymer)

Her Adventurous Night
1946   Universal
Small wonder. ("Junior": Scotty Beckett)

Her Alibi
1989   Warner Brothers
He held her in his arms and kissed her long and hard. He felt he understood this woman completely now. Not a part of her existed that he didn't know. Except of course what she didn't want him to know. ("Phil Blackwood": Tom Selleck)

Herbie Goes to Monte Carlo
1977   Buena Vista
Well, almost. ("Wheely Applegate": Don Knotts)

Here Come the Girls
1953   Paramount
You can go home, folks, I'll never make it. ("Stanley Snodgrass": Bob Hope)

Here Comes Mr. Jordan
1941   Columbia
So long, champ. ("Mr. Jordan": Claude Rains)

Here Comes the Groom
1951   Paramount
That's my Em. ("Pete": Bing Crosby)

Hero and the Terror
1988   Cannon

Oh, Danny. I do, I do. ("Kay Griffith": Brynn Thayer)

Heroes
1977   Universal
You're OK. ("Carol Bell": Sally Field)

Hero's Island
1962   United Artists
That's how you'll end up, Major Bonnett, but I guess that's how we'll all end up after all is said and done. You go on, do what you have to do. I'll stay here and do my best to bring up a family that believes in God and believes in the land. God and us and the land is all I know. God and us and the land. ("Devon Mainwaring": Kate Manx)

He's My Girl
1987   Scotti Brothers
One, two, one, two, three. ("Bryan Peters": David Hallyday)

Hide in Plain Sight
1980   MGM/UA
Let's see. ("Thomas Hacklin, Jr.": James Caan)

Hiding Out
1987   DEG
You know, it's much better the second time. ("Max/Andrew/Eddie Collins": John Cryer)

High Anxiety
1977   20th Century–Fox
Never mind, keep pulling back. Maybe nobody will notice. (Cameraman)

High Ballin'
1978   American International

I'll see you, Tank. ("Rane": Peter Fonda)

The High Commissioner
1968   Cinerama
OK. ("Scobie Malone": Rod Taylor)

High Road to China
1983   Warner Brothers
I should have sold you when I had the chance. ("O'Malley": Tom Selleck)

High Sierra
1941   Warner Brothers
Free? Free. ("Marie Garson": Ida Lupino)

High Society
1956   MGM
End of story. (Louis Armstrong as himself)

High Spirits
1988   Tri-Star
Yeah, happiness. ("Jack": Steve Guttenberg)

High Tide
1987   Tri-Star
OK, well, I'll leave this with you. (Waitress)

Hills of Home
1948   MGM
Come ye blessed of my father, for I was sick and ye visited me. ("Tammas Milton": Tom Drake)

His Brother's Wife
1936   MGM
Now, Chris, be yourself or don't be yourself. ("Rita Wilson": Barbara Stanwyck)

His Girl Friday
1940   Columbia
OK, Duffy. Well, isn't that a coincidence? We're going to Albany. I wonder if Bruce can put us up. Say, why don't you? ("Walter Burns": Cary Grant)

His Kind of Woman
1951   RKO
You know, you could be a handy thing to have around the house if a man went broke. ("Dan Milner": Robert Mitchum)

Hit List
1989   New Line
Hey. ("Frank De Salvo": Leo Rossi)

Hitler's Children
1943   RKO
And that night as I left Germany I thought lots of things weren't quite the same. True, the fires were still burning in the hills, and Hitler's children were still swearing to die for him. But to me the fires didn't seem to burn so brightly, and the voices didn't come up quite so bravely. And perhaps all over Germany people were beginning to ask themselves the same question you must ask yourself tonight as you go home: Can we stop Hitler's children before it's too late? Well, you and I at least know the answer to that question. So long as we have boys like Karl and girls like Anna, the light will always outshine the dark. For as the prophets of old used to say, the memory of virtue is immortal, and we have a long, long memory. ("Professor Nichols": Kent Smith)

The Holcroft Covenant
1985 Universal
Now it works. ("Noel Holcroft":
Michael Caine)

Hold That Ghost
1941 Universal
Now who put that there? ("Ferdinand
Jones": Lou Costello)

Hold Your Man
1933 MGM
All aboard for Cincinnata. (Conductor)

Holiday
1938 Columbia
Right here. ("Johnny Case": Cary
Grant)

Holiday Inn
1942 Paramount
But the world can't do this to us.
("Danny Reed": Walter Abel)

Hollywood Hotel
1937 Warner Brothers
Sure, she believed you. ("Jonesey":
Glenda Farrell)

Hollywood or Bust
1956 Paramount
May I have your autograph, please?
Oh, wonderful. Thank you. (A fan)

Hollywood Shuffle
1987 Goldwyn
Through rain, sleet and snow, I
deliver your mail. I'm a U.S. postman
and you can be one too. I deliver people's dreams and more importantly I
have the respect and admiration of
the entire community, and that makes
me proud. So if you can't take pride in
your job, remember, there's always
work at the post office. ("Bobby Taylor": Robert Townsend)

Hombre
1967 20th Century–Fox
He was called John Russell. ("Men-
dez": Martin Balsam)

Home Alone
1990 20th Century–Fox
Kevin, what did you do to my room?
("Buzz": Devin Ratray)

Home from the Hill
1959 MGM
Not till today, he didn't. Come on.
Let's us go on home. ("Rafe Copley":
George Peppard)

Home Is Where the Hart Is
1987 Atlantic
Now, of course, my compensation will
be the usual twenty percent. Oh, did
I say twenty percent? Crazy me, living in the past. It's twenty-five–eight
percent. ("Carson Boundy": Martin
Mull)

Hondo
1954 Warner Brothers
Yup. The end of a way of life. Too bad.
It's a good way. Wagons forward! Yo!
("Hondo Lane": John Wayne)

Honey, I Shrunk the Kids
1989 Buena Vista
Hey, wait, I get it. French class.
("Nick Szalinski": Robert Oliveri)

Honeymoon
1947 RKO

In accordance with the powers vested in me and all the requirements having been complied with, I declare them legally married. ("Judge Riberol": Charles Trowbridge)

Honeymoon Hotel
1964 MGM
Oh. ("Sherry": Jill St. John)

Honeysuckle Rose
1980 Warner Brothers
Ladies and gentlemen, Buck Bonham. ("Viv": Dyan Cannon)

Honky Tonk
1941 MGM
No, Candy Man. Now, for understanding you so well, what do I get? ("Elizabeth Cotton": Lana Turner)

Hook, Line and Sinker
1968 Columbia
Well, if nothing else, you can tell everybody I died a happy man. A true fisherman. With a smile on my lips and a fish in my heart. ("Peter Ingersoll": Jerry Lewis)

Hooper
1978 Warner Brothers
Roger, as usual, you're wrong. ("Sonny Hooper": Burt Reynolds)

Hoosiers
1986 Orion
I love you guys. ("Coach Norman Dale": Gene Hackman)

Hope and Glory
1987 Columbia
All my life nothing ever quite matched the perfect joy of that moment. My school lay in ruins, the river beckoned with a promise of stolen days. ("Bill Rohan": Sebastian Rice Edwards)

Hopscotch
1980 Avco
Will you never learn? ("Isabel": Glenda Jackson)

The Horizontal Lieutenant
1962 MGM
That's how I won my second purple heart, and along with it, Lieutenant Molly Blue. ("2nd. Lt. Merle Wye": Jim Hutton)

The Horn Blows at Midnight
1945 Warner Brothers
Elizabeth, I just had the craziest dream. You know, if you saw it in the movies, you'd never believe it. ("Athanael": Jack Benny)

Hornets' Nest
1969 United Artists
They, they killed Papa, they killed Mama, too. I killed Carlo, but I didn't mean it. Soldier, I didn't mean it. ("Aldo": Mark Colleano)

Horror Show
1989 MGM/UA
Great. ("Donna McCarthy": Rita Taggart)

Horse Feathers
1932 Paramount
We do. ("Professor Wagstaff": Groucho Marx/"Baravelli": Chico Marx)

The Horsemen
1970 Columbia

Farewell, my son. May Allah sustain thee. May he give you peace. ("Tursen": Jack Palance)

Hostile Guns
1967   Paramount
My regular run is Huntsville. We'll visit, we'll have a lot of time to talk. Mike, let's get on the road. ("Gid McCool": George Montgomery)

Hot Blood
1955   Columbia
All right, I'll be a king, I'll be anything. ("Stephen Torino": Cornel Wilde)

Hot Lead and Cold Feet
1978   Buena Vista
Morning, Mr. Bloodshy. ("Denver Kid": Don Knotts)

Hot Money
1936   Warner Brothers
It's the tops. ("Chick Randall": Ross Alexander)

Hot Pursuit
1987   Paramount
Overboard! ("Mac MacClaren": Robert Loggia)

The Hot Rock
1972   20th Century–Fox
Good morning. ("Dortmunder": Robert Redford)

Hot Stuff
1979   Columbia
OK, you kids! Now stop it! I mean it! The fun's over! It's time to go to bed. ("Ernie Fortunato": Dom DeLuise)

Hot Summer Night
1957   MGM
Sure. ("William Joel Partain": Leslie Nielsen)

Hot to Trot
1988   Warner Brothers
That's all, folks. ("The voice of Don": John Candy)

Houdini
1953   Paramount
I'll come back, Bess. If there's any way, I'll come back. I'll come back. ("Houdini": Tony Curtis)

The Hound of the Baskervilles
1959   United Artists
Oh, thank you. ("Doctor Watson": Andre Morell)

The Hounds of Notre Dame
1980   Pan-Canadian
God, I love those little wonders. ("Father Athol Murray": Thomas Peacocke)

Hour of the Assassin
1987   Concorde
Excuse me. Excuse me please. ("Merrick": Robert Vaughn)

Hour of the Gun
1967   United Artists
Aces. ("Doc Holliday": Jason Robards, Jr.)

House of Dark Shadows
1970   MGM
Jeff. ("Maggie Evans": Kathryn Leigh Scott)

House of Frankenstein
1944   Universal

Don't go this way. Quicksand. Quicksand. Not this way. Quicksand. Not that way. Quicksand. Quicksand. ("Dr. Gustav Niemann": Boris Karloff)

House of Numbers
1957 MGM
Hello, this is the warden. I want you to pick up Arne Judlow at an apartment at three two seven nine Acacia Street. He's unarmed and I want him taken alive. That's an order. ("Warden": Edward Platt)

The House on Carroll Street
1988 Orion
I have nothing to say. ("Emily Crane": Kelly McGillis)

Houseboat
1958 Paramount
I do. ("Cinzia Zaccardi": Sophia Loren)

The Houston Story
1956 Columbia
Frankie, listen to me. You've hurt enough people already. ("Louie": Frank Jenks)

How I Got into College
1989 20th Century–Fox
There's always graduate school. ("'A'": Bruce Wagner)

How the West Was Won
1962 MGM
The West that was won by its pioneers, settlers, adventurers, is long gone now, yet it is theirs forever, for they left tracks in history that will never be eroded by wind or rain, never plowed under by tractors, never buried in the compost of events. Out of the hard simplicity of their lives, out of their vitality, their hopes, their sorrows, grew legends of courage and pride to inspire their children and their children's children. From soil enriched by their blood, out of their fever to explore and build, came lakes where once were burning deserts, came the goods of the earth, mines and wheat fields, orchards and great lumber mills, all the sinews of a growing country. Out of their rude settlements, their trading posts, came cities to rank among the great ones of the world. All the heritage of a people free to dream, free to act, free to mold their own destiny. ("Narrator": Spencer Tracy)

How to Beat the High Cost of Living
1980 American International
But Louise stood up in the canoe so it sunk. Everything was lost and Elaine came up really pissed off and starts yelling at us, and Louise spots the money so we put all the money in. ("Jane": Susan Saint James)

How to Frame a Figg
1971 Universal
I know so. But I'm going to change all that. ("Ema Letha Kusic": Elaine Joyce)

How to Marry a Millionaire
1953 20th Century–Fox
Gentlemen, to our wives. ("Tom Brockman": Cameron Mitchell)

How to Murder a Rich Uncle
1957 Columbia
Cheers. ("Alice": Katie Johnson)

How to Murder Your Wife
1965 United Artists
Oh, well, I suppose if he can put up with her, I can. ("Charles": Terry-Thomas)

How to Steal a Million
1966 20th Century–Fox
Oh, thank you. ("Nicole": Audrey Hepburn)

The Howling
1980 Avco Embassy
Rare. ("Marsha": Elisabeth Brooks)

Huckleberry Finn
1939 MGM
Positively, ma'am, this must be one I forgot about. ("Huckleberry Finn": Mickey Rooney)

Huckleberry Finn
1960 MGM
'Bye, Huck, honey. God bless you. ("Jim": Archie Moore)

Huckleberry Finn
1974 United Artists
If there is a God up there, and I ain't sure if there is or there ain't, he'll hear me praying for you, Jim. ("Huckleberry Finn": Jeff East)

The Hucksters
1947 MGM
Now we're starting out with exactly an even nothing in the world. It's neater that way. ("Victor Albee Norton": Clark Gable)

The Human Comedy
1943 MGM
You see, Marcus, the ending is only the beginning. ("Narrator": Ray Collins)

Human Desire
1954 Columbia
Yes, you understand. You're real bright. Well, see if you can understand this. I'm in love with Jeff and he walked out on me. You know why? Because I wanted him to kill you and he couldn't. You never knew me, you never bothered to figure me out. Well, I'm gonna tell you something. Owens did have something to do with me, but it was because I wanted him to. I wanted that big house he lived in. I wanted him to get rid of that wife of his. But he wasn't quite the fool you are. He knew what I was after. And you know what, I admired him for it. If I'd of been a man, I'd of behaved exactly as he did. Now get out of here and let me unpack. ("Vicki Buckley": Gloria Grahame)

The Hunchback of Notre Dame
1939 RKO
Why was I not made of stone like thee? ("Quasimoto": Charles Laughton)

The Hunt for Red October
1990 Paramount
Is everything all right, sir? Would you like another drink? ("Stewardess": Denise E. James)

The Hunter
1980 Paramount
God bless you. ("Papa Thorson": Steve McQueen)

The Hurricane
1937 United Artists

You're right, Germaine. It's only a floating log. ("Governor Eugene DeLaage": Raymond Massey)

Hurricane
1979   Paramount
No! ("Charlotte Bruckner": Mia Farrow)

Hush ... Hush, Sweet Charlotte
1964   20th Century-Fox
Get back over there. (Police officer)

The Hustler
1961   20th Century-Fox
So do you, Fast Eddie. ("Minnesota Fats": Jackie Gleason)

Hysterical
1983   Embassy
I love you too. Whoever you are. ("Kate": Cindy Pickett)

I Accuse
1958   MGM
Thank you, Colonel Picquart. ("Alfred Dreyfuss": Jose Ferrar)

I Am a Fugitive from a Chain Gang
1932   Warner Brothers
I steal. ("James Allen": Paul Muni)

I Cover the Waterfront
1933   United Artists
That's a swell finish. ("Julie Kirk": Claudette Colbert)

I Dream Too Much
1935   RKO
Yes, I know what you mean. And some people were born to have a baby. ("Annette Monard Street": Lily Pons)

I Love N.Y.
1987   Manley
I can't help it. ("Mario Cotone": Scott Baio)

I Love You Again
1940   MGM
Nothing. You certainly can kick that amnesia around. ("'Doc' Ryan": Frank McHugh)

I Loved a Woman
1933   Warner Brothers
I'm sleepy. ("John Hayden": Edward G. Robinson)

I Ought to Be in Pictures
1982   20th Century-Fox
Me? I'm not sure yet. I'm sort of in a transitional period. ("Libby": Dinah Manoff)

I Shot Jesse James
1949   Screen Guild
I'm sorry for what I done to Jess. I loved him. ("Bob Ford": John Ireland)

I Thank a Fool
1962   MGM
Christine, you gonna give me a lift? ("Stephen Dane": Peter Finch)

I, the Jury
1982   20th Century-Fox
It was easy. ("Mike Hammer": Armand Assante)

I Walk Alone
1947   Paramount
It is. ("Kay Lawrence": Lizabeth Scott)

I Walk the Line
1970   Columbia

Henry. ("Alma McCain": Tuesday Weld)

I Want to Live
1958   United Artists
Dear Mr. Montgomery. There isn't much I can say with words, they always fail me when most needed. But please know that with all my heart I appreciate everything you've done for me. Sincerely, Barbara. ("Barbara Graham": Susan Hayward)

I Wanted Wings
1941   Paramount
Blow hard, Lieutenant, you're a big boy now. ("Carolyn Bartlett": Constance Moore)

I Was a Male War Bride
1949   20th Century–Fox
I'm not going to worry about that until the Statue of Liberty goes past that porthole. ("Capt. Henri Rochard": Cary Grant)

Ice Follies of 1939
1939   MGM
Shh. (Ice show spectators)

The Ice Pirates
1984   MGM/UA
That's right. ("Jason": Robert Urich)

Ice Station Zebra
1968   MGM
Do svidaniya. ("Cdr. James Ferraday": Rock Hudson)

I'd Rather Be Rich
1964   Universal
We'll get married or nothing. ("Cynthia Dulaine": Sandra Dee)

The Idolmaker
1980   United Artists
That's it. ("Vincent Vacarri": Ray Sharkey)

I'll Cry Tomorrow
1955   MGM
For the first time our principal subject knows that this is her life and we have her unqualified permission to tell the whole truth. It's a story of degradation and shame. But when you hear the facts you'll come to realize how much courage it took for her to come here tonight. You'll also realize that it's a story full of hope, hope for many who are living and suffering in a half world of addiction to alcohol, hope for all people wherever and whoever they are. So, this is your life, Lillian Roth. (Ralph Edwards, as himself)

Illegally Yours
1988   MGM/UA
Well, actually, we didn't go to jail. We went to my mother's house instead, where there was a changing of the guard. The press from all over came too, and half the town. Suzanne, you see, finally brought her father into it, and then it turned out that Arnie the blackmailer had been wanted for murder in two states. There were even rewards posted. Mr. Keeler gave us each a very generous one. But the money didn't come soon enough so Molly got evicted anyway, but that was OK because we decided to do a little traveling before we settled down. I guess my mom and the gypsy were both right, love is a gamble, and it is all in the dice. Just sometimes you

really get lucky. ("Richard Dice": Rob Lowe)

I'm Dancing as Fast as I Can
1982   Paramount
Jean Scott Martin died on August twelfth, nineteen eighty-one. This documentary on the last year of her life is dedicated to her memory. And it is ending as she asked it to end. ("Barbara Gordon": Jill Clayburgh)

I'm Gonna Get You, Sucka
1988   MGM/UA
That's my theme music. Every good hero should have some. See you around. ("Jack Spade": Keenen Ivory Wayans)

Imitation General
1958   MGM
Well, get in, boy. ("M/Sgt. Murphy Savage": Glenn Ford)

Imitation of Life
1934   Universal
I can hear you now, "I want my quack quack. I want my quack quack." ("Beatrice 'Bes' Pullman": Claudette Colbert)

Imitation of Life
1959   Universal
Come with us. ("Lora Meredith": Lana Turner)

Immediate Family
1989   Columbia
Do you like it? ("Lucy Moore": Mary Stuart Masterson)

Immortal Battalion
1944   20th Century–Fox

This is not a story of the past, it's a story of the future. It shows us the kind of men democracies have produced and will continue to produce. Those boys who turn their backs upon civilian life, who gave up the quiet joys of peaceful living to accept the discipline, the danger and the glory of army life. It happens that the eight men whose lives we follow in the picture are British Tommys. But those of us who have been with our own troops know that this is the story of our G.I. Joes, too. And that is a story that will never die. (Narrator)

The Impossible Years
1968   MGM
The hell you are. ("Jonathan Kingsley": David Niven)

Impulse
1990   MGM/UA
You know, Lottie, not all habits are bad. ("Stan": Jeff Fahey)

In a Lonely Place
1950   Columbia
I lived a few weeks while you loved me. Good-bye, Dix. ("Laurel Gray": Gloria Grahame)

In Cold Blood
1967   Columbia
My cup runneth over. Surely goodness and mercy will follow me all the days of my life and I will dwell in the house of the lord forever. ("The Rev. James Post": Sheldon Allman)

In Harm's Way
1965   Paramount
I'll be here, Rock. ("Lt. Maggie Haynes": Patricia Neal)

The In-Laws
1979   Warner Brothers
Well, why don't we? ("Vince Ricardo": Peter Falk)

In Like Flint
1967   20th Century–Fox
Flint! Flint! Are you all right? Say something! Flint, are you all right? Say something! ("Cramden": Lee J. Cobb)

In Name Only
1939   RKO
We were both dreaming, darling, but now it's true. ("Julie Eden": Carole Lombard)

In the Good Old Summertime
1949   MGM
Psychologically, I'm very confused but personally I feel just wonderful. ("Veronica Fisher": Judy Garland)

In the Heat of the Night
1967   United Artists
Yeah. ("Virgil Tibbs": Sidney Poitier)

In the Mood
1988   Lorimar
Three weeks later Wendy and I were married. She was perfect for me, same age, same optimistic philosophy; and she didn't already have another husband which I had come to realize was a very important quality in a wife. We got her parents' permission, because I didn't want to break any more laws about this sort of thing. In time California dropped its charges against me, and eventually the newspapers and the public forgot all about me and left us in peace to start a long and happy life together. I never heard from Judy or Francine again but I've never forgotten them, and I hope they're happy. I've also never stopped believing that things really do work out in the end and that love, though sometimes very difficult, is very good. Thank you. ("Ellsworth 'Sonny' Wisecarver": Patrick Dempsey)

In This Our Life
1942   Warner Brothers
No. It's out of our hands. There's nothing more we can do. ("Craig Fleming": George Brent)

In Which We Serve
1942   British Lion
God bless our ships and all who sail in them. (Narrator)

The Incredible Shrinking Man
1957   Universal
If there were other bursts of radiation, other clouds drifting across seas and continents, would other beings follow me into this vast new world, so close, the infinitesimal and the infinite. But suddenly I knew they were really the two ends of the same concept. The unbelievably small and the unbelievably vast eventually meet, like the closing of a gigantic circle. I looked up as if somehow I would grasp the heavens, the universe, worlds beyond number, God's silver tapestry spread across the night. And in that moment I knew the answer to the riddle of the infinite. I had thought in terms of man's own limited dimension. I had presumed upon nature. That existence begins and

ends is man's conception, not nature's. And I felt my body dwindling, melting, becoming nothing. My fears locked away and in their place came acceptance. All this vast majesty of creation, it had to mean something. And then I meant something too. Yes, smaller than the smallest, I meant something too. To God there is no zero. I still exist. ("Scott Carey": Grant Williams)

The Incredible Shrinking Woman
1981   Universal
Here, let me try, sweetheart. ("Pat Kramer": Lily Tomlin)

Indiana Jones and the Last Crusade
1989   Paramount
Yes, sir. Hah! ("Indiana Jones": Harrison Ford)

Indiana Jones and the Temple of Doom
1984   Paramount
Yay. ("Short Round": Ke Huy Quan)

Indiscreet
1958   Warner Brothers
What are you crying about, Anna? Don't cry, Anna. I love you. Everything will be all right. You'll like being married. You will. You'll see. ("Philip Adams": Cary Grant)

Indiscretion of an American Wife
1954   Columbia
No. ("Giovanni Doria": Montgomery Clift)

Inherit the Wind
1960   United Artists
You're wrong, Henry, you'll be there. You're the type. Who else would defend my right to be lonely? ("E. K. Hornbeck": Gene Kelly)

The Innocents
1961   20th Century–Fox
Miles! Miles! ("Miss Giddens": Deborah Kerr)

Inside Detroit
1955   Columbia
The honest, civic-minded men of Detroit staged a resourceful and courageous battle against the forces of gansterism to overcome this very real threat to the country's security. The United Auto Workers union will long stand as a symbol to every other union and guild in the nation of what must be done to preserve this security forever. Well, that's the story, folks. Glad we could get together. This is John Cameron Swayze saying goodbye. (John Cameron Swayze)

Inside Straight
1951   MGM
Good night, Ada. ("Rip MacCool": David Brian)

Inspiration
1930   MGM
But these moments are so precious. I want to keep them. I want to think of this old room and all the places where we've been happy. I want to remember you as you are tonight. ("Yvonne": Greta Garbo)

Interiors
1978   United Artists

Yes. It's very peaceful. ("Renata": Diane Keaton)

Interlude
1957   Universal
No, I mean home, really home. ("Helen Banning": June Allyson)

Interlude
1968   Columbia
No, it's nothing really. I'll tell you when I see you. ("Sally": Barbara Ferris)

Intermezzo: A Love Story
1939   United Artists
Holger, welcome home. ("Margit Brandt": Edna Best)

Into the Night
1985   Universal
Can I have a ride to the airport? ("Diana": Michelle Pfeiffer)

Intruder in the Dust
1949   MGM
Our conscience, Uncle John. ("Chick Mallison": Claude Jarman, Jr.)

Invaders from Mars
1953   20th Century–Fox
Gee whiz. ("David MacLean": Jimmy Hunt)

Invasion of the Body Snatchers
1956   Allied Artists
Operator, get me the Federal Bureau of Investigation. Yes, it's an emergency. ("Dr. Hall": Whit Bissell)

Invasion of the Body Snatchers
1978   United Artists

Matthew. Matthew. ("Nancy Bellicec": Veronica Cartwright)

The Invisible Kid
1988   Taurus
I'm laughing. ("Grover Dunn": Jay Underwood)

The Invisible Man
1933   Universal
Father, come quickly! ("Flora Cranley": Gloria Stuart)

The Invisible Man Returns
1940   Universal
Helen, darling. ("Geoffrey Radcliffe": Vincent Price)

The Ipcress File
1965   Universal
Thank you. ("Harry Palmer": Michael Caine)

The Irish in Us
1935   Warner Brothers
Here's another one for ya. (Ambulance attendant)

Irma La Douce
1963   United Artists
But that's another story. ("Moustache": Lou Jacobi)

The Iron Mistress
1952   Warner Brothers
No woman is worth the lives of eight men. ("Jim Bowie": Alan Ladd)

Ironweed
1987   Tri-Star
It's a mighty nice room. Gets the morning light. ("Francis Phelan": Jack Nicholson)

Irreconcilable Differences
1984   Warner Brothers
Well, me, I'm having a hamburger, fries, a coke and maybe a salad. How about you, Luce? ("Albert Brodsky": Ryan O'Neal)

Isaac Littlefeathers
1984   Lauron
After all, it's not the cards you've been dealt, it's how you play them that counts. And that's how I knew that somehow the kid was going to be OK. ("Jesse Armstrong": Scott Hylands)

It Came from Outer Space
1953   Universal
No, just for now. It wasn't the right time for us to meet. But there'll be other nights, other stars for us to watch. They'll be back. ("John Putnam": Richard Carlson)

It Happened On Fifth Avenue
1947   Allied Artists
Remind me to nail up the board in the back fence. He's coming through the front door next winter. ("Michael O'Connor": Charlie Ruggles)

It Happened One Night
1934   Columbia
Dunno. (Man at motel)

It Happens Every Spring
1949 20th Century–Fox
Yes, sir, Professor, you sure put that methyl, ethyl, propyl, butyl on that ball! ("Schmidt": Alan Hale, Jr.)

It Takes Two
1988   United Artists

Uh, uh, uh, I got it. Watch this. ("Travis Rogers": George Newberg)

It's a Great Feeling
1949   Warner Brothers
Nothing. (Dennis Morgan as himself)

It's a Mad, Mad, Mad, Mad World
1963   United Artists
Don't you mess with me! Get away from me! Leave me alone! Leave me alone! ("Mrs. Marcus": Ethel Merman)

It's a Wonderful Life
1946   RKO
That's right. That's right. Attaboy, Clarence. ("George Bailey": James Stewart)

It's a Wonderful World
1939   MGM
Well, all I can say is, I just thought of a poem. Uh, roses are red, violets are blue, I get a hundred grand for this, but I want you. ("Guy Johnson": James Stewart)

Ivanhoe
1952   MGM
Before me kneels a nation divided. Rise as one man and that one for England. ("King Richard": Norman Wooland)

I've Heard the Mermaids Singing
1987   Miramax
Come here, I'll show you some more. ("Polly Vandersma": Sheila McCarthy)

Jack McCall, Desperado
1952   Columbia
Welcome home, Mrs. McCall. ("Jack McCall": George Montgomery)

Jacknife
1989   Cineplex
Who knows? ("Martha": Kathy Baker)

The Jackpot
1950   20th Century–Fox
See, Phyllis. I told you everything would be all right. ("Tommy Lawrence": Tommy Rettig)

The Jagged Edge
1985   Columbia
Fuck him. He was trash. ("Sam Ransom": Robert Loggia)

Jamaica Run
1953   Paramount
Great House will live again, Mother. We'll make it live in peace and beauty. ("Todd Dacey": Wendell Corey)

Jane and the Lost City
1987   Glen Films
Just the way you are, sweetheart. ("Jungle Jack": Sam Jones)

Jane Eyre
1943   20th Century–Fox
As the months went past, he came to see the light once more, as well as to feel its warmth. To see first the glory of the sun, and then the mild splendor of the moon, and at last the evening star. And then one day when our firstborn was put into his arms, he could see that the boy had inherited his own eyes as they once were, large, brilliant and black. ("Jane Eyre": Joan Fontaine)

The January Man
1989   MGM
Ow. ("Bernadette Flynn": Mary Elizabeth Mastrantonio)

Jason and the Argonauts
1963   Columbia
For the moment, let them enjoy a calm sea, a fresh breeze and each other. The girl is pretty, and I was always sentimental. But for Jason, there are other adventures. I have not yet finished with Jason. Let us continue the game another day. ("Zeus": Niall MacGinnis)

Jassy
1947   Universal
Jassy. ("Barney Hatton": Dermot Walsh)

Jaws
1975   Universal
I used to hate the water. I can't imagine why. ("Brody": Roy Scheider)

Jaws: The Revenge
1987   Universal
And they all started singing "Nearer My God to Thee." ("Hoagie": Michael Caine)

Jaws 2
1978   Universal
Sure, they did. ("Brody": Roy Scheider)

The Jazz Singer
1953   Warner Brothers
You'd make your father very happy. ("Uncle Louie": Alex Gerry)

The Jazz Singer
1980   Associated Film Distribution

My son. ("Cantor Rabinovitch": Laurence Olivier)

Jeremiah Johnson

1972   Warner Brothers
You'll have done well to keep so much hair when so many's after it. I hope you'll fare well. ("Bear Claw": Will Geer)

The Jerk

1979   Universal
I was so glad to be going home. I remembered the days when I sang and danced with my family on the porch of the old house. But, things change and with all the additions to the family we had to tear down the old house even though we loved it. But we built us a bigger one. ("Navin Johnson": Steve Martin)

Jesus Christ Superstar

1973   Universal
Father, into your hands I commit my soul. ("Jesus Christ": Ted Neeley)

Jet Pilot

1957   Universal
Wipe off your chin. ("Col. Shannon": John Wayne)

The Jewel of the Nile

1985   20th Century–Fox
Aw, guys, aw. ("Ralph": Danny De-Vito)

Jezebel

1938   Warner Brothers
God protect you and Pres. ("Amy Bradford Dillard": Margaret Lindsay)

The Jigsaw Man

1984   United Film Distribution
Have a drink. Once in Geneva, you and I and the microfilm, why don't we go into business together. Only this time not for five million dollars but for five million pounds. ("Sir Philip Kimberly": Michael Caine)

Jivaro

1954   Paramount
Good-bye. ("Sylvester's wife": Marian Mosick)

Jo Jo Dancer, Your Life Is Calling

1986   Columbia
Thank you. ("Jo Jo Dancer Alter Ego": Richard Pryor)

Joe Kidd

1972   Universal
Next time I'll knock your damn head off. ("Joe Kidd": Clint Eastwood)

Johnny Come Lately

1943   United Artists
Sure, sure I have. You're my girl. ("Tom Richards": James Cagney)

Johnny Cool

1963   United Artists
No, let's go now. ("Dare Guiness": Elizabeth Montgomery)

Johnny Dangerously

1984   20th Century–Fox
Well, it paid a little. ("Johnny Dangerously": Michael Keaton)

Johnny Eager

1942   MGM
Aw, just another hood, I guess. Well,

whoever he is, he don't mean a thing to anybody now, much less to me. Say, call Mae and tell her I'll be late, will ya? ("Joe Agridowski, Officer No. 711": Byron Shores)

Johnny Tiger
1966   Universal
All right, kids, no school today! ("George Dean": Robert Taylor)

Jolson Sings Again
1949   Columbia
It's your right to hear those bobby-soxers squeal. ("Ellen Clark": Barbara Hale)

The Jolson Story
1946   Columbia
And, Steve, when he gets home nights after the show, don't let him sing too long. ("Julie Benson": Evelyn Keyes)

Jory
1972   Avco Embassy
I've got to do what Roy said. I've got to find a place with my own name on it. I've got to find my promised land. ("Jory": Robby Benson)

Journey for Margaret
1942   MGM
Yes. Yes, you'll see. ("John Davis": Robert Young)

Journey to the Center of the Earth
1959   20th Century–Fox
I warn you, I'm wearing stays again. ("Carla": Arlene Dahl)

Joy of Living
1938   RKO
Oh, that's a great idea. ("Dan Brewster": Douglas Fairbanks, Jr.)

Joyride
1977   American International
I could sure use the sun. ("John": Robert Carradine)

Juarez
1939   Warner Brothers
Forgive me. ("Benito Pablo Juarez": Paul Muni)

Judge Hardy and Son
1939   MGM
Oh, Andy. ("Polly Benedict": Ann Rutherford)

Judith
1965   Paramount
We'll survive. ("Aaron Stein": Peter Finch)

The Juggler
1953   Columbia
Help me. Someone, I'm sick. I need help. ("Hans Muller": Kirk Douglas)

Julia Misbehaves
1948   MGM
Beast. ("Julia Packett": Greer Garson)

Julie
1956   MGM
I wouldn't go through that again. Not for anything. ("Det. Capt. Pringle": Frank Lovejoy)

Julius Caesar
1953   MGM
This was the noblest Roman of them

all. All the conspirators, save only he, did what they did in envy of great Caesar. He only in a general honest thought and common good to all made one of them. His life was gentle and the elements so mixed in him that nature might stand up and say to all the world this was a man. ("Marc Antony": Marlon Brando)

Jumbo
1962   MGM
Jumbo! ("Kitty Wonder": Doris Day/"Pop Wonder": Jimmy Durante/ "Lulu": Martha Raye)

Jumping Jacks
1952   Paramount
Chick! Chick! ("Hap Smith": Jerry Lewis)

Jungle Book
1942   United Artists
That one, mem-sahib, is another story. ("Buldeo, the Storyteller": Joseph Calleia)

Jungle Captive
1945   Universal
Don't know. Harrigan's orders. ("Motorcycle cop": Eddy Chandler)

Junior Bonner
1972   Cinerama
Tell him Junior sent you. ("Junior Bonner": Steve McQueen)

Just Between Friends
1986   Orion
Well, she has terrific taste. But, uh, who picked out the rest of your outfit? ("Sandy Dunlap": Christine Lahti)

Just for You
1952   Paramount
Oh, no. ("Jordan Blake": Bing Crosby)

Just Tell Me What You Want
1980   Warner Brothers
Stella, don't put any calls through till I ring back. I'm negotiating. ("Max Herschel": Alan King)

Just the Way You Are
1984   MGM/UA
Great. And while you're at it, be thinking of what you can take pictures of.... ("Susan": Kristy McNichol)

Just You and Me, Kid
1979   Columbia
The trunk is for surprises. ("Bill": George Burns)

Justine
1969   20th Century–Fox
"There are times I simply adored you." How like Justine to end a love affair with the only really loving thing she ever said to me. I'll never forgive her, but I won't forget her either. I don't want to. ("Darley": Michael York)

The Kansan
1943   United Artists
Mind? ("John Bonniwell": Richard Dix)

Kansas City Princess
1934   Warner Brothers
Oh, cut it out, willya. Can't you see he's all upset? ("Rosie": Joan Blondell)

The Karate Kid
1984   Columbia
Hey! Hey, Mr. Miyagi! We did it! We did it! All right! ("Daniel": Ralph Macchio)

The Karate Kid Part II
1986   Columbia
Wrong. ("Daniel": Ralph Macchio)

The Karate Kid Part III
1989   Columbia
We did it! We did it! ("Daniel": Ralph Macchio)

Kathy O'
1958   Universal
Merry Christmas. ("Kathy O'Rourke": Patty McCormack)

Keep 'Em Flying
1941   Universal
Where? ("Blackie Benson": Bud Abbott)

Kelly
1981   Paramount
Yeah, Dad, did he really give him to you? ("Kelly": Twila-Dawn Vokins)

Kelly's Heroes
1970   MGM
We did it! (A soldier)

Kenner
1971   MGM
I knew it, I knew my mother would come back. ("Saji": Ricky Cordell)

The Kentucky Fried Movie
1977   United Film
I'm not wearing any pants. Film at eleven. ("Newscaster": Neil Thompson)

Key Largo
1948   Warner Brothers
He's all right, Dad. He's coming back to us. ("Nora Temple": Lauren Bacall)

The Keys of the Kingdom
1944   20th Century–Fox
Come along, boy. Wasn't it just fine of God to make all the rivers and fill them all with little fishes and then send you and me here to catch them, Andrew, hm? ("Father Francis Chisholm": Gregory Peck)

The Kid from Brooklyn
1946   RKO
Now something has to be done about this, gentlemen. The record of Sunflower Dairies has been much too good in the past, thank you, to allow. ("Burleigh Sullivan": Danny Kaye)

Kid Millions
1935   United Artists
Somebody left their laundry. ("Eddie Wilson, Jr.": Eddie Cantor)

Kill Me Again
1989   MGM/UA
Can you identify suspect, over. (Voice on police radio)

Kill the Umpire
1950   Columbia
Kill the umpire! Kill the umpire! Kill the umpire! (Spectators at baseball game)

Killer Force
1975   American International
It's a small world, Roberts. I'll find them. ("Harry Webb": Telly Savalas)

The Killers
1946   Universal
Thanks. ("Jim Reardon": Edmond O'Brien)

The Killers
1964   Universal
Oh, no, no. ("Sheila Farr": Angie Dickinson)

The Killing
1956   United Artists
What's the difference? ("Johnny Clay": Sterling Hayden)

The Killing Fields
1984   Warner Brothers
Nothing's forgiven, nothing. ("Dith Pran": Dr. Haing S. Ngor)

The Killing Time
1987   New World
You wouldn't have killed him, would you? ("Sheriff Sam Wayburn": Beau Bridges)

Kind Hearts and Coronets
1949   Eagle Lion
My memoirs. My memoirs. My memoirs. My memoirs. ("Louis Mazzini": Dennis Price)

Kindergarten Cop
1990   Universal
Uh-oh, they're gonna do it. ("Lowell": Ben McCreary)

The King and Four Queens
1956   United Artists
This will be a rare education. ("Dan Kehoe": Clark Gable)

The King and I
1956   20th Century–Fox
There shall be no bowing like toad nor crouching nor crawling. This does not mean, however, you do not show respect for king. You will stand with shoulders back and chin high like this. You will face king with proud expression showing pride in self as well as in king. This is proper way for men to show esteem for one another. By looking upon each other's faces with kindness of spirit, eyes meeting eyes in equal gaze. Bodies upright, standing as men were meant to stand with dignity.... ("Prince Chulalongkorn": Patrick Adiarte)

King Creole
1958   Paramount
Good luck, Danny. ("Nellie": Dolores Hart)

King Kong
1933   RKO
Oh, no, it wasn't the airplanes. It was beauty killed the beast. ("Carl Denham": Robert Armstrong)

King Kong
1976   Paramount
Jack! Jack! ("Dwan": Jessica Lange)

The King of Comedy
1982   20th Century–Fox
Rupert Pupkin, ladies and gentlemen, let's hear it for Rupert Pupkin. Wonderful. Rupert Pupkin, ladies and gentlemen. ("Announcer": Jeff David)

King of Hockey
1936   Warner Brothers
OK, Princess. ("Gabby Dugan": Dick Purcell)

King of the Lumberjacks
1940   Warner Brothers
Yeah and sometimes he can do other people a lot of good too. ("Dominic": Stanley Fields)

King Rat
1965   Columbia
Only hate, Grey, only hate. ("Marlowe": James Fox)

King Solomon's Mines
1950   MGM
It's all right now, it's all over. Seems we're going to live. ("Allan Quatermain": Stewart Granger)

King's Row
1941   Warner Brothers
What was it you wanted, honey, to build a house? We'll move into it in broad daylight. And we'll invite the folks in, too. For Pete's sake, let's give a party. I feel swell. ("Drake McHugh": Ronald Reagan)

Kinjite
1989   Cannon
That's justice. ("Lieutenant Crowe:" Charles Bronson)

The Kiss
1988   Tri-Star
I love you, Daddy. ("Amy Halloren": Meredith Salenger)

Kiss Me Goodbye
1982   20th Century–Fox
Kay. ("Rupert Baines": Jeff Bridges)

Kiss Me Kate
1953   MGM
A pox upon the life that late I led. ("Fred Graham/Petruchio": Howard Keel)

Kiss of Death
1947   20th Century–Fox
Sometimes out of the worst comes the best. Mr. D'Angelo got what he wanted. Nick got what he wanted, and I got all I ever wanted. I got Nick. ("Nettie": Coleen Gray)

Kiss of the Spider Woman
1985   MGM/UA
That can never happen now. This dream is short, but this dream is happy. ("Leni Lamaison/Marta/Spider Woman": Sonia Braga)

Klute
1971   Warner Brothers
I have no idea what's going to happen. I just, I can't, can't stay in the city, you know. Maybe I'll come back. You might see me next week. ("Bree Daniel": Jane Fonda)

Knock on Any Door
1949   Columbia
Look, Nick, I'm afraid I haven't been able to be very much help to you, but you know how I feel. There's one thing I can promise you, I'll do everything I can to keep other fellows like you from, well, to help other fellows like you, as long as I live. ("Andrew   Morton": Humphrey Bogart)

Knock on Wood
1954   Paramount
We'd better get a bigger car. (Man in car)

Kongo
1932 MGM
Well, how about it, Ann? ("Doctor Kingsland": Conrad Nagel)

Krakatoa-East of Java
1969 Cinerama
Want to see the ship? ("Capt. Chris Hanson": Maximilian Schell)

Kramer vs. Kramer
1979 Columbia
You look terrific. ("Ted Kramer": Dustin Hoffman)

The L-Shaped Room
1963 Columbia
Good-bye. ("Girl at End": Nanette Newman)

La Bamba
1987 Columbia
Ritchie! ("Bob Morales": Esai Morales)

Ladies' Man
1961 Paramount
Ma! Ma! Did you see that pussycat? ("Herbert H. Heebert": Jerry Lewis)

The Lady from Shanghai
1948 Columbia
I went to call the cops, but I knew she'd be dead before they got there and I'd be free. Bannister's note to the DA'd fix it so I'd be innocent officially, but that's a big word, innocent, stupid's more like it. Well, everybody is somebody's fool. The only way to stay out of trouble is to grow old, so I guess I'll concentrate on that. Maybe I'll live so long that I'll forget her. Maybe I'll die trying. ("Michael O'Hara": Orson Welles)

Lady in a Cage
1964 Paramount
Get out! ("Mrs. Hilyard": Olivia De Havilland)

The Lady in the Lake
1946 MGM
Yes, but it's wonderful. ("Adrienne Fromsett": Audrey Totter)

The Lady Is Willing
1942 Columbia
He's all right, darling. He smiled at me. ("Dr. Corey T. McBain": Fred MacMurray)

Lady Killer
1933 Warner Brothers
I can't wait that long. ("Dan Quigley": James Cagney)

Lady of the Tropics
1939 MGM
My son, she goes where there's no east or west, and she will be judged by one who alone knows how great or how little were her sins. ("Father Antoine": Ernest Cossart)

Lady Sings the Blues
1972 Paramount
All right, later. ("The Agent": Ned Glass)

The Lady Takes a Flyer
1958 Universal
Mike, I told you! Oh, Mike. ("Maggie Colby": Lana Turner)

Lady with Red Hair
1940 Warner Brothers
Thank you, David. ("Caroline Carter": Miriam Hopkins)

A Lady without Passport
1950 MGM
Karczag. Pete Karczag. A real American name. ("Marianne Lorress": Hedy Lamarr)

Ladyhawke
1985 Warner Brothers
I love you, I love you. ("Isabeau": Michelle Pfeiffer)

The Landlord
1970 United Artists
Come on. ("Lanie": Marki Bey)

Lassie Come Home
1943 MGM
Oh, Lassie. Oh. You're my Lassie. Come home. ("Joe Carraclough": Roddy McDowell)

The Last American Hero
1973 20th Century–Fox
Where you goin' from here, Junior? (Reporter)

The Last American Virgin
1982 Cannon
Sure. ("Victor": Brian Peck)

The Last Angry Man
1959 Columbia
'Bye, Myron. ("Woodrow Wilson Thrasher": David Wayne)

The Last Blitzkrieg
1959 Columbia
Pinwheel, this is Pinwheel three, over. Pinwheel, this is Pinwheel three. Mission accomplished. Crossroads is now secured. We have prisoners and a number of casualties. I'll wait further orders. ("Sergeant Ludwig": Dick York)

The Last Detail
1973 Columbia
Yeah, maybe our fucking orders have come through. ("Buddusky": Jack Nicholson)

The Last Emperor
1987 Columbia
He died in nineteen sixty-seven. (Guide)

The Last Hurrah
1958 Columbia
Like hell I would. ("Frank Skeffington": Spencer Tracy)

The Last Mile
1959 United Artists
You guys do what you want. I'm gonna get me some fresh air. ("'Killer' Mears": Mickey Rooney)

The Last of Mrs. Cheyney
1937 MGM
That's the first of Lady Dilling. ("Lord Arthur Dilling": Basil Rathbone)

Last of the Comanches
1953 Columbia
Thank you, sir, but the credit belongs to a lot of people, some of it belongs right in your own family. Prophet Satterlee, O'Rattigan, Trooper Creel and Little Knife. Belongs to a whole platoon of men and it started way back at Dry Butte. There was young Lieutenant Williams and Corporal Floyd, Martinez, Henry Rupert, Jim Starbuck, Rusty Potter. If there's to be peace, they're the ones who paid for it, and I think they'd like to know that what they died for was worthwhile. ("Sergeant Matt Trainer": Broderick Crawford)

Last of the Red-Hot Lovers
1972   Paramount
I think it's strange of you to think it's strange of me. ("Barney Cashman": Alan Arkin)

The Last Picture Show
1971   Columbia
Never you mind, honey. Never you mind. ("Ruth Popper": Cloris Leachman)

The Last Starfighter
1984   United Artists
Wow! ("Louis Rogan": Chris Hebert)

The Last Temptation of Christ
1988   Universal
It is accomplished! It is accomplished! ("Jesus": Willem Dafoe)

Last Train from Gun Hill
1959   Paramount
That's right: Petey. Raise him right, Matt. ("Craig Belden": Anthony Quinn)

The Last Tycoon
1976   Paramount
I don't want to lose you. ("Monroe Stahr": Robert DeNiro)

The Last Warrior
1989   SVS
Please! Don't! ("Katherine": Maria Holvoe)

Laura
1944   20th Century–Fox
Good-bye, my love. ("Waldo Lydecker": Clifton Webb)

The Law and Jake Wade
1958   MGM
Well, you like me a lot better than I like you. ("Jake Wade": Robert Taylor)

Law and Order
1932   Universal
Tombstone's only one town. ("Frame Johnson": Walter Huston)

The Law vs. Billy the Kid
1954   Columbia
He said no one would ever kill him. ("Nita Maxwell": Betta St. John)

Lawless Frontier
1935   Monogram
Boy, will I go for that. ("John Tobin": John Wayne)

Lean on Me
1989   Warner Brothers
Come on, son. Here. ("Joe Clark": Morgan Freeman)

Leave It to Blondie
1945   Columbia
Why, Dagwood, I haven't finished yet. ("Blondie": Penny Singleton)

The Legacy
1978   Columbia
Anything I want. ("Maggie Walsh": Katharine Ross)

The Legend of the Lone Ranger
1981   Universal
Hi-yo, Silver! Away! ("The Lone Ranger": Klinton Spilsbury)

Legend of the Lost
1957   United Artists
Joe! Joe! They are coming! Look!

They are coming! ("Dita": Sophia Loren)

Legion of the Lawless
1940   RKO
Maybe I should have taken up the law myself. ("Doc Denton": Herbert Heywood)

The Lemon Drop Kid
1951   Paramount
Quiet, Crosby. ("Lemon Drop Kid": Bob Hope)

Leonard Part 6
1987   Columbia
Do it. ("Leonard": Bill Cosby)

Les Girls
1957   MGM
Man, oh, man, here we go again. ("Barry Nichols": Gene Kelly)

Less Than Zero
1987   20th Century–Fox
Good. ("Clay": Andrew McCarthy)

Let It Ride
1989   Paramount
We're having a good day. ("Trotter": Richard Dreyfuss)

Lethal Weapon
1987   Warner Brothers
I'll put five on the mutt. ("Martin Riggs": Mel Gibson)

Lethal Weapon 2
1989   Warner Brothers
Oh, don't make me laugh. ("Martin Riggs": Mel Gibson)

Let's Dance
1950   Paramount
Bon voyage. ("Larry Channock": Barton MacLane)

Let's Do It Again
1975   Warner Brothers
Millions of people betting against Sammy Davis, Junior. Ain't nobody gonna bet on Sammy Davis, Junior. The man don't weigh but about a hundred and eighteen pounds fighting a man weighing two hundred and thirty pounds. Ali be so comfortable he come in weighing three hundred and forty pounds. Come in and hit Sammy dead on top of the head, break both his legs, that'd be the end of the fight. But if you hypnotize him, we'd go in there eight hundred to one odds. . . . ("Billy Foster": Bill Cosby)

Let's Make It Legal
1951   20th Century–Fox
It was the only time in my life, but the stakes were pretty high. ("Hugh": Macdonald Carey)

Let's Make Love
1960   20th Century–Fox
Will they be surprised at night school. ("Amanda": Marilyn Monroe)

Let's Scare Jessica to Death
1971   Paramount
I sit here and I can't believe that it happened. And yet I have to believe it. Nightmares or dreams, madness or sanity, I don't know which is which. ("Jessica": Zohra Lampert)

The Letter
1940   Warner Brothers
With all my heart, I still love the man

I killed. ("Leslie Crosbie": Bette Davis)

Leviathan
1989 MGM
Better, a lot better. ("Beck": Peter Weller)

Liar's Moon
1982 Crown International
I'll bet there's a lover's moon out tonight. ("Ginny Peterson": Cindy Fisher)

Libel
1959 MGM
Mark. ("Lady Maggie Loddon": Olivia De Havilland)

Libeled Lady
1936 MGM
Quiet, people! Please be quiet! ("James B. Allenbury": Walter Connolly)

Licence to Kill
1989 United Artists
So why don't you ask me? ("James Bond": Timothy Dalton)

License to Drive
1988 20th Century–Fox
Don't wait up, guys. ("Les": Corey Haim)

Lt. Robin Crusoe, U.S.N.
1966 Buena Vista
Anyway, dear, that's just the way it happened. I'll be home soon. All my love, Rob. ("Lt. Robin Crusoe": Dick Van Dyke)

Life Begins at 17
1958 Columbia
Peasants. ("Pooky Peck": Cathy O'Neill)

The Life of Riley
1948 Universal
I'm the happiest of all. I've got Gillis back. ("Chester A. Riley": William Bendix)

Life with Father
1947 Warner Brothers
No, I'm going to be baptized. ("Father [Clarence Day]": William Powell)

Lifeboat
1944 20th Century–Fox
Well, maybe they can answer that. ("Connie Porter": Tallulah Bankhead)

Light of Day
1987 Tri-Star
Thank you very much. ("Patti Rasnick": Joan Jett)

The Lighthorsemen
1988 Cinecom
It says we're not going to lose you. ("Anne": Sigrid Thornton)

Li'l Abner
1959 Paramount
This joyful wedding can't be consummated until we pays homage to the one man who made it possible. Who romanticized this boy, who put them back the way they was, and who saved our town from being bombed? None other than that beloved man a-setting up there on an even more beloved horse, Jubilation T. Cornpone. ("Marryin' Sam": Stubby Kaye)

Lili
1952   MGM
Not anymore. ("Lili Daurier": Leslie
Caron)

Lilies of the Field
1963   United Artists
Amen. ("Mother Maria": Lilia Scala/
"Sister Gertrude": Lisa Mann/"Sister
Agnes": Isa Crino/"Sister Albertine":
Francesca Jarvis/"Sister Elizabeth":
Pamela Branch)

Lilith
1964   Columbia
Help me. ("Vincent Bruce": Warren
Beatty)

Limelight
1952   United Artists
And I must see about that ambulance.
(Doctor)

Limit Up
1989   MCEG
Yes, sir, that's something. Hm, I
think I see another lost soul. ("Nike":
Danitra Vance)

The Lion and the Horse
1952   Warner Brothers
See, even Jiminy's glad you two are
coming home. He flocked to welcome
you back. ("Jenny": Sherry Jackson)

The Lion in Winter
1968   Avco Embassy
Do you think there's any chance of it?
("Henry II": Peter O'Toole)

Lion of the Desert
1981   United Film Distribution

We will never surrender. We win or
we die. We will have the next generation to fight, and after the next, the
next. As for me, I will live longer than
my hangman. ("Omar Mukhtar": Anthony Quinn)

The Liquidator
1965   MGM
Rubbish. The department can't afford
to lose men like you, Boysie, not after
what you did today. Take the wheel.
("Mostyn": Trevor Howard)

Listen to Me
1989   Columbia
I trust you now. ("Monica Tomanski":
Jami Gertz)

Little Big Man
1970   National General
Get out. Get out. ("Jack Crabb":
Dustin Hoffman)

Little Boy Lost
1953   Paramount
I'm sorry. ("Bill Wainwright": Bing
Crosby)

Little Caesar
1930   Warner Brothers
Mother of mercy, is this the end of
Rico? ("Cesare Enrico Bandello/Rico –
Little Caesar": Edward G. Robinson)

Little Darlings
1980   Paramount
Wait a minute, sucker. This is my
friend Ferris Whitney. My best
friend. ("Angel": Kristy McNichol)

Little Dorrit
1988   Cannon

I love you. ("Amy Dorrit": Sarah Pickering)

The Little Drummer Girl
1984   Warner Brothers
I'm dead, Jos. You killed me, remember? ("Charlie": Diane Keaton)

The Little Hut
1957   MGM
Can't even juggle anymore. ("Henry Brittingham-Brett": David Niven)

Little Men
1940   RKO
Oh, there's that fox again. ("Willie": Jack Oakie)

Little Monsters
1989   MGM/UA
Um, it's kind of a long story. ("Brian": Fred Savage)

Little Nikita
1988   Columbia
Let's go home. ("Elizabeth Grant": Caroline Kava)

Little Old New York
1940   20th Century-Fox
Oh, Mr. Browne, the pleasure will be mutual. ("Pat O'Day": Alice Faye)

The Little Prince
1974   Paramount
My God, it never happened. He wasn't here. It never happened. ("The Pilot": Richard Kiley)

The Little Princess
1939   20th Century-Fox
My daddy. ("Sara Crewe": Shirley Temple)

A Little Sex
1982   Universal
Good. I said we could start over. I didn't say it would be painless. ("Katherine": Kate Capshaw)

The Little Shepherd of Kingdom Come
1961   20th Century-Fox
You know something. A man's treasure is a loving woman. I found my treasure and I know my belonging place now. ("Chad": Jimmie Rodgers)

Little Shop of Horrors
1986   Warner Brothers
Oh, shit! ("Voice of Audrey II": Levi Stubbs)

Little Women
1933   RKO
Welcome home. ("Jo": Katharine Hepburn)

Little Women
1949   MGM
Oh, Jo. ("Professor Bhaer": Rossano Brazzi)

The Littlest Rebel
1935   20th Century-Fox
There, there, now. All your terrible fears are over. Your father and Colonel Morrison are going free. ("President Lincoln": Frank McGlynn, Sr.)

Lives of a Bengal Lancer
1934   Paramount
His majesty the king emperor has been graciously pleased to confer posthumously the Victoria Cross upon the late Lieutenant McGregor. In accordance with the custom of his

regiment, I place this cross upon the saddlecloth of his horse. ("Col. Stone": Sir Guy Standing)

Living Free
1972   Columbia
Yes, they were free. They would still have their problems to face and dangers to meet, but they were free, living free. ("Joy Adamson": Susan Hampshire)

Living It Up
1954   Paramount
Well, if that's the case, we might as well go to work. ("Homer": Jerry Lewis)

Logan's Run
1976   MGM
Watch it! ("Jessica": Jenny Agutter)

Lone Star
1952   MGM
Oui, mon ami. ("Mizette": William Conrad)

The Loneliness of the Long Distance Runner
1962   Continental
Come on, Smith, get a move on. ("Mr. Craig": Pat Austin)

The Lonely Man
1957   Paramount
Pa. ("Riley Wade": Anthony Perkins)

The Long Hot Summer
1958   20th Century–Fox
Do I know human nature, huh? Didn't I say that fellow Quick was made for my Clara? Am I gonna be a grandfather? I am. Oh, Minnie, it sure is

good to be alive this summer evening. Yeah, alive with friends and family and a big healthy woman to love you. Oh, I like life, Minnie. I like it so much I might just live forever. ("Will Varner": Orson Welles)

Long John Silver
1954   Distributors Corp. of America
Come back. ("Purity Pinker": Connie Gilchrist)

The Long Memory
1952   Rank
Suppose we should. ("Lowther": John McCallum)

The Long Riders
1980   United Artists
I'll kill you. ("Frank James": Stacy Keach)

The Long Ships
1963   Columbia
It, uh, it seems that one of the crowns was adorned with a great jewel, a diamond as big as a gull's egg. Now the three crowns have been lost for many, many years, but I feel, sire, that if we organized a proper expedition it would be quite possible to find those.... ("Rolfe": Richard Widmark)

The Longest Day
1962   20th Century–Fox
OK, run me up the hill, son. ("Brig. Gen. Norman Cota": Robert Mitchum)

The Longest Yard
1974   Paramount
Stick this in your trophy case. ("Paul Crewe": Burt Reynolds)

Longtime Companion

1990　Goldwyn
I just want to be there. ("Willy": Campbell Scott)

Looker

1981　Warner Brothers
Oh, Larry, I don't know if I could take another one of your evenings. ("Cindy": Susan Dey)

Looking for Mr. Goodbar

1977　Paramount
Right? ("Gary Cooper Wright": Tom Berenger)

Loose Cannons

1990　Tri-Star
I knew that. ("Mac": Gene Hackman)

Lord Jeff

1938　MGM
There's hope for you, Albert. And after that, heaven help England, and the mercantile marine. ("'Crusty' Jelks": Herbert Mundin)

Lord Jim

1964　Columbia
I had my chance, father, and I lost. If I lose without honor, if at the last moment I weaken, then it's all without meaning, wasted. ("Lord Jim": Peter O'Toole)

Lord Love a Duck

1966　United Artists
You poor bunny. ("Alan 'Mollymauk' Musgrove": Roddy McDowell)

The Lords of Discipline

1982　Paramount
Go on, take it, you earned it. ("Bear": Robert Prosky)

The Lords of Flatbush

1974　Columbia
I just want to wish you well, both of you. I want you to have a good life, be happy. Salute. ("Wimpy Murgalo": Paul Mace)

Lost and Found

1979　Columbia
Yeah, great. Bye. ("Tricia": Glenda Jackson)

The Lost Boys

1987　Warner Brothers
One thing about living in Santa Carla I never could stomach was all the damn vampires. ("Grandpa": Barnard Hughes)

Lost Horizon

1937　Columbia
Yes. Yes, I believe it. I believe it because I want to believe it. Gentlemen, I give you a toast. Here's my hope that Robert Conway will find his Shangri-La. Here's my hope that we all find our Shangri-La. ("Lord Gainsford": Hugh Buckler)

Lost Patrol

1934　RKO
Speak up, man. Where's your section? (An officer)

The Lost Weekend

1945　Paramount
The way I stood in there, packing my suitcase. Only my mind wasn't on the suitcase and it wasn't on the weekend. Nor was it on the shirts I was putting in the suitcase either. My mind was hanging outside window. It was suspended just about eighteen

inches below. And out there in that great big concrete jungle, I wonder how many others there are like me. Those poor bedeviled guys on fire with thirst. Such comical figures to the rest of the world as they stagger blindly towards another binge, another bender, another spree. ("Don Birnam": Ray Milland)

The Lost World
1960   20th Century–Fox
Well, we'll move out of London as fast as possible. ("Professor Challenger": Claude Rains)

Louisiana Purchase
1941   Paramount
She did. ("Jim Taylor": Bob Hope)

Love and Death
1975   United Artists
Wheat. I'm dead, they're talking about wheat. The question is have I learned anything about life. Only that, only that human beings are divided into mind and body. The mind embraces all the nobler aspirations like poetry and philosophy, but the body has all the fun. The important thing I think is not to be bitter. You know, if, if it turns out that there is a god, I don't think that he's evil. I think that, that the worst you could say about him is that basically he's an underachiever. After all, you know, there are worse things in life than death. I mean, if you've ever spent an evening with an insurance salesman, you, you know exactly what I mean. The, the key here I think is to, to not think of death as an end, but, but think of it more as a very effective

way of, of cutting down on your expenses. Regarding love, huh, you know, uh, what can you say. It's, it's not the, the quantity of your sexual relations that count, it's the quality. On the other hand, if the quantity drops below once every eight months, I would definitely look into it. Well, that's about it for me, folks. Goodbye. ("Boris": Woody Allen)

Love at First Bite
1979   American International
Oh, that's all right with me. I mean, I could never really get my shit together till seven anyway. ("Cindy Sondheim": Susan Saint James)

Love at Large
1990   Orion
I don't know, Harry. I guess there's only one way to find out. ("Stella Wynkowski": Elizabeth Perkins)

Love Child
1982   Warner Brothers
Terry! (Inmates)

Love in the Afternoon
1957   Allied Artists
On Monday, August twenty-fourth of this year, the case of Frank Flannagan and Ariane Chavasse came up before the superior judge in Cannes. They are now married, serving a life sentence in New York, state of New York, U.S.A. ("Claude Chavasse": Maurice Chevalier)

Love Letters
1983   New World
No, not like that. Not like you. ("Anna Winter": Jamie Lee Curtis)

Love Me Tender
1956 20th Century–Fox
Everything's gonna be all right. ("Clinton": Elvis Presley)

Love Story
1970 Paramount
Love. Love means never having to say you're sorry. ("Oliver Barrett, IV": Ryan O'Neal)

Love with the Proper Stranger
1964 Paramount
Come on, come on. (A policeman)

The Loved One
1965 MGM
All first class passengers to your left, sir. (Agent)

Loverboy
1989 Tri-Star
Hey, get your hands off of me, you.... ("Harry Bruckner": Vic Tayback)

The Loves of Carmen
1948 Columbia
No, no, no, no! ("Carmen Garcia": Rita Hayworth)

Loving You
1957 Paramount
I think we'll have to wait a little while. My managers are negotiating a deal of their own. If you'll excuse us, Mr. Taylor, I think this is one deal I can handle by myself. ("Deke Rivers": Elvis Presley)

Lucky Partners
1940 RKO
Case is dismissed. ("Judge": Harry Davenport)

Lucky Stiff
1988 New Line
Yes, yes, yes! ("Ron Douglas": Joe Alaskey)

Lucy Gallant
1955 Paramount
What store? ("Lucy Gallant": Jane Wyman)

Lullaby of Broadway
1951 Warner Brothers
Oh. Oh, Mother, my bag. ("Melinda Howard": Doris Day)

Lust for Life
1956 MGM
Oh, it's not, Sister. It happens in the bright daylight, the sun flooding everything in a light of pure gold. ("Vincent Van Gogh": Kirk Douglas)

MAC and Me
1988 Orion
Now may I extend a warm congratulation. You are now citizens of the United States of America. ("Judge": J. Jay Saunders)

Macao
1952 RKO
You better start getting used to me fresh out of the shower. ("Nick": Robert Mitchum)

MacArthur
1977 Universal
The shadows are lengthening for me. the twilight is here. My days of old have vanished, tone and tint; they have gone glimmering through the dreams of things that were. Their memory is one of wondrous beauty,

watered by tears, and coaxed and caressed by the smiles of yesterday. I listened vainly, but with thirsty ears, for the witching melody of faint bugles blowing reveille, of far drums beating the long roll. In my dreams I hear the crash of drums, the rattle of musketry, the strange mournful mutter of the battlefield. But in the evening of my memory, always I return to West Point, always there echoes and re-echoes Duty, Honor, Country. Today marks my final roll call with you. I want you to know that when I cross the river, my last conscious thoughts will be of the Corps, and the Corps, and the Corps. I bid you farewell. ("Gen. Douglas MacArthur": Gregory Peck)

McGuire, Go Home!
1965   Continental
So you better get your loyalties sorted out. After all, it is a kind of justice. ("Major McGuire": Dirk Bogarde)

Mackenna's Gold
1969   Columbia
Find a hole, old friend. Make it deep. ("Mackenna": Gregory Peck)

Mad Love
1935   MGM
My darling. ("Stephen Orlac": Colin Clive)

Mad Wednesday
1950   RKO
That must be what I was doing all day Wednesday. ("Harold Diddlebock": Harold Lloyd)

Madame Sousatzka
1988   Universal
All right, I've got it now. (A workman)

Madame X
1937   MGM
She was a wonderful woman, father. Whoever she was. ("Raymond Fleuriot": John Beal)

Made for Each Other
1971   20th Century–Fox
Hey, you could have fun with all kinds of girls, am I right? And that's what you're doing. You go out and have fun until you meet up with your type and that's when you'll get married, am I right? ("Gig's father": Paul Sorvino)

Made in Paris
1966   MGM
Oh, no. ("Maggie Scott": Ann-Margret)

Madhouse
1990   Orion
I'll be back. ("Mark Bannister": John Larroquette)

The Madwoman of Chaillot
1969   Warner Brothers
Yes, Ragpicker, I think it's time I moved on to another year. ("Countess Aurelia, the Madwoman of Chaillot": Katharine Hepburn)

The Magic of Lassie
1978   International
Lassie! Lassie! Lassie! ("Chris": Michael Sharrett)

Magic Town
1947   RKO
Hey! Hey, there's Senator Wilton! ("Rip Smith": James Stewart)

The Magnificent Ambersons
1942   RKO

He's going to be all right. Fanny, I wish you could have seen George's face when he saw Lucy. You know what he said to me when we went into that room. He said, "You must have known my mother wanted you to come here today so that I could ask you to forgive me." We shook hands. I never noticed before how much like Isabel George looks. You know something, Fanny, I wouldn't tell this to anyone but you, but it seemed to me as if someone else was in that room and that through me she brought her boy under shelter again and that I'd been through at last to my true love. ("Eugene Morgan": Joseph Cotten)

The Magnificent Doll
1946 Universal
Mr. Madison, I love you very much. ("Dolly Payne Madison": Ginger Rogers)

Magnificent Obsession
1954 Universal
Once you find the way you'll be bound. It'll obsess you. But believe me it'll be a magnificent obsession. ("Dr. Giraud": Paul Cavanaugh)

The Magnificent Seven
1960 United Artists
The old man was right, only the farmers won. We lost. We'll always lose. ("Chris": Yul Brynner)

Magnum Force
1973 Warner Brothers
A man's got to know his limitations. ("Harry Callahan": Clint Eastwood)

Mahogany
1975 Paramount

Then, mister, you've got my vote. ("Tracy/Mahogany": Diana Ross)

Maid to Order
1987 Vista
Hey, where have you been? I've been looking for you everywhere. ("Nick McGuire": Michael Ontkean)

Mail Order Bride
1963 MGM
Good-bye, Annie. ("Will Lane": Buddy Ebsen)

The Main Event
1979 Warner Brothers
Don't worry, we will. ("Hillary Kramer": Barbra Streisand)

The Major and the Minor
1942 Paramount
Come, Philip. ("Susan Applegate": Ginger Rogers)

Major Dundee
1965 Columbia
April nineteenth, eighteen sixty-five, after a brief but costly battle with French irregulars, we crossed the Rio Grande and reentered the United States. ("Timothy Ryan": Michael Anderson, Jr.)

Major League
1989 Paramount
We did it! (Spectator at baseball game)

A Majority of One
1961 Warner Brothers
Aleichem, Mrs. Jacoby. ("Koichi Asano": Alec Guinness)

Making Love
1982 20th Century-Fox
So long, Zack. ("Claire": Kate Jackson)

Making Mr. Right
1987 Orion
No. You see, I'm, I'm, not very good with people. ("Dr. Jeff Peters": John Malkovich)

Making the Grade
1984 MGM/UA
Are you sure? I mean I'm not exactly, uh, Mr. Alligator Shirt. ("Eddie Keaton": Judd Nelson)

Malaya
1949 MGM
Good night. ("The Dutchman": Sydney Greenstreet)

The Male Animal
1942 Warner Brothers
Hooray! ("Michael Barnes": Herbert Anderson)

The Maltese Falcon
1941 Warner Brothers
The, uh, stuff that dreams are made of. ("Sam Spade": Humphrey Bogart)

Mama Loves Papa
1945 RKO
Can't I even watch? (Parrot)

Mame
1974 Warner Brothers
She hasn't changed. She's the pied piper. ("Older Patrick": Bruce Davison)

Man and Boy
1972 Levitt-Pickman

Yes, she is. Let's get on with it. ("Caleb Revers": Bill Cosby)

The Man I Love
1946 Warner Brothers
Here's looking at you, baby. ("Sam Thomas": Bruce Bennett)

The Man in the Gray Flannel Suit
1956 20th Century-Fox
Would you mind if I tell you I worship you? ("Tom Rath": Gregory Peck)

Man of a Thousand Faces
1957 Universal
And he asked of us all forgiveness. ("Creighton Chaney": Roger Smith)

Man-Trap
1961 Paramount
Thanks, Lieutenant. ("Liz Adams": Elaine Devry)

The Man Who Broke the Bank at Monte Carlo
1935 20th Century-Fox
Yes but don't, don't, for heaven's sake, don't call waiter. ("Paul Gallard": Ronald Colman)

The Man Who Came to Dinner
1941 Warner Brothers
Hello? Hello, hello? Oh, dear, something must have happened to Sherry. Operator? Operator? (Voice of "Eleanor Roosevelt")

The Man Who Knew Too Much
1956 Paramount
I'm sorry we were gone so long, but

we had to go over and pick up Hank. ("Dr. Ben McKenna": James Stewart)

The Man Who Loved Women
1983   Columbia
Well, there you have it, it's finally over. And, David, these women have walked for you for the very last time. How I wish you were here to enjoy it. Your delight in women was so passionate, so generous, that miraculously we were all transformed, molded and sculpted by your love as if we were soft clay bent to your quiet will and then set firm in the fires of your passion, with memories as powerful and rich and graceful as the sculpted images you created to beautify the world around us. Good-bye, David. God bless. ("Marianna": Julie Andrews)

The Man Who Wasn't There
1983   Paramount
Thanks, comrade. ("Sam Cooper": Steve Guttenberg)

The Man Who Would Be King
1975   Columbia
You knew, most worshipful brother, Daniel Dravot, Esquire. Well, he became the king of Kafiristan, with a crown on his head. And that's all there is to tell. I'll be on my way now, sir. I've got urgent business in the South. I have to meet a man at Marwar Junction. ("Peachy Carnahan": Michael Caine)

The Man with Bogart's Face
1980   20th Century-Fox
Yeah, well, here's looking at you, kid. ("Sam Spade": Robert Sacchi)

The Man with One Red Shoe
1985   20th Century-Fox
Well, since you're no longer director of CIA, and I am, it doesn't matter what you think. ("Brown": Ed Herman)

Man, Woman and Child
1982   Paramount
I love you too. ("Bob Beckwith": Martin Sheen)

The Manchurian Candidate
1962   United Artists
Made to commit acts too unspeakable to be cited here by an enemy who had captured his mind and soul. He freed himself at last, and in the end heroically and unhesitatingly gave his life to save his country. Raymond Shaw. Hell. Hell. ("Ben Marcum": Frank Sinatra)

Mandingo
1975   Paramount
Papa! Papa! Papa! ("Hammond": Perry King)

Manhattan
1979   United Artists
Why couldn't you have brought this up last week? Six months isn't so long. Not everybody gets corrupted. You have to have a little faith in people. ("Tracy": Mariel Hemingway)

Manhattan Melodrama
1934   MGM
May I try with you? ("Eleanor": Myrna Loy)

Mannequin
1987   20th Century-Fox

My bills, my dress, my, my, new watch, oh, my God, I. . . . ("Roxie": Carole Davis)

Man's Castle
1933   Columbia
Aw, you don't have to be afraid of that no more, Whosis. ("Bill": Spencer Tracy)

Many Rivers to Cross
1955   MGM
Doggone. There was times I didn't think I'd make it. ("Bushrod Gentry": Robert Taylor)

Mara of the Wilderness
1965   Allied Artists
Thank you, Mara. ("Ken Williams": Adam West)

Marathon Man
1976   Paramount
Go get them! ("Babe Levy": Dustin Hoffman)

Mardi Gras
1958   20th Century–Fox
I said I'll never let you go. ("Michelle Marton": Christine Carere)

Marie
1985   MGM/UA
I'm gonna give it. I'm gonna give it to my lawyer. ("Marie Ragghianti": Sissy Spacek)

Marie Antoinette
1938   MGM
Oh, Mama, think of it. I shall be queen. I shall be queen of France. ("Marie Antoinette": Norma Shearer)

Marjorie Morningstar
1958   Warner Brothers
Yes, I think I have. ("Marjorie Morningstar": Natalie Wood)

The Mark of Zorro
1940   20th Century–Fox
Well, we're going to marry and raise fat children and watch our vineyards grow. ("Don Diego Vega": Tyrone Power)

Marooned
1969   Columbia
Ten, nine, eight, seven, six, five, four, three, two, one. (Console operators)

Marriage on the Rocks
1965   Warner Brothers
Well, if you're going to have a baby, I guess I better get married. ("Dan Edwards": Frank Sinatra)

Married Bachelor
1941   MGM
I did. ("Mother with baby": Connie Gilchrist)

Married to the Mob
1988   Orion
I'll think about it. ("Angela de Marco": Michelle Pfeiffer)

Mary of Scotland
1936   RKO
Even as thine arms were spread upon the cross, so receive me into the arms of mercy, and forgive me my sins. ("Mary Stuart": Katharine Hepburn)

Mary, Queen of Scots
1971   Universal
Lord, into your hands I commend my

spirit. ("Mary, Queen of Scots": Vanessa Redgrave)

M*A*S*H
1970   20th Century-Fox
That is all. (Voice over PA)

Mask
1985   Universal
These things are good: ice cream and cake, a ride on a Harley, seeing monkeys in the trees, the rain on my tongue and the sun shining on my face. These things are a drag: dust in my hair, holes in my shoes, no money in my pocket and the sun shining on my face. ("Rusty Dennis": Cher)

The Mask of Fu Manchu
1932   MGM
Well, as I was saying, wherever you are, Genghis Kahn, I give you back your sword. ("Nayland Smith": Lewis Stone)

Massacre River
1949   Allied Artists
Laura! Laura! ("Larry Knight": Guy Madison)

Masters of the Universe
1987   Cannon
I have the power. ("He-Man": Dolph Lundgren)

Mata Hari
1931   MGM
God save her, protect her, and if you must take her, take me too. ("Lt. Alexis Rosanoff": Ramon Novarro)

The Mating Game
1959   MGM
Perfect. Everything's just perfect. ("Pop Larkin": Paul Douglas)

Max Dugan Returns
1983   20th Century-Fox
So long, Pop. ("Nora McPhee": Marsha Mason)

Maxie
1985   Orion
It's five minutes to a motel. ("Jan/Maxie": Glenn Close)

Me, Natalie
1969   National General
Dear David, I love you and I guess I always will love you because you were the one who taught me I could be loved. I intended to be here, I really did. I thought about it all night, how I wanted you. But I didn't know why it bothered me about anything else. And I thought what a jerk I was to be thinking about anything else because what else was there? I mean what else was there in the future if there wasn't you. But the funny thing was that because there was you I wasn't afraid of that. I mean even when I thought of Betty and how miserable she was gonna be and Shirley what she said about holding on when you find it, no matter what, because that was the only way to be happy. It didn't make any difference because that was Betty's miserable and that was Shirley's happy. I only know I have to say goodbye. And if I'm miserable today tomorrow maybe I'll be happy and maybe I won't. But if I'm miserable it'll be my miserable and if I'm happy it will be my happy and I can't do it

any other way. Because this is me, me Natalie, and I really never knew it before. ("Natalie Miller": Patty Duke)

The Mean Season
1985   Orion
Let's go. ("Malcolm Anderson": Kurt Russell)

Mean Streets
1973   Warner Brothers
Thank you. Thank you. (Voice on radio)

The Mechanic
1972   United Artists
Steve, if you read this it means I didn't make it back. It also means you've broken a filament to go to a thirteen-second-delay trigger. End of game. Bang, you're dead. ("Arthur Bishop": Charles Bronson)

Meet John Doe
1941   Warner Brothers
There ya are, Norton, the people. Try and lick that. ("Henry Connell": James Gleason)

Meet Me in St. Louis
1944   MGM
I can't believe it. Right here where we live. Right here in St. Louis. ("Esther Smith": Judy Garland)

Meet the People
1944   MGM
It is? ("William 'Swanee' Swanson": Dick Powell)

Melanie
1982   Embassy
Come on, it's my wife! ("Carl Daniel": Don Johnson)

The Member of the Wedding
1952   Columbia
Sure, baby. ("Berenice Sadie Brown": Ethel Waters)

Memories of Me
1988   MGM/UA
Now's the time to go to sleep, time to slip away, time to say sweet dreams to the things that I loved today. Sweet dreams to the stars, sweet dreams to the breeze, sweet dreams to belly buttons that go in and belly buttons that go out. Sweet dreams to all the tushies in the world, little ones and the big fat ones like the waitress at the bowling alley. Sweet dreams. ("Abbie": Billy Crystal)

Memphis Belle
1990   Warner Brothers
What's wrong, Cap? (Man at airfield)

The Men
1950   United Artists
Please. ("Ken": Marlon Brando)

Men Don't Leave
1990   Warner Brothers
I remember once we went out on some boats and I got to drive one by myself. That was good. Most of all I just remember being together 'cause then I was saved. ("Matt Macauley": Charlie Korsmo)

Mermaids
1990   Orion
Mom. ("Kate Flax": Christina Ricci)

Merton of the Movies
1947   MGM
Mr. Rupert, we thank you, and I'll

treasure this cane always and carry it in all of my pictures as an inspiration to rise to the heights. ("Merton Gill": Red Skelton)

A Message to Garcia
1936　20th Century-Fox
Thank you. This message means the liberation of our people. ("General Garcia": Enrique Acosta)

Messenger of Death
1988　Cannon
God have mercy. ("Homer Foxx": Laurence Luckinbill)

Metalstorm: The Destruction of Jared-Syn
1983　Universal
Well, now, I can see why you were so hot to find Jared-Syn's camp. Hop in, princess, we're going to town. ("Dogen": Jeffrey Byron)

Mexican Hayride
1948　Universal
I love you, Joe. That's me. Dagmar, I'm going to give you a kiss, baby, that—oh, what a kiss. ("Joe Bascom/Humphrey Fish": Lou Costello)

Miami Blues
1990　Orion
Got my teeth back. ("Sergeant Hoke Moseley": Fred Ward)

Micki and Maude
1984　Columbia
Wait, wait, wait. Oh, oh. ("Rob Salinger": Dudley Moore)

Midnight
1939　Paramount
What? ("The Judge": Monty Wooley)

Midnight
1989　SVS Films
How was that for a test, huh? I'm a terrific actress. ("Midnight": Lynn Redgrave)

Midnight Cowboy
1969　United Artists
OK, folks, just a little illness. We'll be in Miami in a few minutes. ("Bus driver": Al Stetson)

Midnight Crossing
1988　Vestron
Yeah. ("Jeffrey Schubb": John Laughlin)

Midnight Express
1978　Columbia
. . . No! No! No! No! No! ("Billy Hayes": Brad Davis)

Midnight Lace
1960　Universal
The world always underestimates the British. How could I have made the same mistake? ("Anthony Preston": Rex Harrison)

Midnight Run
1988　Universal
Looks like I'm walking. ("Jack Walsh": Robert DeNiro)

A Midsummer Night's Sex Comedy
1982　Warner Brothers
That's incredible. ("Andrew": Woody Allen)

Midway
1976   Universal
I don't know, but I think I know what he'd have said. It doesn't make any sense, Admiral. Yamamoto had everything going for him, power, experience, confidence. Were we better than the Japanese or just luckier? ("Admiral Chester W. Nimitz": Henry Fonda)

The Mighty Barnum
1934   20th Century–Fox
Bailey. Bailey. That's it, Barnum and Bailey. That's right. Take a partner. You know, a hundred years from now people are liable to be talking about us. Barnum and Bailey, the greatest show on earth. ("Phineas T. Barnum": Wallace Beery)

The Mighty Quinn
1989   MGM
I don't know. ("Xavier": Denzel Washington)

The Milagro Beanfield War
1988   Universal
Fiesta, there's a fiesta. ("Amarante Cordova": Carlos Riquelme)

The Milkman
1950   Universal
That's my boy. ("Breezy Albright": Jimmy Durante)

Millennium
1989   20th Century–Fox
This is not the beginning of the end. It is the end of the beginning. ("Sherman, the Robot": Robert Joy)

Million Dollar Mermaid
1952   MGM

It doesn't belong to you, either. ("Annette Kellerman": Esther Williams)

Million Dollar Mystery
1987   DEG
Bob, you take care of yourself. There's a lot of that stuff going around. ("Fred": Mark Dryden)

Mine Own Executioner
1948   20th Century–Fox
Hello, Charlie. How's life? ("Felix Milne": Burgess Meredith)

Minnie and Moskowitz
1971   Universal
Wilt thou, Minnie Moore. ("Minister": David Rowlands)

Miracle on 34th Street
1947   20th Century–Fox
Maybe. Maybe I didn't do such a wonderful thing after all. ("Fred Gailey": John Payne)

The Mirror Crack'd
1980   Associated Film Dist.
She's given the performance of her life. ("Miss Marple": Angela Lansbury)

Miss Firecracker
1989   Corsair
Yeah, oh, yeah. As nice as they come. ("Carnelle Scott": Holly Hunter)

Missing
1982   Universal
No, that's my right. I just thank God that we live in a country where we can still put people like you in jail. ("Ed Horman": Jack Lemmon)

The Missionary
1983   Columbia
Got no money. ("The Rev. Charles Fortescue": Michael Palin)

Mississippi
1935   Paramount
That's better. ("Lucy Rumford": Joan Bennett)

Mississippi Burning
1988   Orion
Yeah. ("Rupert Anderson": Gene Hackman)

Mr. and Mrs. Bridge
1990   Miramax
Hello? Hello? Is anybody there? Is anybody there? ("India Bridge": Joanne Woodward)

Mr. and Mrs. Smith
1941   RKO
Oh, David. Oh, David. Oh, David. ("Ann Smith/Ann Krausheimer": Carole Lombard)

Mr. Belvedere Goes to College
1949   20th Century-Fox
Yes, it is. ("Lynn Belvedere": Clifton Webb)

Mr. Belvedere Rings the Bell
1951   20th Century-Fox
Nonsense, my dear fellow. And stop breathing on my carnation. ("Lynn Belvedere [Oliver Erwenter]": Clifton Webb)

Mr. Blandings Builds His Dream House
1948   RKO
Yeah, do that. ("Bill Cole": Melvyn Douglas)

Mister 880
1950   20th Century-Fox
Skipper. Good-bye. I'll come to see you very soon. ("Ann Winslow": Dorothy McGuire)

Mr. Imperium
1951   MGM
I'll be seeing you. ("Fredda Barlo": Lana Turner)

Mr. Mom
1983   20th Century-Fox
My fellow Americans, I am Howard Humphries, president of Schooner Tuna. All of us here at Schooner Tuna sympathize with those of you hit so hard by these trying economic times. In order to help you, we are reducing the price of Schooner Tuna by fifty cents a can. When this crisis is over we will go back to our regular prices. Until then, remember, we're all in this together. Schooner Tuna, the tuna with a heart. ("Humphries": Graham Jarvis)

Mr. Music
1950   Paramount
Oh, Paul, darling. ("Katherine Holbrook": Nancy Olson)

Mister Roberts
1955   Warner Brothers
Captain, it is I, Ensign Pulver, and I just threw your stinkin' palm tree overboard. Now what's all this crud about no movie tonight? ("Ens. Frank Thurlowe Pulver": Jack Lemmon)

Mr. Smith Goes to Washington
1939   Columbia
Yippee! ("Saunders": Jean Arthur)

Mr. Winkle Goes to War
1944   Columbia
She helped, too, Mr. Winkle. ("Barry": Ted Donaldson)

Mitchell
1975   Allied Artists
All right, let's get your coat. ("Mitchell": Joe Don Baker)

Moby Dick
1956   Warner Brothers
The coffin, drowned Queequeg's coffin, was my lifebuoy. For one whole day and night it sustained me on that soft and dirge-like main. Then a sail appeared. It was the *Rachel*. The *Rachel* who in her long, melancholy search for her missing children found another orphan. The drama's done. All are departed away. The great shroud of the sea rolls over the *Pequod*, her crew, and Moby Dick. I only am escaped, alone, to tell thee. ("Ishmael": Richard Basehart)

Modern Romance
1981   Columbia
I can't believe it. I love you. Now you watch. It's going to be perfect. I promise. Oh, Mary. Perfect. Perfect. ("Robert Cole": Albert Brooks)

Mogambo
1953   MGM
I said, take good care of her. ("Victor Marswell": Clark Gable)

Mommie Dearest
1981   Paramount
Does she? Does she? ("Christina Crawford [Adult]": Diana Scarwid)

Money from Home
1954   Paramount
So do me somethin'. ("Virgil Yokum": Jerry Lewis)

The Money Pit
1986   Universal
My wife. Auf wiedersehen. Hasta la vista. ("Carlos": John van Dreelen)

Monkey Business
1931   Paramount
I'm looking for a needle in the haystack. ("Groucho": Groucho Marx)

Monkey Business
1952   20th Century–Fox
What time did you order the table? ("Prof. Barnaby Fulton": Cary Grant)

Monkey on My Back
1957   United Artists
Oh, Cathy. ("Barney Ross": Cameron Mitchell)

Monkeys, Go Home!
1967   Buena Vista
Our olives? ("Hank Dussard": Dean Jones)

Monsieur Beaucaire
1946   Paramount
Look what happened on the way over. ("Mons. Beaucaire": Bob Hope)

Monsieur Verdoux
1947   United Artists
No, thank you. Uh, uh, just a moment. I've never tasted rum. ("Henri Verdoux": Charlie Chaplin)

Montenegro
1981   Atlantic

They all lived happily ever after. ("Marilyn Jordan": Susan Anspach)

The Moon Is Blue
1953 United Artists
Imagine. A dollar twenty just to go to the top of an old building. ("Patty O'Neill": Maggie McNamara)

Moon over Miami
1941 20th Century–Fox
Well, it may be perfect for all of you but how about my hundred and fifty bucks? ("Jack O'Hara": Jack Haley)

Moon over Parador
1988 Universal
Thanks. Thank you. Thank you so much. ("Jack Noah": Richard Dreyfuss)

Moonfleet
1955 MGM
He's my friend. ("John Mohune": Jon Whiteley)

Moonraker
1979 United Artists
Why not? ("James Bond": Roger Moore)

Moonstruck
1987 MGM
Alla famiglia salute. (Family member)

More Than a Secretary
1936 Columbia
I can't believe it. ("Carol Baldwin": Jean Arthur)

The More the Merrier
1943 Columbia

Aw, don't cry, baby. ("Joe Carter": Joel McCrea)

The Morning After
1986 20th Century–Fox
You, oh, you make me happy. ("Alex Sternbergen": Jane Fonda)

Morning Glory
1933 RKO
Nellie, they've all been trying to frighten me. They've been trying to frighten me into being sensible, but they can't do it, not now, not yet. They've got to let me be as foolish as I want to be. I, I want to ride through the park. I want to. I want a white ermine coat, and I'll buy you a beautiful present, and Mr. Hedges. I'll buy Mr. Hedges a little house, and I'll have rooms full of white orchids. And they've got to tell me that I'm much more wonderful than anyone else. Oh, Nellie, Nellie, I'm not afraid. I'm not afraid of being left a morning glory. I'm not afraid. I'm not afraid. I'm not afraid. Why should I be afraid? I'm not afraid. ("Eva Lovelace": Katharine Hepburn)

Morocco
1930 Paramount
Good luck, Legionnaire Brown. ("Le Bessier": Adolphe Menjou)

Moscow on the Hudson
1984 Columbia
This is a free country welcome to almost anyone, and I hope that someday you will join me here. Of course, I'll continue to write to you every week. Yes, in America anything is possible. Good-bye for now, beloved

family. I love you. Volya. ("Vladimir Ivanoff": Robin Williams)

Mother Carey's Chickens
1938   RKO
Hooray for us. ("Peter Carey": Donnie Dunagan)

Mother Is a Freshman
1948 20th Century–Fox
Twice. ("Abigail 'Abby' Fortitude Abbott": Loretta Young)

Mother Wore Tights
1947   20th Century–Fox
A kiss. ("Frank Burt": Dan Dailey)

Moulin Rouge
1952   United Artists
Good-bye. Good-bye. Good-bye, Henri. (Woman's voice)

The Mountain Men
1980   Columbia
God damn you, Henry Frapp. ("Bill Tyler": Charlton Heston)

The Mouse That Roared
1959   Columbia
Oh, fine, fine. All right, carry on. ("Will": William Hartnell)

Mrs. Brown, You've Got a Lovely Daughter
1968   MGM
That's life, isn't it? What you lose on the swing, you gain on the roundabouts. ("Herman": Peter Noone)

Mrs. Miniver
1942   MGM
We in this quiet corner of England have suffered the loss of friends very dear to us, some close to this church. George West, choir-boy, James Ballard, stationmaster and bell-ringer, and the proud winner, only an hour before his death of the Beldon cup for his beautiful Miniver Rose, and our hearts go out in sympathy to the two families who share the cruel loss of a young girl who was married at this altar only two weeks ago. The homes of many of us have been destroyed, and the lives of young and old have been taken; there's scarcely a household that hasn't been struck to the heart. And why? Surely you must have asked yourselves this question. Why, in all conscience should these be the ones to suffer? Children, old people, a young girl at the height of her loveliness, why these? Are these our soldiers? Are these our fighters? Why should they be sacrificed? I shall tell you why. Because this is not only a war of soldiers in uniform. It is a war of the people, of all the people, and it must be fought not only on the battlefield but in the cities and in the villages, in the factories and on the farms, in the home and in the heart of every man, woman and child who loves freedom. Well, we have buried our dead, but we shall not forget them. Instead, they will inspire us with an unbreakable determination to free ourselves and those who come after us from the tyranny and terror that threaten to strike us down. This is the people's war. It is our war. We are the fighters. Fight it, then. Fight it with all that is in us, and may God defend the right. ("Vicar": Henry Wilcoxon)

Mrs. Soffel
1984   MGM/UA

Just a little violet / From across the way / Came to cheer a prisoner / In his cell one day. / Just a little flower / Sent by loving hand / Has a kindly meaning / That true hearts understand. / Just a little flower / Plucked with loving care. / God has smiled upon it / And the sender fair. / And soon that little token / Wrapped in hands so neat / Rests quietly within a grave / For which a heart that's true does beat. ("Ed Biddle": Mel Gibson)

The Mummy
1932   Universal
Helen! Come back! It's Frank! Come back! ("Frank Whemple": David Manners)

Munster, Go Home
1966   Universal
Hurry up, Marilyn. ("Herman Munster": Fred Gwynne)

Murder Ahoy
1964   MGM
You know, the moment I clapped eyes on her, I said to meself, what an old darling. ("Captain Rhumstone": Lionel Jeffries)

Murder by Death
1976   Columbia
Ah, let idiots find out for themselves. Drive, please. ("Sidney Wang": Peter Sellers)

Murder, He Says
1945   Paramount
Oh. No hurry, sheriff. ("Pete Marshall": Fred MacMurray)

The Murder Man
1935   MGM

Don't feel too badly. I've been around for thirty years, and I want to tell you something. It's a long step from here to the finish. You know, juries take a lot of things into consideration. ("Captain Cole": Lionel Atwill)

Murder One
1988   Miramax
And I was right there by their side in the movie with them. All the shooting and the killing and the robbing was gonna end. And when Carl and Wayne, they were done, all those dead people [would] get up and take a bow. But they didn't. And they never will. ("Billy Isaacs": Henry Thomas)

Murphy's Law
1986   Cannon
Guess I'll make that a case of soap. ("Jack Murphy": Charles Bronson)

Murphy's Romance
1985   Columbia
How do you like your eggs? ("Emma": Sally Field)

Muscle Beach Party
1964   American International
No place. It's people for people I see. ("Julie": Lucianna Paluzzi)

Music Box
1989   Tri-Star
Go forward. Good, good. That's good. Yeah, Mikey, that's good. ("Michael Laszlo": Armin Mueller-Stahl)

My Best Friend Is a Vampire
1988   King's Road
Unbelievable. ("Ralph": Evan Mirand)

My Blue Heaven
1990   Warner Brothers
You know, sometimes I even amaze myself. ("Vinnie": Steve Martin)

My Bodyguard
1980   20th Century-Fox
Wait a minute. ("Linderman": Adam Baldwin)

My Cousin Rachel
1952   20th Century-Fox
Blessed Rachel, only you can know now this burden that I must carry to the end of my days. This question that I must ask myself again and again every day of my life, never to be answered now until we meet at last in Purgatory. Were you innocent or were you guilty? Rachel, my torment. My blessed, blessed torment. ("Philip Ashley": Richard Burton)

My Darling Clementine
1946   20th Century-Fox
Ma'am, I sure like that name Clementine. ("Wyatt Earp": Henry Fonda)

My Dear Secretary
1948   United Artists
Oh, Ronnie, don't. Oh, Ronnie. ("Mrs. Reeves": Florence Bates)

My Dinner with Andre
1981   New Yorker
I treated myself to a taxi. I rode home through the city streets. There wasn't a street; there wasn't a building that wasn't connected to some memory in my mind. There I was buying a suit with my father. There I was having an ice cream soda after school. When I finally came in, Debby was home from work. I told her everything about my dinner with Andre. ("Wally": Wallace Shawn)

My Fair Lady
1964   Warner Brothers
Eliza? Where the devil are my slippers? ("Prof. Henry Higgins": Rex Harrison)

My Favorite Brunette
1947   Paramount
Boy, he'll take any kind of a part. ("Jackson": Bob Hope)

My Favorite Wife
1940   RKO
Merry Christmas. ("Ellen Arden": Irene Dunne)

My Favorite Year
1982   MGM/UA
The way you see him here, like this, this is the way I like to remember him. I think if you had asked Alan Swann what was the single most gratifying moment in his life, he might have said this one right here. The next day I drove up to Connecticut with him and Alfie. This time he knocked on the door, and when he and Tess saw each other it was like they'd never been apart. Like Alfie says, with Swann you forgive a lot, you know. I know. ("Benny Stone": Mark Linn-Baker)

My Foolish Heart
1949   RKO
You don't have to, El, it's all right. After all, I could have been the girl in the brown and white dress. Anybody could have. ("Mary Jane": Lois Wheeler)

My Friend Irma
1949 Paramount
I was wrong. Anything can happen if you live with my friend Irma. ("Jane Stacey": Diana Lynn)

My Geisha
1962 Paramount
Keep bowing, you little ham. ("Paul Robaix": Yves Montand)

My Girl Tisa
1948 Warner Brothers
Welcome to America, Papa. ("Tisa Kepes": Lilli Palmer)

My Left Foot
1989 Miramax
Because Christy Brown was born there. ("Mary Carr": Ruth McCabe)

My Little Chickadee
1939 Universal
Oh, yeah, yeah. I'll do that, my little chickadee. ("Flower Belle Lee": Mae West)

My Man Godfrey
1936 Universal
Stand still, Godfrey, it'll all be over in a minute. ("Irene Bullock": Carole Lombard)

My Mom's a Werewolf
1989 Crown International
Stacey, you gotta come over, and bring Issue forty-three. ("Jennifer Shaber": Katrina Caspary)

My Pal Trigger
1946 Republic
Wait till Trigger sees this! ("Roy Rogers": Roy Rogers)

My Reputation
1946 Warner Brothers
I'll never be lonely again. ("Jessica Drummond": Barbara Stanwyck)

My Sister Eileen
1955 Columbia
Well, on behalf of my sister Eileen and me, I, me, uh, I'd like to thank you and your wonderful country for this great honor. Actually, we didn't do anything to deserve this. All I did was say something about the conga. ("Ruth Sherwood": Betty Grant)

My Six Loves
1963 Paramount
I did not. ("Sonny": Teddy Eccles)

My Stepmother Is an Alien
1988 Columbia
Yes! ("Jessie Mills": Alyson Hannigan)

My Wild Irish Rose
1947 Warner Brothers
I don't think you will. ("William 'Duke' Muldoon": George O'Brien)

The Mysterious Doctor
1943 Warner Brothers
You're right, Ruby, what price Hitler now? ("Dr. Frederick Holmes": Lester Matthews)

The Mystery of Mr. X
1934 MGM
Oh, oh, I beg your pardon. ("Revel": Robert Montgomery)

Mystery Street
1950 MGM
We got our man. He showed up. Turned

out to be a guy named Harkley. He's under arrest. Well, I guess that's about all, except I think your husband will be with you very soon now. And, Mrs. Shanway, I wanted to tell you that. . . . Hello? Hello, Mrs. Shanway? ("Lt. Peter Morales": Ricardo Montalban)

Nadine
1987   Tri-Star
Vernon, trust me. ("Nadine Hightower": Kim Basinger)

The Naked City
1948   Universal
There are eight million stories in the Naked City. This has been one of them. ("Narrator": Mark Hellinger)

The Naked Gun: From the Files of Police Squad!
1988   Paramount
Oh, Frank, everyone should have a friend like you. ("Jane Spencer": Priscilla Presley)

The Naked Jungle
1954   Paramount
Christopher! ("Joanna": Eleanor Parker)

The Naked Spur
1953   MGM
I'll fix some of Jesse's coffee for you. ("Lina Patch": Janet Leigh)

Nana
1934   United Artists
Now I can go, and I'm glad I'm going. Very glad. ("Nana": Anna Sten)

Nancy Goes to Rio
1950   MGM

Yes, come on. ("Frances Elliott": Ann Sothern)

Narrow Margin
1990   Tri-Star
Let the record state that the witness has pointed to Mr. Leo Watts. Thank you, Miss Hunnicut. No further questions. ("Caulfield": Gene Hackman)

Nate and Hayes
1983   Paramount
Row! Row! ("Captain Bully Hayes": Tommy Lee Jones)

National Lampoon's Animal House
1978   Universal
No prisoners! ("John 'Bluto' Blutarsky": John Belushi)

National Lampoon's Christmas Vacation
1989   Warner Brothers
I did it. ("Clark Griswold": Chevy Chase)

National Lampoon's European Vacation
1985   Warner Brothers
Yep, the Griswalds are back. ("Rusty Griswald": Jason Lively)

National Lampoon's Vacation
1983   Warner Brothers
What'd I tell you? Did I say trust me, huh? ("Clark Griswold": Chevy Chase)

National Velvet
1945   MGM
Mi! Mi! ("Velvet Brown": Elizabeth Taylor)

Native Son
1986   Cinecom
I will, Bigger. Good-bye. ("Max": John Karlen)

The Natural
1984   Tri-Star
Way back, way, way, way back, up high into the right field. That ball is still going. It's way back, high up in there. He did it. Hobbs did it. (Announcer)

Neighbors
1981   Columbia
Well, Enid never did like to come home to a dark house. ("Earl Keese": John Belushi)

Network
1976   MGM/UA
This was the story of Howard Beale, the first known instance of a man who was killed because he had lousy ratings. ("Narrator": Lee Richardson)

The Nevadan
1950   Columbia
Yeah, that's right. Horse? ("Dyke Merrick": Charles Kemper)

Never a Dull Moment
1967   Buena Vista
You sure do. ("Sally Inwood": Dorothy Provine)

Never Give a Sucker an Even Break
1941   Universal
My Uncle Bill. But I still love him. ("His niece, Gloria": Gloria Jean)

Never on Sunday
1959   Lopert
Because with love, it's possible. ("The Captain": Mitsos Liguisas)

Never Steal Anything Small
1958   Universal
Dan, the world is loony. ("Linda Cabot": Shirley Jones)

The Neverending Story
1984   Warner Brothers
Bastian made many other wishes, and had many other amazing adventures before he finally returned to the ordinary world. But that's another story. (Narrator)

The New Adventures of Pippi Longstocking
1988   Columbia
Come on, let's go home. ("Pippi": Tami Erin)

The New Centurians
1972   Columbia
Please! Would somebody throw a blanket! ("Gus": Scott Wilson)

New Girl in Town
1977   New World
You know what you can do with your contract. You can take your contract and shove it up your ass. ("Jamie": Monica Gayle)

A New Leaf
1970   Paramount
Come, I think we'd better go. ("Henry Graham": Walter Matthau)

A New Life
1988   Paramount
Hey, what are you talking about? I

said she would burp, you said. . . .
("Steve Giardino": Alan Alda)

New Moon
1940 MGM
Citizeness de Beaumanoir. ("Charles":
Nelson Eddy)

New York, New York
1977 United Artists
OK, I'm there. ("Jimmy Doyle":
Robert De Niro)

New York Stories
1989 Buena Vista
Well, it was a little better. Here I am.
We're on the beach here. ("Mother":
Mae Questel)

The Next One
1982 Allstar
Don't talk, OK. I'm a friend. A friend.
I'll teach you a few very important
things quickly and then I want you to
meet a very nice lady. ("Tim Johnson": Jeremy Licht)

Niagara
1952 20th Century-Fox
And had it answered. ("Ray Cutler":
Casey Adams)

Nick Carter, Master Detective
1939 MGM
Now, if I'm wrong, I'll, ouch! ("Nick
Carter/Robert Chalmers": Walter
Pidgeon)

Nickelodeon
1976 Columbia
Action! (Director)

Night and the City
1950 20th Century-Fox

All right, stop it, Kristo. There you
are, Kristo. Give her the blood money.
She cut my throat for you. ("Harry
Fabian": Richard Widmark)

The Night Before
1988 King's Road
Sorry. ("Winston Connelly": Keanu
Reeves)

A Night in the Life of Jimmy Reardon
1988 20th Century-Fox
It sure made me feel good to say it.
Hell, I might even do it. ("Jimmy
Reardon": River Phoenix)

Night into Morning
1951 MGM
This is our last hour together. I'm not
going to keep you for it. But I'll
remember every one of your faces for
the rest of my life. And I rather imagine you'll remember mine. Because
we've gone a journey together. There
were times when I lost my way, and
somewhere along the road you and
others became the teacher and I the
student. You taught me that as long
as one man is without an answer all
men are without an answer. You
taught me that only he who chooses to
be alone is alone. And so even though
our small journey is over and we go
our separate ways, we'll never really
be apart. Till the end of time we'll
carry in our hearts the things that
we've shared together. I'm sure someone somewhere said that much better
than I, probably Shakespeare, surely
the Bible. But I think it's something
that a man should say at last to himself. As you know, I teach English,

but there are some things very hard to say in it. So if you don't mind I'll use my first-year Spanish. Vaya con Dios. Go with God. Let's all go with God. ("Phillip Ainley": Ray Milland)

Night Key
1937 Universal
Oh, Joan. ("Dave Mallory": Boris Karloff)

'Night, Mother
1986 Universal
Thelma, are you all right? Hold on a minute, Thelma, I'll go find him. ("Loretta Cates": Carol Robbins)

Night of the Cobra Woman
1974 New World
I'm ready to join you, Lena. I only want to be with you now. ("Duff": Roger Garrett)

The Night of the Iguana
1964 MGM
I'll get you back up, baby. I'll always get you back up. ("Maxine Faulk": Ava Gardner)

The Night of the Living Dead
1968 Continental
Hey, Randy, light these torches over here. (Police Chief)

Night People
1954 20th Century–Fox
We interrupt this program for an announcement from American military headquarters here. The return of Corporal John J. Leatherby of Toledo, Ohio, who was picked up by the Russians ten days ago has been ef-

fected through regular channels. The promptness with which the Russians responded to diplomatic conversations is interpreted by many here as still further indication that they are now genuinely anxious for the resumption of normal peaceful relations with the Western powers. (Radio announcer)

Night Song
1947 RKO
Sorry. ("Chick": Hoagy Carmichael)

Night Time in Nevada
1948 Republic
Just stand back. ("Roy Rogers": Roy Rogers)

A Night to Remember
1943 Columbia
Well, he is. And that's why I love him. Jeff, Jeff, get up. Get up, that's your good suit. Aw, honey, come on. There. He'll be all right. ("Nancy Troy": Loretta Young)

Nightfall
1956 Columbia
It does now. Let's go keep it company. ("James Vanning": Aldo Ray)

Nightmare at Shadow Woods
1987 Film Concept Group
I'm Todd. ("Maddy": Louise Lasser)

Nightstick
1987 Production Distribution Co.
This is Calhoun. I have the map. Bomb squads to the following locations. Sixty-ninth Street branch at Lexington, second stall in the ladies room. The Harlem branch at one hundred

twenty-eighth, assistant manager's office, behind the bar that looks like a computer terminal. Broadway, eleventh street branch, ha, ha, you're not gonna believe this one. ("Jack Calhoun": Bruce Fairbairn)

Nightwing
1979   Columbia
He summoned the eternal fires. ("Youngman Duran": Nick Mancuso)

Nine to Five
1980   20th Century–Fox
Holy merde. ("Roz": Elizabeth Wilson)

1984
1984   Atlantic
I love you. ("Winston Smith": John Hurt)

1941
1979   Universal
It's going to be a long war. ("Gen. Stilwell": Robert Stack)

Ninja Academy
1990   Omega
Try not to wake the others on the way out, OK? ("Josh": Will Egan)

Ninotchka
1939   MGM
Darling. ("Count Leon Dolga": Melvyn Douglas)

No Deposit, No Return
1976   Buena Vista
Now we're even. ("J. W. Osborne": David Niven)

No Down Payment
1957   20th Century–Fox

Good-bye. ("Betty Kreitzer": Barbara Rush)

No Holds Barred
1989   New Line
Randy. ("Rip": Hulk Hogan)

No Leave, No Love
1946   MGM
May I? ("Sgt. Michael Hanlon": Van Johnson)

No Man of Her Own
1932   Paramount
Well, let's see. Look, I picked this guy up in Rio. Named him Glendale. Yeah, honey, lucky he didn't die on board. Oh, such a rough trip. Oh, no kidding. The third day out the wind blew off the top deck, on a great big ocean liner, would you believe it? You should have seen the excitement on board. Why, they even had the passengers put on their life jackets. . . . ("Jerry 'Babe' Stewart": Clark Gable)

No Man's Land
1987   Orion
Fuck you! ("Ted Varrick": Charlie Sheen)

No Mercy
1986   Tri-Star
So what do you say, huh? What do you say? ("Eddie Jillette": Richard Gere)

No Questions Asked
1951   MGM
It's all right, she's with him. ("Inspector Matt Duggan": George Murphy)

No Sad Songs for Me
1950 Columbia
No, I only remember she smiled.
("Polly Scott": Natalie Wood)

No Small Affair
1984 Columbia
I'll never love anybody but Laura,
never. I'll never make love to anyone
again. That's almost definite. ("Charles
Cummings": John Cryer)

No Time for Sergeants
1958 Warner Brothers
It gives me great pleasure to award
this air medal, which through a
regrettable error was previously
awarded posthumously, to Private
Benjamin B. Whitledge, U.S. Army
infantry. ("Maj. Gen. Eugene Bush":
Howard Smith)

No Way Out
1950 20th Century–Fox
Don't cry, white boy. You're gonna
live. ("Dr. Luther Brooks": Sidney
Poitier)

No Way Out
1987 Orion
He will return. Where else does he
have to go? (Russian agent)

No Way to Treat a Lady
1968 Paramount
Please. ("Christopher Gill": Rod
Steiger)

Nobody's Fool
1986 Island
Yeah, well, how about we start with a
fish or a turtle or maybe something
you don't have to feed. ("Riley": Eric
Roberts)

Nobody's Perfekt
1981 Columbia
No nuns, no skates, no strippers.
("Carol": Susan Clark)

Nocturne
1946 RKO
You know, I've got a mother that's
anxious to meet you. ("Lt. Joe
Warne": George Raft)

None But the Lonely Heart
1944 RKO
Good-bye, Dad. ("Ernie Mott": Cary
Grant)

Norma Rae
1979 20th Century–Fox
Norma, what I've had from you has
been sumptuous. ("Reuben": Ron
Leibman)

North by Northwest
1959 MGM
I know, but I'm sentimental. ("Roger
Thornhill": Cary Grant)

North Dallas Forty
1979 Paramount
Yeah. ("Phillip Elliott": Nick Nolte)

North from Lone Star
1941 Columbia
So long, Cannonball! ("Wild Bill
Hickock": Bill Elliott)

North Star
1943 RKO
Yes. It'd be different for us. Wars
don't leave people as they were. All
people will learn this and come to see
that wars do not have to be. We'll

make this the last war. We'll make a free world for all men. The earth belongs to us, the people, if we fight for it. And we will fight for it. ("Marina": Anne Baxter)

Northwest Mounted Police
1940   Paramount
Come on, sweetheart. ("Dusty Rivers": Gary Cooper)

Northwest Passage
1940   MGM
Hear from him? Every time we look across a river we'll hear his voice, calling us through the wind. And he'll be within us, Elizabeth, no matter where we are or he may be, for that man will never die. ("Langdon Towne": Robert Young)

Norwood
1969   Paramount
Norwood, do you know what I want? I want to live in a trailer and listen to you play and sing every day. ("Rita Lee Chipman": Kim Darby)

Not as a Stranger
1955   United Artists
Kris, help me. For God's sake, help me. ("Lucas": Robert Mitchum)

Not of This Earth
1988   Concorde
Yeah, come on. ("Harry": Roger Lodge)

Not with My Wife, You Don't
1966   Warner Brothers
Secret agent. ("'Tank' Martin": George C. Scott)

Nothing But a Man
1965   Cinema V
Baby, I feel so free inside. ("Duff Anderson": Ivan Dixon)

Nothing in Common
1986   Tri-Star
You're the last person I thought would ever come through for me. ("Max": Jackie Gleason)

Nothing Sacred
1937   United Artists
Run for your life! Run for your life! The hotel is flooded. Flooded. ("Doctor Enoch Downer": Charles Winninger)

Now, Voyager
1942   Warner Brothers
Oh, Jerry, don't let's ask for the moon. We have the stars. ("Charlotte Vale": Bette Davis)

Nowhere to Go
1958   MGM
Too early, I'd say. (Man on tractor)

The Nude Bomb
1980   Universal
Don't be ridiculous, Chief. There is no fallout from a nude bomb. Fallout from a nude. ("Maxwell Smart": Don Adams)

Number One with a Bullet
1987   Cannon
Nicholas, I am not a well woman. ("Mrs. Barzak": Doris Roberts)

Nuts
1987   Warner Brothers
Out! ("Claudia Draper": Barbara Streisand)

The Nutty Professor
1963 Paramount
Yes, actually, Stella. What's right is right. Let's split. ("Prof. Julius Ferris Kelp/Buddy Love": Jerry Lewis)

O. C. and Stiggs
1987 MGM/UA
Kopa one hundred's advanced weather's got us trapped in a three-day heat streak with all intentions of breaking the one-eighteen mark wide open today. Just stay inside, forget the electric bill, turn up the air. Tomorrow a reprieve at one fifteen, low tonight seventy-seven, right now one sixteen in the valley of the sun, and Kopa one hundred. (Voice on radio)

O Lucky Man!
1973 Warner Brothers
What's there to smile about? ("Mick Travis": Malcolm McDowell)

Objective Burma
1944 Warner Brothers
We'll have you out of here right away. And some jeeps to take you down to the planes. I'll see you back at the base. ("Col Carter": Warner Anderson)

The Odd Couple
1968 Paramount
Ante a quarter, fellows. ("Speed": Larry Haines)

Ode to Billy Joe
1976 Warner Brothers
Now that would be right neighborly of you, Mr. Barksdale, sir. ("Bobbie Lee Hartley": Glynnis O'Connor)

The Odessa File
1974 Columbia
I bear no hatred, no bitterness towards the German people. Peoples are not evil, only individuals are evil. If, after my death, this diary should be found and read, will some kind friend please say Kaddish for me? ("Tauber's voice": Cyril Shaps)

Of Human Bondage
1934 RKO
Yes. ("Philip": Leslie Howard)

Of Unknown Origin
1983 Warner Brothers
I had a party. ("Bart Hughes": Peter Weller)

Off Limits
1953 Paramount
Go. Go, girl. ("Wally Hogan": Bob Hope)

Off Limits
1988 20th Century–Fox
Peace. ("Albaby Perkins": Gregory Hines)

An Officer and a Gentleman
1982 Paramount
Way to go, Paula! Way to go! ("Lynette Pomeroy": Lisa Blount)

The Offspring
1987 TMS
Welcome to Oldfield. ("Julian White": Vincent Price)

Oh, God
1977 Warner Brothers
I'll tell you what. You talk, I'll listen. ("God": George Burns)

Oh God, Book II
1980   Warner Brothers
Good-bye, Tracy. Go ahead, Tracy. there's nothing worse than cold egg foo yung. ("God": George Burns)

Oh, God, You Devil
1984   Warner Brothers
Sing. ("God": George Burns)

Oh Heavenly Dog
1980   20th Century–Fox
Better stick with B.J. You're not the, uh, Benji type. ("Jackie Howard": Jane Seymour)

Oh, Men! Oh, Women!
1957   20th Century–Fox
Oh, darling, how could I have been so stupid. That's what I meant, you know, finesse, smooth stuff, god-like. ("Myra Hagerman": Barbara Rush)

O'Hara's Wife
1983   Davis-Panzer
Thanks, Harry. Thanks for everything. ("Bob O'Hara": Edward Asner)

Oklahoma!
1955   Magna
Thank you. Good-bye. Hah! ("Curly": Gordon MacRae)

Oklahoma Crude
1973   Columbia
Noble. ("Lena Doyle": Faye Dunaway)

Old Acquaintance
1943   Warner Brothers
Let's drink to that, Millie. ("Kitty Marlowe": Bette Davis)

Old Enough
1984   Orion
Yeah, I like it. ("Lonnie": Sarah Boyd)

The Old Fashioned Way
1934   Paramount
It cures hoarseness. Who will be the first to buy a bottle? ("The Great McGonigle": W. C. Fields)

Old Gringo
1989   Columbia
He told me I would forget. But how could I not remember. The young general who wanted to change the world. The old writer who wanted to bid it farewell. I am the one who will live to remember them both. ("Harriet Winslow": Jane Fonda)

The Old Man and the Sea
1958   Warner Brothers
Up the road in his shack the old man was sleeping again. He was still sleeping on his face, and the boy was sitting by him watching him. The old man was dreaming about the lions. ("Narrator": Spencer Tracy)

Old Yeller
1957   Buena Vista
He's big enough to learn. He's big enough to act like Old Yeller. ("Travis Coates": Tommy Kirk)

Oliver's Story
1978   Paramount
Only the living need each other. Only the living can carry life on. Part of me was trying to die because I thought I owed that to Jenny. I owe her something else, something much harder to give. A new life, another try. A set-

ting free. ("Oliver Barrett, IV": Ryan O'Neal)

Omega Syndrome
1987 New World
Oh, well, we were just –. ("Jack Corbett": Ken Wahl)

The Omen
1976 20th Century-Fox
Yes, sir. ("Secret serviceman": Burnell Tucker)

On a Clear Day You Can See Forever
1970 Paramount
Well, so long, doctor. See you later. ("Daisy Gamble": Barbra Streisand)

On an Island with You
1948 MGM
Looks like we're gonna have a weddin' after all, Pineapple. ("Buckley": Jimmy Durante)

On Borrowed Time
1939 MGM
Coming, Grandma. ("Pud": Bobs Watson)

On Dangerous Ground
1951 RKO
Jim. ("Mary Malden": Ida Lupino)

On Golden Pond ,
1981 Universal
Yeah, just the two of them now. Babies all grown up and moved to Los Angeles or somewhere. ("Norman Thayer, Jr.": Henry Fonda)

On Moonlight Bay
1951 Warner Brothers

Here's your hat. Keep your head up and breathe through your nose. ("Wesley Winfield": Billy Gray)

On the Beach
1959 United Artists
God, God forgive us. Peter, I think I'll have that cup of tea now. ("Mary Holmes": Donna Anderson)

On the Right Track
1981 20th Century-Fox
Did I tell you I can pick the stock market? ("Lester": Gary Coleman)

On the Waterfront
1954 Columbia
Where you guys going? Wait a minute! I'll remember this! I'll remember every one of ya! I'll be back, don't you forget that! I'll be back! ("Johnny Friendly": Lee J. Cobb)

Once Before I Die
1967 Goldstone
No, please, don't. Please, no. ("Alex": Ursula Andress)

Once More, with Feeling
1960 Columbia
Look, Mr. Wilbur, look. ("Maxwell Archer": Gregory Ratoff)

Once Upon a Time in the West
1969 Paramount
Go away. Go away. Go away. I don't want you to see me die. ("Cheyenne": Jason Robards, Jr.)

The One and Only
1978 Paramount
Come here, lover. If there are panties

under there, I'm going back to Ohio. ("Mary Crawford": Kim Darby)

The One and Only, Genuine, Original Family Band
1968   Buena Vista
That's statesmanship! ("Grandpa Bower": Walter Brennan)

One Crazy Summer
1986   Warner Brothers
Thank you so much. ("Egg Stork": Bobcat Goldthwait)

One Flew over the Cuckoo's Nest
1975   United Artists
Let's go. ("Chief Bromden": Will Sampson)

One Foot in Heaven
1941   Warner Brothers
Yes, dear, I know. ("William Spence": Fredric March)

100 Rifles
1969   20th Century–Fox
All right! All right! ("Yaqui Joe": Burt Reynolds)

One More Saturday
1986   Columbia
That's hard to say. I'll tell you one thing: whoever marries Tobi is going to be a very lucky man. ("Larry": Tom Davis)

One on One
1977   Warner Brothers
All the way up with a red-hot poker. I can play anywhere I want. ("Henry Steele": Robby Benson)

One Woman's Story
1949   Universal
If you want to, that is. ("Howard Justin": Claude Rains)

Only Angels Have Wings
1939   Columbia
Son of a gun. Hey! Hey, Geoff! ("Bonnie Lee": Jean Arthur)

The Only Game in Town
1969   20th Century–Fox
All right now, one, two, three. ("Joe Grady": Warren Beatty)

Only Two Can Play
1962   British Lion
It's quite a long drive home, isn't it? ("John Lewis": Peter Sellers)

Only When I Laugh
1981   Columbia
Oh, God, you're terrible. Wait till I tell Toby. I'll call her in a few minutes. Maybe we can all have lunch together. The whole world can go to hell as long as the three of us can have lunch together. I even reserved a nice little table in heaven, Italian, of course. Oh, thank God the three of us have each other to lean on. ("Jimmy": James Coco)

Operation Mad Ball
1957   Columbia
Wait a minute. I'm still half an officer. ("Lt. Betty Bixby": Kathryn Grant)

Operation Pacific
1950   Warner Brothers
Let's go get blitzed. ("'Duke' Gifford": John Wayne)

Operation Petticoat
1959 Universal
Strange, still that number one engine. I guess they were never able to fix that. ("Lt. Comdr. M. T. Sherman": Cary Grant)

Operator 13
1934 MGM
And remember only loyalty and love. ("Gail Loveless/'Ann Claibourne'": Marion Davies)

Opposing Force
1987 Orion
They kept the pressure up for an answer that would get them off the hook. All I really wanted to know was did I qualify. When they said yes, that was good enough for me. Sort of. ("Lt. Casey": Lisa Eichhorn)

The Opposite Sex
1956 MGM
Hope it's a little boy. ("Edith": Joan Blondell)

Ordinary People
1980 Paramount
I love you, too. ("Calvin": Donald Sutherland)

Orphans
1987 Lorimar
I am a dead-end kid. I am a fucking dead-end kid. ("Treat": Matthew Modine)

Oscar Wilde
1959 Vantage
Will you play something gay? ("Oscar Wilde": Robert Morley)

The Osterman Weekend
1983 20th Century–Fox
Am I still on? ("John Tanner": Rutger Hauer)

The Other
1972 20th Century–Fox
Niles, wash up now. Time for lunch. ("Aunt Vee": Norma Connolly)

The Other Side of Midnight
1977 20th Century–Fox
Thank you, Sister. ("Constantin Demeris": Raf Vallone)

Our Little Girl
1935 20th Century–Fox
Oh, that's just fine. Now I can take a picture. ("Molly Middleton": Shirley Temple)

Out of the Past
1947 RKO
You can tell me. You knew him better than I did. Was he going away with her? I have to know. Was he going away with her? ("Ann": Virginia Huston)

The Out-of-Towners
1970 Paramount
Oh, my God. ("Gwen Kellerman": Sandy Dennis)

The Outing
1987 TMS
Stop. ("Alex Wallace": Andra St. Ivanyi)

The Outlaw
1943 RKO
Yes. ("Rio": Jane Russell)

Outlaw Blues
1977   Warner Brothers
Dear Channel Two news. I have got a solid-gold, guaranteed, sure-fire story just for you: news film of the Bobby Ogden wedding in Mexico. Now, it can be yours on an absolutely exclusive basis, no radio or other TV. The price is eight hundred dollars for color, six hundred dollars for black and white. But hurry because we're going with the first offer. Also extend our warmest congratulations to Mayor Cavenaugh on his inspiring victory. See you all soon. Mrs. Tina Waters Ogden. P.S. Hope Gar's other leg heals real soon. ("Tina Waters": Susan Saint James)

The Outlaw Josey Wales
1976   Warner Brothers
I reckon so. I guess we all died a little in that damn war. ("Josey Wales": Clint Eastwood)

Outpost in Morocco
1949   United Artists
In the name of the French government, I accept your word, and thank you for your good offices in helping to restore order. ("Capt. Paul Gerard": George Raft)

The Outriders
1950   MGM
He said he was out of bullets. ("Will Owen": Joel McCrea)

Over the Brooklyn Bridge
1983   Cannon
What do you say we try something tonight that even we'll be ashamed of in the morning. ("Albie Sherman": Elliott Gould)

Over 21
1945   Columbia
OK, boss. ("Robert Gow": Charles Coburn)

Overboard
1987   MGM
A little girl. ("Joanna Stayton/Annie Profitt": Goldie Hawn)

The Overlanders
1946   Universal
My word. ("Bill Parsons": John Nugent Hayward)

The Owl and the Pussycat
1970   Columbia
Yeah. It's too damn enervating. ("Doris": Barbra Streisand)

The Ox-Bow Incident
1943   20th Century–Fox
He said he wanted his wife to get this letter, didn't he? He said there was nobody to look after the kids, didn't he? ("Gil Carter": Henry Fonda)

P.K. and the Kid
1987   Lorimar
You could use a little luck yourself. ("William 'Kid' Kane": Paul LeMat)

P.O.W. The Escape
1986   Cannon
You weren't the only one. ("Colonel Cooper": David Carradine)

The Pack
1977   Warner Brothers
Come on. That's a good boy. ("Jerry": Joe Don Baker)

Paid in Full
1949   Paramount

Little Jane. Hello, little Jane. ("Jane Langley": Lizabeth Scott)

Paint Your Wagon
1969 Paramount
Do you think he'll be all right, Pardner? Where's he going. ("Elizabeth": Jean Seberg)

The Painted Hills
1951 MGM
Hey, Shep. ("Tommy Blake": Gary Gray)

The Painted Veil
1934 MGM
I love you. ("Katherine Koerber Fane": Greta Garbo)

Pale Rider
1985 Warner Brothers
Thank you. Good-bye. ("Megan Wheeler": Sydney Penney)

The Paleface
1948 Paramount
What do you want, a happy ending? ("'Painless' Peter Potter": Bob Hope)

The Palm Beach Story
1942 Paramount
Well, nothing, it seems. ("Gerry Jeffers": Claudette Colbert)

Papa's Delicate Condition
1963 Paramount
You do and I won't let him in the house. ("Jack 'Papa' Griffith": Jackie Gleason)

The Paper Chase
1973 20th Century–Fox
Aren't you going to open your grades? ("Susan Kingfield": Lindsay Wagner)

Paperhouse
1989 Vestron
He's all right now, Mom. I know he is. ("Anna Madden": Charlotte Burke)

Papillon
1973 Allied Artists
Hey, you bastards. I'm still here. ("Henri 'Papillon' Charriere,": Steve McQueen)

Paradise
1982 Embassy
Yeah, we better. ("Sarah": Phoebe Cates)

Paradise Hawaiian Style
1966 Paramount
I didn't want to spoil your fun, and mine. ("Rick Richards": Elvis Presley)

The Parallax View
1974 Paramount
Ladies and gentlemen, you've been invited here today for the official announcement of the inquiry into the death of George Hammond. A complete transcript of the investigation is in preparation. This committee has spent nearly six months of investigation followed by eleven weeks of hearings. After careful deliberation it has concluded that George Hammond was assassinated by Joseph Frady. An overwhelming body of evidence has revealed that Frady was obsessed with the Carroll assassination and in his confused and distorted mind seems to have imagined that Hammond was

responsible for the senator's death. He was equally convinced that Hammond was somehow plotting to kill him, and it is for those reasons that Frady assassinated him. Although I'm certain that it will do nothing to discourage conspiracy peddlers, there is no evidence of a conspiracy in the assassination of George Hammond. Those are our findings, the evidence will be available to you as soon as possible. This is an announcement, gentlemen, there will be no questions. ("Commission spokesman": Ford Rainey)

Paramedics
1988   Vestron
Need a ride, young lady? ("Captain Prescott": John P. Ryan)

Pardners
1956   Paramount
Good-bye. Now the end. Not that way. That's better. ("Wade Kingsley, Jr.": Jerry Lewis)

The Parent Trap
1961   Buena Vista
You and I were marching on real slow, sort of funny like, in organdy dresses. And there was music coming from someplace, and there were flowers and people. ("Sharon McKendrick/Susan Evers": Hayley Mills)

Parenthood
1989   Universal
That's great. (Family member)

Paris Blues
1961   United Artists
I want to do something, though. I'd like to give you a going-away present. You may not like, but I don't care. It's just this, you're never gonna forget me. You're gonna walk down the street of wherever you happen to be and you're gonna see me, even when you know I'm not there. And nobody in this whole world is ever gonna be as right for you as I was, for twelve days in Paris in autumn, 'cause that's been your gift to me. ("Lillian Corning": Joanne Woodward)

Paris, Texas
1984   20th Century–Fox
Oh. ("Jane": Nastassja Kinski)

The Parson and the Outlaw
1957   Columbia
Billy! ("Tonya": Marie Windsor)

A Passage to India
1984   Columbia
I do not think I will ever see them again. ("Doctor Aziz": Victor Banerjee)

Passage to Marseille
1944   Warner Brothers
That letter will be delivered. ("Capt. Freycinet": Claude Rains)

Passport to Pimlico
1949   Eagle Lion
Ladies and gentlemen. We're back in England. ("Arthur Pemberton": Stanley Holloway)

Pat and Mike
1952   MGM
And take you right down with me, Shorty. ("Mike": Spencer Tracy)

A Patch of Blue
1965   MGM
She's ready. ("Gordon Ralfe": Sidney Poitier)

Paternity
1981   Paramount
Hallelujah, man. ("Buddy Evans": Burt Reynolds)

Paths of Glory
1957   United Artists
Yes, sir. ("Sgt. Boulanger": Bert Freed)

The Patsy
1964   Paramount
Which reminds me. I'm having nuts and whipped cream for lunch. Would you join me, please. Crew, that's lunch. One hour for the actors and seven days for the technicians. It's a movie set breaking once and for all to go to have lunch. ("Stanley Belt": Jerry Lewis)

Patti Rocks
1988   Film Dallas
Billy, there's a word for that. ("Eddie": John Jenkins)

Patton
1970 20th Century–Fox
For over a thousand years, Roman conquerors returning from the wars enjoyed the honor of a triumph, a tumultuous parade. In the procession came trumpeteers and musicians and strange animals from the conquered territories, together with carts laden with treasure and captured armaments. The conqueror rode in a triumphal chariot, the dazed prisoners walking in chains before him. Sometimes his children, robed in white, stood with him in the chariot or rode the trace horses. A slave stood behind the conqueror holding a golden crown and whispering in his ear a warning that all glory is fleeting. ("General George S. Patton, Jr.": George C. Scott)

Patty Hearst
1988   Atlantic
Yeah. Pardon my French, Dad, but fuck 'em. Fuck them all. ("Patricia Hearst": Natasha Richardson)

The Pawnbroker
1965   Alllied Artists
Back it up. Back it up. Stand back. Stand back. (Police officer)

The Pearl of Death
1944   Universal
And when that time comes, perhaps even the pearl will be washed clean again. ("Sherlock Holmes": Basil Rathbone)

Pee-wee's Big Adventure
1985   Warner Brothers
I don't have to see it, Dottie. I lived it. (Pee-wee Herman, as himself)

Peggy Sue Got Married
1986   Tri-Star
Charlie, uh, I'd like to invite you over to your house for dinner on Sunday with your kids. I'll make a strudel. ("Peggy Sue": Kathleen Turner)

The Penitent
1988   New Century

For what? I told you I would not die on a cross. ("Juan Matco": Armand Assante)

Penitentiary
1979 MGM/UA
Good-bye, Too. ("'Seldom Seen'": Floyd Chatman)

Pennies from Heaven
1936 Columbia
Hey, hey, hey, get out there! Hey, hey, look, out! Look out! ("Larry": Bing Crosby)

Pennies from Heaven
1982 MGM/UA
I'm Arthur and I love you. ("Arthur Parker": Steve Martin)

Penny Serenade
1941 Columbia
And over in that corner I could, I could put a little electric train. ("Roger Adams": Cary Grant)

Penrod and Sam
1937 Warner Brothers
Good night. . . . ("Penrod Schofield": Billy Mauch)

People Will Talk
1951 20th Century–Fox
Professor Elwell, you're a little man. It's not that you're short. You're little, in the mind and in the heart. Tonight you tried to make a man little whose boots you couldn't touch if you stood on tiptoe on top of the highest mountain in the world. And, as it turned out, you're even littler than you were before. ("Shunderson": Finlay Currie)

Perfect
1985 Columbia
Now, where were we? ("Adam Lawrence": John Travolta)

The Perils of Pauline
1947 Paramount
I guess I'll never learn. ("Pearl White": Betty Hutton)

Permanent Record
1988 Paramount
I made a decision about that. I decided to write about my own experiences. I like my own experiences, all in all. ("M.G.": Michelle Meyrink)

Personal Best
1982 Warner Brothers
Are you shittin' me? Hey. ("Chris Cahill": Mariel Hemingway)

Pet Sematary
1989 Paramount
No! ("Louis Creed": Dale Midkiff)

Pete 'n' Tillie
1972 Universal
I like your attitude, Mrs. Seltzer. ("Pete Seltzer": Walter Matthau)

The Petrified Forest
1936 Warner Brothers
"God bids me tend it with good husbandry. This is the end for which we twain are met." ("Gabrielle Maple 'Gabby'": Bette Davis)

The Phantom of the Opera
1943 Universal
After you, m'sieu. ("Anatole Garron": Nelson Eddy)

Phantom Raiders
1940   MGM
Well, if I'm wrong, I'll apologize. ("Nick Carter": Walter Pidgeon)

The Phenix City Story
1955   Allied Artists
The devices that cheated them were broken up and burned, but how long would it last. The evil men who ruled our lives for so long were still out there, waiting their moment to come back. We'd won a battle, but had we won the war? That is the question that I, John Patterson, and all of our good friends had to consider. The people of Alabama elected me attorney general in my father's place with two sacred duties to perform: to seek out and bring to justice the murderers of my father and to keep the gambling hells of Phenix City closed, firmly closed forever. With God's help I shall not fail. ("John Patterson": Richard Kiley)

Phffft
1954   Columbia
Whoosh. ("Robert Tracy": Jack Lemmon)

The Philadelphia Experiment
1984   New World
I've got it all figured out. The Navy owes me forty years back pay. ("David Herdeg": Michael Pare)

The Philadelphia Story
1940   MGM
Feels though I lived through all this before in another life. ("Uncle Willie": Roland Young)

Physical Evidence
1989   Columbia

Jesus, Joe, can't you do anything right? ("Jenny Hudson": Theresa Russell)

Pick a Star
1937   MGM
Rinaldo. ("Rinaldo Lopez": Mischa Auer)

The Pick-Up Artist
1987   20th Century–Fox
Come on, let's eat. ("Jack Jericho": Robert Downey)

A Piece of the Action
1977   Warner Brothers
No. ("Dave Anderson": Bill Cosby/ "Manny Durrell": Sidney Poitier)

Pillars of the Sky
1956   Universal
And Jesus said, "I am the resurrection and the life. He that believeth in me though he were dead yet shall he live and whosoever liveth and believeth in me shall never die." Blessed be the God and father of our lord Jesus Christ. Father of mercies and God of all comforts. Comfort of us in all our afflictions that we may be able to comfort them that are in any affliction with the comfort wherewith we ourselves are comforted. Hear my prayer, oh lord, and with thine ears consider my calling. ("First Sergeant Emmett Bell": Jeff Chandler)

Pillow Talk
1959   Universal
Wait! Jonathan! Jonathan! ("Brad Allen": Rock Hudson)

The Pilot
1979   New Line

Where my heart is. Where my heart is, Doc. ("Mike Hagan": Cliff Robertson)

Pimpernel Smith
1942   United Artists
We shall all be back. ("Prof. Horatio Smith": Leslie Howard)

Pink Cadillac
1989   Warner Brothers
Sweetheart, if there's any justice on this planet, they'll never make you give back that red dress. ("Tommy Nowak": Clint Eastwood)

The Pink Jungle
1968   Universal
Well, no, it's not official, but uh you might call it undercover activity. I'll see you in about a week, Clyde. ("Ben Morris": James Garner)

The Pink Panther
1963   United Artists
Well, you know, it wasn't easy. ("Inspector Jacques Clouseau": Peter Sellers)

The Pink Panther Strikes Again
1976   United Artists
What? Kato, you imbecile, not now! ("Inspector Jacques Clouseau": Peter Sellers)

Pinky
1949   20th Century–Fox
Fine, he's in the old dining room. ("Pinky [Patricia Johnson]": Jeanne Crain)

Piranha
1978   New World

There's nothing left to fear. ("Dr. Mengers": Barbara Steele)

Pirates
1986   Cannon
Would you do me a kindness and sing a little while I nod off. And mind you, sing, don't bray like a donkey. Sing that little French ditty I've a liking for. ("Captain Kidd": Walter Matthau)

Pittsburgh
1942   Universal
I love ya, Cash. So help me, I love ya. ("Pittsburgh 'Pitt' Markham": John Wayne)

Places in the Heart
1984   Tri-Star
Peace of God. ("Edna Spalding": Sally Field)

Plain Clothes
1988   Paramount
Yeah, actually, I can't wait to get back to school. ("Matt Dunbar": Loren Dean)

Planet of the Apes
1968   20th Century–Fox
Oh, my God. I'm back. Back home. All the time. You finally really did it. You maniacs! You blew it up! Damn you! God damn you all to hell! ("George Taylor": Charlton Heston)

Platoon
1986   Orion
I think now, looking back, we did not fight the enemy, we fought ourselves, and the enemy was in us. The war is over for me now, but it will always be

there the rest of my days, as I'm sure Elias will be, fighting with Barnes for what Rhah called possession of my soul. There are times since when I've felt like a child born of those two fathers. But be that as it may, those of us who did make it have an obligation to build again, to teach others what we know, and to try with what's left of our lives to find a goodness and meaning to this life. ("Chris Taylor": Charlie Sheen)

Play It Again, Sam
1972   Paramount
Here's looking at you, kid. ("Humphrey Bogart": Jerry Lacy)

Plaza Suite
1971   Paramount
She was better off in the bathroom. You hear me? Better off in the bathroom. ("Roy Hubley": Walter Matthau)

Please Don't Eat the Daisies
1960   MGM
I beg your pardon. ("Lawrence Mackay": David Niven)

The Pleasure of His Company
1961   Paramount
I'll sue you, Pogo, I'll sue you! Toy, come back here! Toy! ("James Dougherty": Gary Merrill)

Plenty
1985   20th Century–Fox
There will be days and days and days like this. ("Susan Traherne": Meryl Streep)

The Plunderers
1960   Allied Artists

No, the boy Davy would not forget. Nor would we who stood watching as he rode away. None of us would ever forget what had happened and why. For none of us were without blame. But even as we shared the guilt we shared also the knowledge of a new hope, a new understanding. We had taken note that day that there are none who trespass against us as we trespass against ourselves. ("Sam Christy": Jeff Chandler)

Plymouth Adventure
1952   MGM
Aye, sir. (A sailor)

Point Blank
1967   MGM
Leave it. ("Fairfax/'Yost'": Keenan Wynn)

Police Academy
1984   Warner Brothers
Thank you, Commandant Lassard, Chief Hurst, Madame Mayor, Mr. President, His Holiness the Pope, the King of Norway, and our other honored guests. ("Carey Mahoney": Steven Guttenberg)

Police Academy 2: Their First Assignment
1985   Warner Brothers
Good-bye. (Wedding guest)

Poltergeist
1982   MGM/UA
Don't look back! ("Steve Freeling": Craig T. Nelson)

Poltergeist II
1986   MGM/UA

The car needs me! ("Steve Freeling": Craig T. Nelson)

Poltergeist III
1988   MGM/UA
She did it. She saved us. ("Patricia Gardner": Nancy Allen)

Pony Express
1953   Paramount
I know. ("Denny": Jan Sterling)

The Pope of Greenwich Village
1984   MGM/UA
Absolutely. ("Paulie": Eric Roberts)

Popeye
1980   Paramount
Oh, Popeye. Oh, my hero. ("Olive Oyl": Shelley Duvall)

Popi
1969   United Artists
Those lousy kids. ("Abraham Rodriguez": Alan Arkin)

Poppy
1936   Paramount
Never give a sucker an even break. ("Prof. Eustace McGargle": W. C. Fields)

Portnoy's Complaint
1972   Warner Brothers
See you tomorrow. ("Alexander Portnoy": Richard Benjamin)

Portrait in Black
1960   Universal
David! David, don't! Don't! ("Sheila Cabot": Lana Turner)

Portrait of Jennie
1948   Selznick

Oh, heavens, is it really me? I think someday it will hang in a museum, and people will come from all over the world to see it. ("Jennie Appleton": Jennifer Jones)

The Poseidon Adventure
1972   20th Century–Fox
No. (Rescuer)

Posse
1975   Paramount
I'll hunt you down! ("Marshal Howard Nightingale": Kirk Douglas)

Possessed
1931   MGM
I don't care what they do to me back there. If I win it'll be with you. And if I lose it'll still be with you. ("Mark Whitney": Clark Gable)

Postcards from the Edge
1990   Columbia
End mark. (Man with clap-stick)

The Postman Always Rings Twice
1946   MGM
The truth is you always hear him ring the second time, even if you're way out in the back yard. Father, you were right, it all works out. I guess God knows more about these things than we do. Somehow or other, Cora paid for Nick's life with hers. And now I might. Father, would you send up a prayer for me and Cora, and if you could find it in your heart, make it that we're together, wherever it is. ("Frank Chambers": John Garfield)

The Postman Always Rings Twice
1981   Paramount
You do. ("Frank Chambers": Jack Nicholson)

Pot o' Gold
1941   United Artists
Ladies and gentlemen, the reason she's so happy is that we're going to be married any second now. All right, Miss McCorkle, trick your way out of that one. ("Jimmy Haskell": James Stewart)

The Power and the Prize
1956   MGM
Oh, no, a piano! You didn't! You! ("Miriam Linka": Elizabeth Mueller)

Powwow Highway
1989   Warner Brothers
You are my brother. ("Philbert Bono": Gary Farmer)

Predator
1987   20th Century–Fox
My God. ("Mac": Bill Duke)

The President's Lady
1953   20th Century–Fox
Well, here, here we are, Rachel. Look at them. Some of those good people feel sorry for me. More fools, they. They don't know what memories I've brought with me. They can't see the way you looked that first day when we met when our whole lives lay ahead of us. I remember the way the wind blew your hair back sittin' there in the prow of that old riverboat, and the look of trust that was always there when there was danger to face.

What a vision you were at the top of those stairs. And the way you looked with Lincoya crowdin' his poor little life into a few short years. And the way you always ran to me when I came home again. The way you ran to me. Why, I have enough memories to sustain me all the days of my life. ("Andrew Jackson": Charlton Heston)

Presidio
1988   Paramount
Come on. ("Lt. Colonel Alan Caldwell": Sean Connery)

Presumed Innocent
1990   Warner Brothers
The murder of Carolyn Polhemus remains unsolved. It is a practical impossibility to try two people for the same crime. Even if it wasn't, I couldn't take his mother from my son. I'm a prosecutor, I have spent my life in the assignment of blame. With all deliberation and intent, I reached for Carolyn. I cannot pretend it was an accident. I reached for Carolyn and set off that insane mix of rage and lunacy that led one human being to kill another. There was a crime, there was a victim, and there is punishment. ("Rusty Sabich": Harrison Ford)

Pretty Baby
1978   United Artists
Make sure you get Violet. ("Hattie": Susan Sarandon)

Pretty Maids All in a Row
1971   MGM
My place or yours? ("Ponce": John David Carson)

Pretty Poison
1968   20th Century–Fox
Now about these people I live with. What we've got to plan is, mm, something. . . . ("Sue Ann": Tuesday Weld)

Pretty Woman
1990   Buena Vista
Welcome to Hollywood! Wha's your dream? Everybody comes here. This is Hollywood, land of dreams. Some dreams come true, some don't. But keep on dreaming. This is Hollywood, always time to dream. So keep on dreamin'. ("Happy Man": Abdul Salaam El Razzac)

Prettykill
1987   Spectrafilm
How do you say "start over" in French? ("Larry Turner": David Birney)

The Pride of St. Louis
1952   20th Century–Fox
Well, I don't know, I . . . . Out with you. ("Patricia Nash Dean": Joanne Dru)

Pride of the Bluegrass
1939   Warner Brothers
I know, Mr. Danny. If you is listening, Mr. Mack, I reckon everything's squared now. ("Domino Jones": Sam McDaniels)

Pride of the Marines
1945   Warner Brothers
Home. ("Al Schmid": John Garfield)

The Pride of the Yankees
1942   RKO
Play ball! (Umpire)

Prime Cut
1972   National General
Well, it's uh windy, and calm, and peaceful as any place anywhere. ("Nick Devlin": Lee Marvin)

The Prime of Miss Jean Brodie
1969   20th Century–Fox
Little girls, I am in the business of putting old heads on young shoulders, and all my pupils are the crème de la crème. Give me a girl at an impressionable age and she is mine for life. ("Jean Brodie": Maggie Smith)

The Prince and the Pauper
1937   Warner Brothers
This is good for cracking nuts, isn't it? ("Prince Edward": Bobby Mauch)

The Prince of Pennsylvania
1988   New Line
I used to be a prince. ("Rupert Marshetta": Keanu Reeves)

Prince of Players
1955   20th Century–Fox
Good night. Good night. Parting is such sweet sorrow, that I shall say good night till it be morrow. ("Mary Devlin Booth": Maggie McNamara)

Prince of the City
1981   Warner Brothers
I don't think I have anything to learn from you. (Recruit)

The Princess and the Pirate
1944   RKO
Go sell your rack shellac. (Bing Crosby, as himself)

The Princess Bride
1987   20th Century–Fox

As you wish. ("The Grandfather": Peter Falk)

Princess O'Rourke
1943   Warner Brothers
Come. ("Princess Maria": Olivia De Havilland)

The Principal
1987   Tri-Star
I'm the principal, man. ("Rick Latimer": Jim Belushi)

Private Benjamin
1980   Warner Brothers
Don't call me stupid. ("Judy Benjamin": Goldie Hawn)

The Private Files of J. Edgar Hoover
1978   American International
Within two years of the death of J. Edgar Hoover, the vice president was forced to resign facing criminal indictment, the closest aides to the president of the United States were dismissed and indicted because of alleged illegal activities; two attorney generals were removed from office and faced criminal conspiracy charges and the president of the United States resigned his office for the first time in history under the threat of impeachment. The sources of information that brought about this upheaval in government have never been fully disclosed, and some have been heard to speculate that if the hand of J. Edgar Hoover had reached back from beyond the grave, he couldn't have done it any better himself. (Narrator)

Private Lessons
1981   Jensen Farley
Excellent. Can we discuss it over dinner, then? Why don't I have my chauffeur pick you up at eight? ("Philly": Eric Brown)

The Private Life of Henry VIII
1933   United Artists
Six wives. And the best of them's the worst. ("Henry VIII": Charles Laughton)

The Private War of Major Benson
1955   Universal
Well, Sister Theresa, shall we join the ladies? ("Mother Redemption": Nana Bryant)

A Prize of Gold
1955   Columbia
OK. ("Sgt. Joe Lawrence": Richard Wydmark)

Prizzi's Honor
1985   20th Century-Fox
How about it? Holy cow, Charley, just tell me where you want to meet. ("Maerose Prizzi": Anjelica Huston)

The Prodigal
1955   MGM
My sons, my rock, my future. ("Eli": Walter Hampden)

The Producers
1967   Avco
Sing out, men! ("Max Bialystock": Zero Mostel)

The Professionals
1966   Columbia
Yes, sir. In my case, an accident of birth; but you, sir, you're a self-made

man. ("Henry Rico Farden": Lee Marvin)

Protocol
1984   Warner Brothers
We won! ("Sunny Davis": Goldie Hawn)

Prudence and the Pill
1968   20th Century–Fox
No, but seriously. Don't you think I'm right? ("Gerald Hardcastle": David Niven)

Psycho
1960   Universal
It's sad when a mother has to speak the words that condemn her own son, but I couldn't allow them to believe that I could commit murder. They'll put him away now as I should have years ago. He was always bad and in the end he intended to tell them I killed those girls and that man as if I could do anything except just sit and stare like one of his stuffed birds. Oh, they know I can't even move a finger, and I won't. I'll just sit here and be quiet just in case they do suspect me. They're probably watching me. Well, let them. Let them see what kind of person I am. I'm not even going to swat that fly. I hope they are watching. They'll see. They'll see and they'll know and they'll say, "Why, she wouldn't even harm a fly." ("Mother's Voice": Virginia Gregg)

Psycho II
1983   Universal
Remember, Norman, I'm the only one who loves you. Only your mother truly loves you. (Voice of mother)

Psycho III
1986   Universal
But I'll be free. I'll finally be free. ("Norman Bates": Anthony Perkins)

Pulp
1972   United Artists
I'll get the bastards yet. Oh, I wish my leg didn't itch. ("Mickey King": Michael Caine)

Pump Up the Volume
1990   New Line
Turn on the truth. (Voice on radio)

The Pumpkin Eater
1964   Columbia
Yes. I'll have one. ("Jo": Anne Bancroft)

Pumpkinhead
1988   MGM/UA
Kill me. ("Ed Harley": Lance Henriksen)

Punchline
1988   Columbia
All the family stuff. ("Lilah Krytsick": Sally Field)

The Purple Heart
1944   20th Century–Fox
The defendants and each of them are found guilty of the crime of murder as set forth in the indictment. They will be removed from the courtroom and given into the custody of the military prison until such time as the sentence of death is executed upon their bodies. ("Mitsuro Toyama": Peter Chong)

The Pursuit of Happiness
1970   Columbia

Throw that luggage behind the seat. ("Pilot": William Devane)

Pursuit to Algiers
1945   Universal
Yes, Watson, let me advise you. If you ever consider taking up another profession, never even think of becoming an actor. ("Sherlock Holmes": Basil Rathbone)

Pygmalion
1938   MGM
Where the devil are my slippers, Eliza? ("Prof. Henry Higgins": Leslie Howard

Q & A
1990   Tri-Star
I want us to marry. And I'll sit by your side till you're ready. If you tell me you'll never be ready, well, I'll just leave right now and never bother you again. Otherwise I'm here, as long as it takes. ("Al Reilly": Timothy Hutton)

Quackser Fortune Has a Cousin in the Bronx
1970   UMC
And did you know that Messiah's Handel had its world premiere here? ("Quackser Fortune": Gene Wilder)

Quality Street
1937   RKO
Thank you. ("Susan Throssel": Fay Bainter)

Quebec
1951   Paramount
I don't know. It's only the candle for my mother, the candle for Stephanie, they're the same. ("Mark Douglas": John Barrymore, Jr.)

Queen Bee
1955   Columbia
The sun is shining. Funny, I didn't expect the sun to be shining. ("John Avery Phillips": Barry Sullivan)

Queen Christina
1933   MGM
All hands on deck. (A sailor)

Quicksilver
1986   Columbia
Wait, wait, I know the perfect place. ("Jack Casey": Kevin Bacon)

The Quiet Man
1952   Republic
Hold on to your hats. ("Michaeleen Flynn": Barry Fitzgerald)

Quigley Down Under
1990   MGM/UA
Matthew Quigley. ("Crazy Cora": Laura San Giacomo)

R.P.M.
1970   Columbia
Boo! (Spectator)

Race with the Devil
1975   20th Century–Fox
You know, you are definitely a charmer, Frank. Hey, everybody, lighten up, it's all over. Frank, go on ahead and open up that vermouth in two seconds. ("Roger": Peter Fonda)

Racing with the Moon
1984   Paramount
Ready. ("Nicky": Nicholas Cage)

The Rack
1956   MGM

This isn't going to be an extenuation but I want to say it anyway. Captain Miller came to my hotel this morning just about dawn. He's the witness who was tortured. He said he'd read the papers and he'd seen my testimony there and he wanted to talk. So we sat down and we started talking about the men we knew who were prisoners over there. He said he thought that every man has a moment in his life when he's got to choose. If he chooses right, then it's a moment of magnificence. If he chooses wrong, then it's a moment of regret that will stay with him for the rest of his life. I wish that every soldier, I wish that everybody could feel the way I feel now. Because if they did they'd know what it's like to be a man who sold himself short and who lost his moment of magnificence. I pray to God that they find theirs. Amen. ("Capt. Edward W. Hall, Jr.": Paul Newman)

Radio Days
1986   Orion
I never forgot that New Year's Eve, when Aunt Bea awakened me to watch nineteen forty-four come in. And I've never forgotten any of those people, or any of the voices we used to hear on the radio. Although the truth is, with the passing of each New Year's Eve, those voices do seem to grow dimmer and dimmer. ("Narrator": Woody Allen)

Rage at Dawn
1955   RKO
I know. ("Laura Reno": Mala Powers)

Rage in Heaven
1941   MGM
Poor Philip. Too many people have looked into his secrets. We must let him rest now. ("Sheila Bergen": Ingrid Bergman)

Raging Bull
1980   United Artists
Go get 'em, champ. ("Jake La Motta": Robert De Niro)

The Raid
1954   20th Century-Fox
If they burned down St. Albans would you understand why it had to be done? Do you think you'd be able to forgive them for that? ("Maj. Neal Benton": Van Heflin)

Raiders of the Lost Ark
1981   Paramount
Well, I know what I've got here. Come on, buy you a drink. You know, a drink. ("Marion Ravenwood": Karen Allen)

Rain
1932   United Artists
I'm sorry for everybody in the world I guess. ("Sadie Thompson": Joan Crawford)

Rain Man
1988   MGM/UA
Yeah. ("Raymond Babbitt": Dustin Hoffman)

The Rainbow
1989   Vestron
Hey, look, it's a rainbow. ("Will Brangwen": Christopher Gable)

Raising Arizona
1987   20th Century-Fox

And I don't know, you tell me, this whole dream, was it wishful thinking? Was I just fleeing reality, like I know I'm liable to do? But me and Ed, we can be good too, and it seemed real, it seemed like us, and it seemed like, well, our home. If not Arizona, then a land not too far away where all parents are strong, and wise and capable, and all children are happy and beloved. I dunno. Maybe it was Utah. ("H. I. McDonnough": Nicholas Cage)

Rambo: First Blood Part II
1985   Tri-Star
Day by day. ("John Rambo": Sylvester Stallone)

Rancho De Luxe
1974   United Artists
Whatever you say, Ceese. We can find a way. ("Jack McKee": Jeff Bridges)

Random Harvest
1942   MGM
Paula! ("Charles Rainier": Ronald Colman)

Ratboy
1986   Warner Brothers
Eugene. ("Nikki Morrison": Sondra Locke)

The Raven
1935   Universal
So you're the big, bad raven, huh? ("Jean Thatcher": Irene Ware)

The Razor's Edge
1984   Columbia
America. ("Larry Darrell": Bill Murray)

Real Genius
1985   Tri-Star
I like it. ("Mitch Taylor": Gabe Jarret)

Real Men
1987   United Artists
Try to be more sensitive. ("Bob Wilson": John Ritter)

Reap the Wild Wind
1942   Paramount
Yes. ("Stephen Tolliver": Ray Milland)

Rear Window
1954   Paramount
Oh, honey, come on. ("Newlywed": Harris Davenport)

Rebecca
1940   United Artists
Look! The west wing! (Spectator at fire)

Rebel Without a Cause
1955   Warner Brothers
He's–. ("Jim's Mother": Ann Doran)

Reckless
1935   MGM
Encore! (Audience member)

The Red Badge of Courage
1951   MGM
So it came to pass that as he trudged from the place of blood and wrath his soul changed. He had been to touch the Great Death and found that, after all, it was but the Great Death. Scars faded as flowers and the youth saw that the world was a world for him. He had rid himself of the red sickness of the battle and the sultry nightmare

was in the past. He turned now with a lover's thirst to images of tranquil skies, fresh meadows, cool brooks, an existence of soft and eternal peace. ("Voice": James Whitmore)

Red Ball Express
1952   Universal
As a matter of fact, take twenty. Cup of coffee, Red? ("Lt. Campbell": Jeff Chandler)

The Red House
1947   United Artists
Looking forward's much better than looking back. ("Nath Storm": Lon McCallister)

Red Mountain
1951   Paramount
A house divided against itself cannot stand. Your president said that. Our president. ("Capt. Brett Sherwood": Alan Ladd)

Red River
1948   United Artists
You've earned it. ("Tom Dunson": John Wayne)

Red Scorpion
1989   Shapiro
Fuckin' A. ("Nikolai": Dolph Lundgren)

The Red Shoes
1948   Eagle Lion
Take off the red shoes. ("Victoria Page": Moira Shearer)

Red Sonja
1985   MGM/UA
Aw, come along, Falkon. ("Tarn": Ernie Reyes, Jr.)

Red Sun
1972   National General
Now, that's the Cristina I'll always like to remember. ("Link": Charles Bronson)

The Redhead and the Cowboy
1950   Paramount
Well, maybe I'll still be able to keep that date with a bottle of wine, and a good-looking redhead. ("Gil Kyle": Glenn Ford)

Reds
1981   Paramount
Spasibo. ("Louise Bryant": Diane Keaton)

The Reincarnation of Peter Proud
1975   Avco Embassy
Marcia, no. Marcia, no. No, no, Marcia, no. ("Peter Proud": Michael Sarrazin)

The Reivers
1969   National General
Lucius Priest McCaslin Hoggenbeck. Only name he could have. ("Boon Hoggenbeck": Steve McQueen)

The Reluctant Astronaut
1967   Universal
I hope she has a good time. ("Roy Fleming": Don Knotts)

The Reluctant Debutante
1958   MGM
Later, darling. ("Jimmy Broadbent": Rex Harrison)

The Remarkable Mr. Pennypacker
1958   20th Century–Fox

Cleave only unto her. As long as we both shall live. ("Pa Pennypacker": Clifton Webb)

Rembrandt
1936   United Artists
Vanity of vanities, all is vanity. ("Rembrandt": Charles Laughton)

Remo Williams:
The Adventure Begins
1985   Orion
No, I am better than that. ("Chiun": Joel Grey)

Rent-a-Cop
1988   Kings Road
You got it. ("Church": Burt Reynolds)

Repeat Performance
1947   Eagle Lion
Happy new year to Sheila. ("William Williams": Richard Basehart)

Requiem for a Heavyweight
1962   Columbia
Boo! (Audience member)

Resurrection
1980   Universal
Thank you. ("Edna McCauley": Ellen Burstyn)

The Return of Daniel Boone
1941   Columbia
Good-bye, and thanks. ("Ellen Brandon": Betty Miles)

The Return of Frank James
1940   20th Century–Fox
'Bye. ("Frank James": Henry Fonda)

Return of the Bad Men
1948   RKO

Well, come on then. Don't fool around here. ("John Pettit": George "Gabby" Hayes)

Return of the Jedi
1983   20th Century–Fox
No, it's not like that at all. He's my brother. ("Princess Leia": Carrie Fisher)

The Return of the Swamp Thing
1989   Miramax
Not necessarily. ("Swamp Thing": Dick Durock)

Return to Horror High
1987   New World
Dad. ("Arthur Lynan Kastleman": Richard Bristoff)

Return to Peyton Place
1961   20th Century–Fox
Good-bye. Good-bye, darling. ("Allison": Carol Lynley)

A Return to 'Salem's Lot
1987   Warner Brothers
Don't let his mother find out. ("Joe Weber": Michael Moriarty)

Reunion in Vienna
1933   MGM
I don't think that'll ever happen again, Father. ("Anton": Frank Morgan)

Revenge of the Pink Panther
1978   United Artists
What? ("Chief Inspector Clouseau": Peter Sellers)

The Revengers
1972   National General

I've had worms in my heart, Mr. Hoop. That's been my trouble. ("John Benedict": William Holden)

Reversal of Fortune
1990   Warner Brothers
Just kidding. ("Claus von Bulow": Jeremy Irons).

The Revolt of Mamie Stover
1956   20th Century–Fox
Thank you. ("Mamie Stover": Jane Russell)

Rhinestone
1984   20th Century–Fox
It's got to be love. ("Nick": Sylvester Stallone)

Rhubarb
1951   Paramount
What a cat. A litter from three wives. ("Man in Park": Paul Douglas)

Rich and Famous
1981   MGM/UA
It's New Year's Eve. I want the press of human flesh. And you're the only flesh around. Kiss me. ("Liz Hamilton": Jacqueline Bisset)

Richest Girl in the World
1934   RKO
It may take longer than you think. ("Tony Travis": Joel McCrea)

Ride Beyond Vengeance
1966   Columbia
That's just a song, and home is just a word. ("The Bartender": William Bryant)

Ride the High Country
1962   MGM

I'll see ya later. ("Gil Westrum": Randolph Scott)

Ride the Pink Horse
1947   Universal
Bueno! (One of Pila's friends)

Ride, Vaquero
1953   MGM
Let me take you home. ("Cordelia Cameron": Ava Gardner)

Riders of Destiny
1933   MGM
I'm going to bake a hundred biscuits. ("Fay Denton": Cecilia Parker)

Riding High
1950   Paramount
Hey, wait for me! ("J. L. Higgins": Charles Bickford)

Riff Raff
1935   MGM
Sure, Pops ain't never home. I'll put you in his room. ("Lil": Una Merkel)

Right Cross
1950   MGM
Gump, have you ever been to Haggerty's? Get the station wagon. ("Rick Gavery": Dick Powell)

Rikky and Pete
1988   MGM/UA
Move it out. Come on, let's go. ("Pete Menzies": Stephen Kearney)

Ringside Maisie
1941   MGM
Darling. ("Maisie Ravier": Ann Sothern)

The Rise and Fall of Legs Diamond
1960 Warner Brothers
A lot of people loved my husband, but he never loved anybody. That's why he's dead. ("Alice Shiffer": Karen Steele)

Risky Business
1983 Warner Brothers
My name is Joel Goodsen. I deal in human fulfillment. I grossed over eight thousand dollars in one night. Time of your life, huh, kid? ("Joel": Tom Cruise)

River of No Return
1954 20th Century-Fox
Mark! ("Kay Weston": Marilyn Monroe)

River's Edge
1987 Island
Because there is no hope for him. There is no hope at all. He didn't love her. He didn't feel a thing. I, uh, at least loved her, I cared for her. I mean, it, you understand, don't you. Sure you do. I don't, uh, like killing people, but sometimes it's necessary. That's enough for now. I, I'd like you all to leave now. I'm very tired and sort of depressed. I lost a good friend today, you know. ("Feck": Dennis Hopper)

Road House
1948 20th Century-Fox
Come on, Lily. ("Susie Smith": Celeste Holm)

The Road Hustlers
1968 American International

Well, Jack, I want to tell you, this sure as hell ain't. Boy. ("Noah Reedy": Jim Davis)

Road to Morocco
1942 Paramount
You had to open your big mouth and ruin the only good scene I got in the picture. I might have won an Academy Award. ("Turkey Jackson": Bob Hope)

Road to Rio
1947 Paramount
Deep. Deep. ("Hot Lips Barton": Bob Hope)

Road to Utopia
1945 Paramount
We adopted him. ("Chester Hooton": Bob Hope)

The Roaring Twenties
1939 Warner Brothers
He used to be a big shot. ("Panama Smith": Gladys George)

The Robe
1953 20th Century-Fox
For the Big Fisherman. ("Diana": Jean Simmons)

Roberta
1935 RKO
Gee, that's swell. ("John Kent": Randolph Scott)

Robinson Crusoe on Mars
1964 Paramount
Hey! Hey! Hey! Yoo-hoo! ("Commander Christopher 'Kit' Draper": Paul Mantee)

RoboCop
1987   Orion
Murphy. ("Alex J. Murphy/RoboCop":
Peter Weller)

Rock-a-bye Baby
1958   Paramount
Five! Five! We had five! Carla went to
Mexico! She only had three! We had
five! I'm better than the bullfighter!
Ole! Ole! ("Clayton Poole": Jerry
Lewis)

Rocket Gibraltar
1988   Columbia
Their whole life was the sea, the sea
and their boats. And so in celebrating
death (yes, you can say celebrating),
they used both. The families of the
great Vikings would put the body of
their loved one on the ship, covered
with straw, and then as the sun was
setting cast it away into the water.
They would light huge bonfires on the
beach, then the Vikings would light
the tips of their arrows in the bonfire
and shoot them at the ship. Oh, it must
have been so beautiful, fire on the
water. Legend has it that if the color
of the setting sun and the color of the
burning ship were the same, then that
Viking had led a good life and in
the afterlife he would go to Viking
heaven. Yes, all night long the Viking
men, women and children watched as
the ship with the body burned in the
water. By dawn all that was left was
ashes, complete obliteration, carried
by the currents to the four corners of
the earth, fresh and beautiful, vanished completely, like a dream. ("Levi
Rockwell": Burt Lancaster)

Rocky
1976   United Artists

I love you. I really do. ("Adrian": Talia
Shire)

Rocky II
1979   United Artists
Rocky! Rocky! Rocky! Rocky! Rocky!
(Fight spectators)

Rocky III
1982   MGM/UA
Come on, watch yourself. Ready?
("Apollo": Carl Weathers)

Rocky IV
1985   MGM/UA
I just want to say, I want to say to my
kid, who should be home sleeping,
Merry Christmas, kid. ("Rocky
Balboa": Sylvester Stallone)

Rocky V
1990   MGM/UA
Oh, yeah. Well, I love almost everybody. ("Rocky": Sylvester Stallone)

Roll on Texas Moon
1946   Republic
Well, I ain't the most beautiful sight
you've ever seen, but I've sure been
misguided. ("Gabby Whittaker":
George "Gabby" Hayes)

Roman Holiday
1953   Paramount
Good afternoon. ("Princess Anne":
Audrey Hepburn)

Romance
1930   MGM
Don't be an idiot, Harry. If you love
her and she loves you, don't let your

mother or anybody else in the world come between you. Don't lose it, my boy. It's the greatest thing in the world, romance. ("Tom Armstrong": Gavin Gordon)

Romance of a Horsethief
1971   Allied Artists
You've orders to return to barracks. ("Stoloff": Yul Brynner)

Romance on the High Seas
1948   Warner Brothers
You need practice. ("Peter Virgil": Jack Carson)

Romantic Comedy
1983   MGM/UA
Stop talking and collaborate. ("Phoebe": Mary Steenburgen)

Romero
1989   Four Seasons
I've often been threatened with death. If they kill me, I shall arise in the Salvadoran people. Let my blood be a seed of freedom and a sign that hope will soon be a reality. A bishop will die, but the church of God, which is the people, will never perish. ("Archbishop Oscar Romero": Raul Julia)

Rooftops
1989   New Visions
Let's see what you can do, home boy. ("Squeak": Alexis Cruz)

Room for One More
1952   Warner Brothers
Well, we were so busy raising a family I guess I just didn't have time. But I happen to love you very much, Mrs. Rose. ("'Poppy' Rose": Cary Grant)

Rooster Cogburn
1975   Universal
I'll be damned if she didn't get the last word in again. Well. ("Rooster Cogburn": John Wayne)

The Rosary Murders
1987   New Line
Dear Father, I'm sitting at your desk writing this. Mother is downstairs somewhere. Soon I will go back to my room and close the door for the last time. I just can't keep hating myself. I wish to God I knew where I'm going. I'm afraid. Good-bye, Father. Please forgive me as I now forgive you. May the lord bless you and keep you forever and ever. Love, Cathy. ("Cathy Jarison": Janet Smith)

Rose Marie
1954   MGM
Go ahead, answer him. He'll wait for you. ("Mike Malone": Howard Keel)

Rose of Cimarron
1952   20th Century–Fox
Get up. ("Rose of Cimarron": Mala Powers)

The Rose Tattoo
1955   Paramount
Now we can go on with our conversation, hm? ("Serafina Delle Rose": Anna Magnani)

Rosemary's Baby
1968   Paramount
Aren't you his mother? ("Roman Castevet": Sidney Blackmer)

Rough Night in Jericho
1967   Universal

Dolan, don't take less than fifty-one percent. ("Alex Flood": Dean Martin)

Roxanne
1987   Columbia
Locked! Locked! Oh! Oh, thank God I have the key. ("C. D. Bales": Steve Martin)

Royal Wedding
1951   MGM
They didn't have to go to all this trouble. A small wedding would have been all right. ("Tom Bowen": Fred Astaire)

Rude Awakening
1989   Orion
Smoked fish. ("Voice of fish": Aaron Russo)

Ruggles of Red Gap
1935   Paramount
My friends, thank you very much. ("Marmaduke Ruggles": Charles Laughton)

Rumpelstiltskin
1987   Cannon
Rumpelstiltskin. ("Emily": Yael Uziely)

Runaway
1984   Tri-Star
Try me. ("Thompson": Cynthia Rhodes)

Running Brave
1983   Buena Vista
Billy, look, man, the cover of "Life," huh. ("Frank": Denis Lacroix)

The Running Man
1987   Tri-Star

Well, that hit the spot. ("Ben Richards": Arnold Schwarzenegger)

Running on Empty
1988   Warner Brothers
Good-bye, Danny! ("Anne Pope": Christine Lahti)

Running Scared
1986   MGM/UA
Um hm, yep, we owe it to this fine city. Hey, do you guys want to buy a bar? ("Danny Castanzo": Billy Crystal)

Running Wild
1973   Golden Circle
Hey, how about that for a background, huh? ("Jeff": Lloyd Bridges)

Russkies
1987   Vista
It was time for Prince Vasily to go and the comrades with whom he had campaigned so valiantly drew close. About them the sound of the weary men hung in the cold air as the soldiers tended their horses. The man they had come to call their friend smiled. "You must remember what I have done here today," he said, "and keep it close to your heart. There are those who may think it dishonorable but I succeeded in uniting all parties and besides my idea is single and clear. I say let those who love what is right join hands, and let our whole watchword be action and virtue." Prince Vasily nodded once to his company, and without a further word, he turned and walked away. ("Danny": Leaf Phoenix)

Ruthless People
1986 Buena Vista
Barbara! ("Sam Stone": Danny DeVito)

Ryan's Daughter
1970 MGM
I don't know. I don't know at all. Come on, Michael. ("Father Collins": Trevor Howard)

Sabrina
1954 Paramount
Merci beaucoup. ("Ship Steward": David Ahdar)

Saddle the Wind
1958 MGM
Well, you better be getting back to your place and let them know that the Sinclairs are still in business. ("Mr. Deneen": Donald Crisp)

Sahara
1943 Columbia
Yeah. They'd want to know. Halliday, Doyle, Tambul, Williams, Stegman, Frenchie, Clarkson. We stopped them at El Alamein. ("Sgt. Joe Gunn": Humphrey Bogart)

St. Elmo's Fire
1985 Columbia
Guess what! You guys will never believe. I found out that it only costs two hundred and fifty dollars to bury a cat. So I figured why don't I just put my stepmonster into a large cat suit. ("Jules": Demi Moore)

Saint Jack
1979 New World

How ya doing, there, sonny, huh, huh? ("Jack Flowers": Ben Gazzara)

The Salamander
1983 ITC
Mister, hey, mister, the ball. (Boy on steps)

Salsa
1988 Cannon
I missed you. ("Rico": Bobby Rosa)

Salvador
1986 Hemdale
Get in there. ("Immigration Officer on Bus": Joshua Gallegos)

Sam Whiskey
1969 United Artists
Sam, you can try, can't you? ("Laura Breckenridge": Angie Dickinson)

Same Time Next Year
1978 Universal
Look, I don't even want to discuss it. I'm back and I'm going to keep coming back every year until our bones are too brittle to risk contact. ("George": Alan Alda)

Sanctuary
1960 20th Century-Fox
Believe. Believe. Believe. Believe. ("Temple Drake": Lee Remick)

The Sand Pebbles
1966 20th Century-Fox
I was home. What happened? What the hell happened? ("Holman": Steve McQueen)

Sands of Iwo Jima
1949 Republic

All right! Saddle up! Let's get back in the war! ("Pfc. Peter Conway": John Agar)

Sangaree
1953 Paramount
He was wise enough to let us find love for ourselves. ("Carlos": Fernando Lamas)

Santa Fe Trail
1940 Warner Brothers
Before this company. And there to have given and pledged their troth each to the other and have declared the same by giving and receiving of rings and by joining hands. I pronounce that they are man and wife. United forever with ties that no man shall break asunder nor the years disturb, whose shining paths shall run together from this day hence unto eternity. (Minister)

Sapphire
1959 Universal
We didn't solve anything, Phil, we just picked up the pieces. ("Superintendent": Nigel Patrick)

Saratoga
1937 MGM
Fritzi, I love you. ("Duke Bradley": Clark Gable)

Satan Met a Lady
1936 Warner Brothers
Uh huh. ("Ted Shayne": Warren William)

Saturday Night Fever
1978 Paramount
Friends then. ("Stephanie": Karen Lynn Gorney)

Savage Wilderness
1956 Columbia
Fine, soldier, just fine. ("Capt. Riordan": Guy Madison)

Save the Tiger
1973 Paramount
You can't play with us, mister. (A child)

Say Anything
1989 20th Century–Fox
Any second now. ("Lloyd Dobler": John Cusack)

Say One for Me
1959 20th Century–Fox
OK. ("Holly": Debbie Reynolds)

Sayonara
1957 Warner Brothers
Yeah. Tell 'em we said sayonara. ("Maj. Lloyd Gruver": Marlon Brando)

Scandal
1989 Miramax
Seven, nine, eleven, twelve, thirteen, fourteen, fifteen. ("Stephen Ward": John Hurt)

Scandal at Scourie
1953 MGM
Oh, yes, we do. I mean that we know you didn't mean to cause all that trouble. Everything's going to be all right now, Edward. We forgot all about the whistle. ("Mrs. Patrick J. McChesney": Greer Garson)

Scandalous
1984 Orion
Everything's just perfect. ("Frank Swedlin": Robert Hays)

Scanners
1981   Avco Embassy
It's me, Kim, Cameron. I'm here. We've won. We've won. ("Cameron Vale": Stephen Lack)

Scaramouche
1952   MGM
Cute. ("Aline de Gavrillac": Janet Leigh)

The Scarlet Claw
1944   Universal
Yes, Watson, Churchill. ("Sherlock Holmes": Basil Rathbone)

The Scarlet Clue
1945   Monogram
Oh, that's me. Let me see this thing. I think I'd rather take this one. Goodbye. ("Birmingham Brown": Mantan Moreland)

Scarlet Empress
1934   Paramount
There is no emperor. There is only an empress. ("Gregory Orloff": Gavin Gordon)

Scarlet Pimpernel
1935   United Artists
Look, Marguerite, England. ("Sir Percy Blakeney": Leslie Howard)

Scarlet Street
1945   Universal
Johnny. Oh, Johnny. Jeepers, I love you, John. ("Kitty March": Joan Bennett)

Scenes from the Class Struggle in Beverly Hills
1989   Cinecom

Oh, Sidney, you're so full of shit. (Voice of "Bojangles")

School Daze
1988   Columbia
Please, wake up. ("Vaughn 'Dap' Dunlap": Larry Fishburne)

Screaming Eagles
1956   Allied Artists
Yes, sir, real pretty. ("Pvt. Mason": Tom Tryon)

Scrooge
1970   National General
Hello. I don't know whether you can hear me, old Jacob Marley, but I don't know whether or not I imagined the things I saw. Between the two of us, we made a merry Christmas, didn't we. Have to leave you now. Must go and get ready. I'm going to have Christmas dinner with my family. ("Ebenezer Scrooge": Albert Finney)

The Sea Bat
1930   MGM
Oh, chiquito lindo, I'll wait near you, always. ("Nina": Raquel Torres)

The Sea of Grass
1947   MGM
It was a hard thing for her to go through, but she's one in a thousand. No one else will ever be like her. ("Col. Jim Brewton": Spencer Tracy)

Sea Wife
1957   20th Century-Fox
No one ever looks at the face of a nun. ("Sea Wife [Sister Therese]": Joan Collins)

The Sea Wolf
1941   Warner Brothers
Oh, no. ("Ruth Brewster": Ida Lupino)

The Search
1948   MGM
Mamita. ("Karel Malik": Ivan Jandl)

Season of Fear
1989   MGM/UA
Fred Drummond is back in the news today. Reunited with his twenty-four-year-old son Mick, the two will begin building the largest wind turbine factory in the world. An optimistic quote from Mick, "It's never too late." (Reporter)

Second Chance
1953   RKO
What a beautiful disaster. ("Cable Car Conductor": Sandro Giglio)

Second Chorus
1940   Paramount
Was perfect. ("Danny O'Neill": Fred Astaire)

Secret Admirer
1985   Orion
Michael! ("Toni": Lou Loughlin)

The Secret Life of Walter Mitty
1947   RKO
Bruce? ("Walter Mitty": Danny Kaye)

The Secret Partner
1961   MGM
Begonias, chum, begonias. ("Det. Supt. Hanbury": Bernard Lee)

See No Evil, Hear No Evil
1989   Tri-Star
I'm not handicapped, I have you. ("Dave Lyons": Gene Wilder)

See You in the Morning
1989   Warner Brothers
Come on. Beth, come on. Petey. ("Larry Livingston": Jeff Bridges)

Seems Like Old Times
1980   Columbia
I need help! ("Glenda": Goldie Hawn)

Semi-Tough
1977   United Artists
Pair of fives. ("Barbara Jane Bookman": Jill Clayburgh)

Seminole
1953   Universal
He loved all people, Lance. That's what made him great. ("Revere": Barbara Hale)

Send Me No Flowers
1964   Universal
No. Oh. ("Judy Kimball": Doris Day)

Senior Week
1988   Vestron
You're gonna really like Florida. I've got a big palm tree in my front yard. ("Lifeguard": Joe Calabria)

A Separate Peace
1972   Paramount
I didn't cry then or ever about Finny. I didn't even cry when he was being lowered into the burial ground outside of Boston. I couldn't escape the feeling that it was my own funeral, and you don't cry in that case. ("Gene": Parker Stevenson)

Separate Vacations
1986 RSL
Yeah! ("Richard Moore": David Naughton)

September Affair
1950 Paramount
Passengers for flight two-oh-one for Rio de Janeiro and Buenos Aires will please go aboard. (Announcer)

Sergeant York
1941 Warner Brothers
Come on. ("Gracie Williams": Joan Leslie)

Serpico
1973 Paramount
Through my appearance here today, I hope that police officers will not experience the same frustration and anxiety that I was subjected to for the past five years at the hands of my superiors because of my attempt to report corruption. I was made to feel that I had burdened them with an unwanted task. The problem is that the atmosphere does not exist in which an honest police officer can act without fear of ridicule or reprisals from fellow officers. Police corruption cannot exist unless it is at higher levels in the department. Therefore the most important result that can come from these hearings is a conviction by police officers that the department will change. In order to ensure this, an independent, permanent investigative body dealing with police corruption like this commission is essential. ("Frank Serpico": Al Pacino)

Sesame Street Presents: Follow That Bird
1985 Warner Brothers
Bruno, come on. ("Oscar": Caroll Spinney)

The Set Up
1949 RKO
We both won tonight. We both won tonight. ("Julie": Audrey Totter)

Seven Angry Men
1955 Allied Artists
No. I am now quite certain that I am worth inconceivably more to hang than for any other purpose. ("John Brown": Raymond Massey)

Seven Brides for Seven Brothers
1954 MGM
I now pronounce you men and wives. ("The Rev. Elcott": Ian Wolfe)

Seven Faces of Dr. Lao
1964 MGM
Mike, the whole world is a circus if you look at it the right way. Every time you pick up a handful of dust and see not the dust but a mystery, a marvel, there in your hand. Every time you stop and think, I'm alive and being alive is fantastic. Every time such a thing happens, Mike, you are part of the circus of Dr. Lao. ("Voice of Dr. Lao": Tony Randall)

Seven Hours to Judgment
1988 Trans World
No! No! Oh, God, oh! No! ("Lisa Eden": Julianne Phillips)

The Seven Per-Cent Solution
1976 Universal
I hope it will not seem too short.

("Sherlock Holmes": Nicol William-son)

7 Women
1966   MGM
So long, you bastard. ("Dr. D. R. Cart-wright": Anne Brancroft)

The Seven Year Itch
1955   20th Century–Fox
Hey! ("The Girl": Marilyn Monroe)

The Seventh Cross
1944   MGM
Good-bye, Toni. ("George Heisler": Spencer Tracy)

The Seventh Voyage of Sinbad
1958   Columbia
I shall try, Captain, I shall try. ("Baronni the Genie": Richard Eyer)

Sex and the Single Girl
1964   Warner Brothers
Driver, follow that plane. ("Motorcy-cle cop": Larry Storch)

Sex, Lies, and Videotape
1989   Miramax
Yeah. ("Ann": Andie MacDowell)

Sextette
1978   Crown International
Well, I'm looking forward to saying the same thing he said. Oh, the British are coming. ("Marlo Man-ners": Mae West)

Shadow of the Thin Man
1941   MGM
So's this one. ("Nick Charles": William Powell)

Shaft's Big Score
1972   MGM
Yeah, adios, mother – Captain Bollin. ("John Shaft": Richard Roundtree)

Shag
1989   Tri-Star
What would I want to go to New Haven for? Pivo? ("Carson McBride": Phoebe Cates)

The Shaggy D.A.
1976   Buena Vista
Come on. ("Tim": Tim Conway)

The Shaggy Dog
1959   Buena Vista
What do you mean you've got a dog? We've got a dog. ("Wilson Daniels": Fred MacMurray)

Shaker Run
1985   Mirage
Well, it was just an idea. ("Judd Pher-son": Cliff Robertson)

Shampoo
1975   Columbia
Well, the puppies are in the car. I can't think of anything else, so why don't we just take off, huh? OK? ("Lester Carr": Jack Warden)

Shamus
1972   Columbia
I, uh, I don't want you to go out of my life. ("Shamus McCoy": Burt Rey-nolds)

Shane
1953   Paramount
'Bye, Shane. ("Joey": Brandon de Wilde)

Shanghai Surprise
1986 MGM/UA
Wave, Gloria! ("Glendon Wasey": Sean Penn)

She
1965 MGM
When it comes back, it'll find me waiting. ("Leo Vincey": John Richardson)

She Married Her Boss
1935 Columbia
OK. ("Franklin": Raymond Walburn)

She Wore a Yellow Ribbon
1949 RKO
If you'll excuse me, Miss Dandridge, I, uh, got to make my report first. Ladies and gentlemen, thank you. ("Capt. Nathan Brittles": John Wayne)

Sherlock Holmes Faces Death
1943 Universal
And God willing, we'll live to see that day, Watson. ("Sherlock Holmes": Basil Rathbone)

Sherlock Holmes in Washington
1943 Universal
Not with me, with Mr. Winston Churchill. I was quoting from a speech he made not so long ago. In that very building. ("Sherlock Holmes": Basil Rathbone)

She's Having a Baby
1988 Paramount
And in the end I realized that I took more than I gave, that I was trusted more than I trusted, that I was loved more than I loved. And what I was looking for was not to be found but to be made. ("Jake Briggs": Kevin Bacon)

She's Out of Control
1989 Columbia
We'll discuss it Thursday night on the air. ("Dr. Fishbinder": Wallace Shawn)

The Shining
1980 Warner Brothers
Oh, oh, Danny! ("Wendy Torrance": Shelley Duvall)

Ship Ahoy
1942 MGM
Skipper Owens, taxpayer in arrears. ("'Skip' Owens": Bert Lahr)

Ship of Fools
1965 Columbia
Oh, I can just hear you saying what has all this to do with us? Nothing. ("Glocken": Michael Dunn)

Shirley Valentine
1989 Paramount
Nah. Thanks. ("Joe Bradshaw": Bernard Hill)

A Shock to the System
1990 Corsair
Boom. ("Graham Marshall": Michael Caine)

The Shocking Miss Pilgrim
1946 20th Century–Fox
Well, naturally, I felt I couldn't. ("John Pritchard": Dick Haymes)

Shockproof
1949 Columbia

Throw those people out of here. ("Harry Wesson": John Baragrey)

Shoot Out
1971 Universal
Dominokee. ("Clay Lomax": Gregory Peck)

Shoot to Kill
1988 Buena Vista
Every damn day. ("Warren Stantin": Sidney Poitier)

The Shop Around the Corner
1940 MGM
Yes, well, would you mind very much if I ask you to pull them up now? ("Klara Novak": Margaret Sullavan)

Shopworn Angel
1938 MGM
Come on. ("Sam Bailey": Walter Pidgeon)

Short Circuit
1986 Tri-Star
Give me five. (Voice of robot)

Short Circuit 2
1988 Tri-Star
How do I feel? I feel alive! ("Voice of Johnny Five": Tim Blaney)

Short Time
1990 20th Century-Fox
I'd kind of like to go home. ("Carolyn Simpson": Teri Garr)

Show Boat
1936 Universal
There's another Ravenal here tonight, Gaylord Ravenal, my first leading man. ("Magnolia Hawks": Irene Dunne)

Show of Shows
1929 Warner Brothers
Hey! (The chorus line)

Showdown at Boot Hill
1958 20th Century-Fox
Oh, you ought to see the other fellow. Not a mark on him. ("Luke Welsh": Charles Bronson)

The Shrike
1955 Universal
Come on, Ann, let's try again. ("Jim Downs": Jose Ferrer)

Sibling Rivalry
1990 Columbia
How's your heart? ("Marjorie Turner": Kirstie Alley)

Sidewalks of London
1940 Paramount
And myself. ("Charles Saggers": Charles Laughton)

Sierra Stranger
1957 Columbia
It's not your fault. I guess it's nobody's fault. ("Bert": Dick Foran)

Siesta
1987 Lorimar
Augustine, tell me. If it wasn't her who was killed, if it was me, why do I still feel such love? ("Claire": Ellen Barkin)

The Sign of the Cross
1932 Paramount
Well, come then. You'll have to go on teaching me, leading me. Sometime I'll know. Stay close. Give me your hand. I can't sing the hymn. I shan't

look up either. I'll be looking at you and believing you're my wife. ("Marcus Superbus": Fredric March)

The Sign of Zorro
1960 Buena Vista
Bravo! ("Zorro, Don Diego": Guy Williams)

Signpost to Murder
1964 MGM
That won't be necessary, Mrs. Thomas. Mrs. Thomas. ("Supt. Bickley": Leslie Denison)

The Silencers
1966 Columbia
You didn't do one single wrong thing. ("Matt Helm": Dean Martin)

Silent Assassins
1988 Panache
Yes, General, I do agree. ("Colonel": Bill Wallace)

Silent Movie
1976 20th Century–Fox
No! (Marcel Marceau)

Silkwood
1983 20th Century–Fox
'Bye. ("Karen Silkwood": Meryl Streep)

The Silver Chalice
1954 Warner Brothers
It will be restored. But for years and for hundreds of years it will lie in darkness, where I know not. When it is brought out into the light again, there will be great cities and mighty bridges and towers higher than the Tower of Babel. It will be a world of evil and long, bitter wars. In such a world as that, the little cup will look very lonely. But it may be in that age, when man holds lightning in his hands and rides the sky as Simon the magician strove to do, it will be needed more than it is needed now. ("Peter": Lorne Greene)

Silver City
1951 Paramount
I got some figuring to do, I'll talk to you later. ("Larkin Moffatt": Edmond O'Brien)

Silver Streak
1976 20th Century–Fox
Yeah, I want to lie back on the grass and have you teach me some more about gardening. ("Hilly": Jill Clayburgh)

Silverado
1985 Columbia
We'll be back. ("Jake": Kevin Costner)

Simba
1955 Lippert
No. ("Allan Howard": Dirk Bogarde)

The Sin of Madelon Claudet
1931 MGM
Oh, you darling. ("Larry": Neil Hamilton)

Sinbad and the Seven Seas
1990 Cannon
And now to our wonderful honeymoon. ("Ali": Roland Wybenga)

Sinbad the Sailor
1947 RKO
It's here and here and here. ("Sinbad": Douglas Fairbanks, Jr.)

Sing
1989   Tri-Star
Yeah. (Audience member)

The Singer Not the Song
1961   Warner Brothers
The singer, the singer, not the song.
("Anacleto": Dirk Bogarde)

Singin' in the Rain
1952   MGM
Kathy. ("Don Lockwood": Gene Kelly)

The Singing Fool
1928   Warner Brothers
Thanks, honey, and if you'll only
stick, well, I know that everything is
gonna be all right. ("Al Stone": Al
Jolson)

Sink the Bismark
1960   20th Century–Fox
You know, Arby, these boys worry
me. Four stripes on his arm and he
don't even know what time of the day
it is. (British seaman)

Sister, Sister
1987   New World
Yes, hurry up. ("Charlotte Bonnard":
Judith Ivey)

Sisters
1973   American International
I'm fine! I, I'm, there's absolutely
nothing wrong with me! All I know is
there was no body because there was
no murder! ("Danielle Breton": Margot Kidder)

The Sisters
1938   Warner Brothers
You look as if you're in love again.
("Helen Elliott": Anita Louise)

Sitting Pretty
1948   20th Century–Fox
And you'll find me of great service,
Mrs. King. I was also an obstetrician.
("Lynn Belvedere": Clifton Webb)

Sixteen Candles
1984   Universal
It already came true. ("Samantha":
Molly Ringwald)

The Ski Bum
1971   Avco Embassy
Please, Johnny, don't make it difficult. It's about night out anyway.
Look, in a couple of days he'll be gone,
Johnny. Johnny? Johnny, are you still
there? ("Samantha": Charlotte Ramp-
ling)

Skin Deep
1989   20th Century–Fox
OK, but you're not being very patri-
otic. ("Zach Hutton": John Ritter)

The Skin Game
1971   Warner Brothers
Would you feel any better if I said I
loved you? Come back here! ("Quincy":
James Garner)

The Skipper Surprised His Wife
1950   MGM
Oh, I haven't done anything to him.
Bill. Bill. ("Daphne Lattimer": Joan
Leslie)

Sky High
1952   Lippert
You hear that, Sally. Oh, Major, I'm
your man. I won't let you down.
What's the job? ("Herbert": Sid
Melton)

Sky Murder
1940 MGM
Honey, let's forget all about Chris and Buster. Beeswax, cut yourself a piece of cake. ("Nick Carter": Walter Pidgeon)

Skyscraper Souls
1932 MGM
Yeah, you're sorry, you're sorry. But who's gonna pay for it? (Man with packages)

Slam Dance
1987 Island
Drop dead. ("Helen Drood": Mary Elizabeth Mastrantonio)

Slander
1956 MGM
That's right, Seth, maybe. Maybe. ("Scott Ethan Martin": Van Johnson)

Slap Shot
1977 Universal
Oh, for sure. ("Reggie Dunlop": Paul Newman)

Slaughterhouse Five
1972 Universal
You hungry? Huh? Here, here. There it is. Take it, take it, take it. Ouch. ("Montana Wildhack": Valerie Perrine)

Slave Girls from Beyond Infinity
1987 Urban Classics
Our universe is vast, full of wonders. We'll explore, find strange new worlds, together. ("Daria": Elizabeth Cayton)

Sleeper
1973 United Artists

Sex and death. Two things that come once in a lifetime. But at least after death you're not nauseous. ("Miles Monroe": Woody Allen)

Sleuth
1972 20th Century–Fox
Andrew, don't forget. Be sure and tell them it was just a bloody game. ("Milo Tendle": Michael Caine)

Slim
1937 Warner Brothers
Slim, I'll be waiting for you. ("Cally": Margaret Lindsay)

Slither
1972 MGM
It's free and clear, Mary, choice lakefront lots. We'll sell half-acre plots, mineral rights, space and more space. It's property management, it's vacation homes, subdivisions and maybe resort properties. Tax shelters, that's it, tax shelters. This could be. . . . ("Barry Fenaka": Peter Boyle)

Smart Woman
1948 Allied Artists
He doesn't eat very much. ("Paula": Constance Bennett)

Smash-up, the Story of a Woman
1947 Universal
Ken, I'm going to tell you something. It had to happen the way it did. I needed to hit rock bottom before I could change. Now I, I'm never going to be afraid again. We're going to have a wonderful life together, darling. And, darling, it's wonderful to

rise each day and fear not, to sleep each night and dream not, and to give one's heart and hurt not. ("Angie Evans": Susan Hayward)

Smokey and the Bandit
1977   Universal
Daddy, wait for me! Don't leave me! Who's gonna hold your hat? ("Junior Justice": Mike Henry)

Smokey and the Bandit II
1980   Universal
You're not getting away from me, Bandit. I'll chase you in hot pursuit. To the ends of the earth, you son of a bitch. ("Sheriff Buford T. Justice": Mr. Jackie Gleason)

Smokey and the Bandit III
1983   Universal
Wait, Daddy! Wait for me! Don't leave me, Daddy! ("Junior": Mike Henry)

Smoky
1946   20th Century–Fox
No. Go ahead, Smoke. ("Clint Barkley": Fred MacMurray)

Smorgasbord
1983   Warner Brothers
Well, uh, since you're so interested, I, I'll tell you. It's really good. You don't have to. . . . ("Warren Nefron/Dr. Perks": Jerry Lewis)

Snow Job
1972   Warner Brothers
Yes, a little sad about the lady. ("Christian Biton": Jean-Claude Killy)

The Snows of Kilimanjaro
1952   20th Century–Fox

Well, I'll be hanged. They've gone. They're gone. ("Harry": Gregory Peck)

So Proudly We Hail
1943   Paramount
John. ("Lt. Janet Davidson": Claudette Colbert)

Soldier of Fortune
1955   20th Century–Fox
I'll always love him. But I've discovered there's a big difference between loving someone and being in love. ("Jane Hoyt": Susan Hayward)

A Soldier's Story
1984   Columbia
Eyes, hut. ("Captain Taylor": Dennis Lipscomb)

Soldiers Three
1951   MGM
Oh, no, no, no, gentlemen, to the, to the three of us, the queen's hard bargainers. ("Colonel Brunswick": Walter Pidgeon)

The Solid Gold Cadillac
1956   Columbia
And so our Cinderella and her Prince Charming went home to their palatial estate on Long Island. But they didn't go in a coach drawn by six white horses. They went in the little stockholders' wedding gift to the bride, a solid gold Cadillac. Well, what else can you give a girl who has everything? ("The narrator": George Burns)

Some Girls
1988   MGM/UA

This is last call for Air Canada flight five five. (Announcer)

Some Kind of Wonderful
1987   Paramount
You look good wearing my fortune. ("Keith Nelson": Eric Stoltz)

Some Like It Hot
1959   United Artists
Well, nobody's perfect. ("Osgood E. Fielding, III": Joe E. Brown)

Somebody Killed Her Husband
1978   Columbia
There's a police station on Thirty-fifth, Eighth Avenue. Oh, God, it just occurred to me. On account of recording this maniac I erased all of my notes on the caterpillar book. ("Jerry Green": Jeff Bridges)

Somebody Loves Me
1952   Paramount
All right. My closing chorus. You know, in show business you gotta quit when you can't top yourself, and I can't because now I've got the billing I've always really wanted, Mrs. Benny Fields. ("Blossom Seeley": Betty Hutton)

Someone to Watch over Me
1987   Columbia
I love you too, Michael. ("Ellie Keegan": Lorraine Bracco)

Something Big
1971   National General
I love him. ("Dover MacBride": Carol White)

Something of Value
1957   MGM

Take him home. Elizabeth has a boy. Raise them together. Maybe this time it'll be better. It's not too late. ("Peter McKenzie": Rock Hudson)

Sometimes a Great Notion
1971   Universal
He's got his kid brother, that goddam family. (Man on shore)

Somewhere in the Night
1946   20th Century–Fox
I found out why tonight. You see, if you have to shoot a man, you don't want to be holding a hat in your hand. It seems that the movies are right. ("Lieutenant Donald Kendall": Lloyd Nolan)

Somewhere in Time
1980   Universal
We've got to keep him going until they get here. ("Doctor": Paul M. Cook)

Son of a Sailor
1933   Universal
No, no, it's my brother's kid. The cutest little redheaded guy you ever saw in your life. Just about that high. He's got eyes just like yours. ("Handsome Callahan": Joe E. Brown)

Son of Flubber
1963   Buena Vista
Oh, I guess I'll have to go along with that. ("Prof. Ned Brainard": Fred MacMurray)

Son of Frankenstein
1939   Universal
Good-bye, Baron von Frankenstein. (Townspeople)

Son of Fury
1942   20th Century–Fox
Eve. ("Benjamin Blake": Tyrone Power)

Son of Paleface
1952   Paramount
Let's see 'em top this on television. ("Junior": Bob Hope)

Son of the Border
1933   RKO
Did I ever tell you about me and the mountain lion? ("Frankie": David Durand)

A Song Is Born
1948   RKO
My goodness. Hobart, remember my advice. ("Professor Oddly": O. Z. Whitehead)

Song of Norway
1970   Cinerama
Nina. ("Edvard Grieg": Toralv Maurstad)

Song of the Thin Man
1947   MGM
That reminds me. ("Nora Charles": Myrna Loy)

Sons and Lovers
1960   20th Century–Fox
I was wrong. I did belong to my mother, but now she's dead, and I don't want her to live again in you. Not even in you, Miriam. I'm sure I'll never find anyone as good as you, or any love as good as yours, but I don't want to find it, because I want to be free. I don't ever want to belong to anyone again. Never any more. And perhaps I'll understand at last what it means to live. Good-bye. ("Paul Morel": Dean Stockwell)

Sophie's Place
1970   Warner Brothers
I mean, what could I say. On behalf of my colleagues, Mr. Marty Miller and myself, I really want to thank you from the bottom of my heart. And I also want to say that the tables are open. ("Herbie Hassler": Telly Savalas)

Sorrowful Jones
1949   Paramount
OK. What a way to spend a honeymoon. ("Sorrowful Jones": Bob Hope)

Sorry, Wrong Number
1948   Paramount
Sorry, wrong number. (Man's voice)

The Sound of Music
1965   20th Century–Fox
What is this sin, my children? ("Mother Abbess": Peggy Wood)

Sounder
1972   20th Century–Fox
I think I really could have made it in the big leagues if I really wanted to. ("Nathan Lee Morgan": Paul Winfield)

South Pacific
1958   20th Century–Fox
Papa! Papa! ("Ngana, Emile's Daughter": Candace Lee/"Jerome, Emile's Son": Warren Hsieh)

A Southern Yankee
1948   MGM

Sallyann, hey, Sallyann! Sallyann, wait for me! Sallyann! ("Aubrey Filmore": Red Skelton)

Southwest Passage
1954 United Artists
Just raise your fingers in the air and rub 'em together. That gritty feeling between 'em is gold dust. ("Tall Tale": Guinn "Big Boy" Williams)

Soylent Green
1973 MGM
You can tell everybody. Listen to me, Hatcher. You've got to tell them solyent green is people. We've got to stop them somehow. ("Detective Thorn": Charlton Heston)

Spaceballs
1987 MGM/UA
Well, good-bye, virgin alarm. ("Voice of Matrix": Joan Rivers)

Spacehunter: Adventures in the Forbidden Zone
1983 Columbia
Sure, kid. ("Wolff": Peter Strauss)

The Spanish Gardener
1956 Rank
Go on. ("Jose": Dirk Bogarde)

The Spanish Main
1945 RKO
He's dead. ("Francisca": Maureen O'Hara)

Sparkle
1976 Warner Brothers
Thank you. Thank you. You're, you're all making us feel real good up here. My friends and I want to sing this next song that goes back with me a long time. I'd like to sing it for my sister, no I'd like to sing it for all my sisters, especially for my man, Stix. He's out there somewhere. I hope they can all hear me. Thank you. ("Sparkle Williams": Irene Cara)

Speed Zone
1989 Orion
Yeah. ("Charlie Cronyn": John Candy)

Spellbound
1945 United Artists
Good-bye. ("Dr. Constance Peterson": Ingrid Bergman)

Spencer's Mountain
1963 Warner Brothers
Right far. ("Clayboy Spencer": James MacArthur)

Spies Like Us
1985 Warner Brothers
Eastern Europe ("Emmett Fitz-Hume": Chevy Chase)

Spinout
1966 MGM
All right. ("Mike McCoy": Elvis Presley)

The Spiral Road
1962 Universal
Els. Els. Els. Oh, thank God. Els. Oh, thank God. ("Dr. Anton Drager": Rock Hudson)

The Spiral Staircase
1945 RKO
One, eight, nine. Dr. Parry, come. It's I, Helen. ("Helen Capel": Dorothy McGuire)

The Spiral Staircase
1975   Warner Brothers
It's, it's Helen. ("Helen": Jacqueline Bisset)

The Spirit Is Willing
1966   Paramount
Forget it. ("Steve Powell": Boone Gordon)

The Spirit of St. Louis
1957   Warner Brothers
There were 200,000 people there that night. And when we came back home there were 4,000,000 people waiting. ("Charles A. Lindbergh": James Stewart)

Spitfire
1934   RKO
Maybe I'll be back soon. ("Trigger Hicks": Katharine Hepburn)

Splash
1984   Buena Vista
Madison! ("Allen Bauer": Tom Hanks)

Splendor in the Grass
1961   Warner Brothers
No, nothing can bring back the hour of splendor in the grass, glory in the flower. We will grieve not, rather find strength in what remains behind. ("Wilma Dean Loomis": Natalie Wood)

Split Decisions
1988   Vista
Eddie McGuinn. ("Announcer at Eddie-Pedroza fight": Danny Valdivia)

Split Second
1953   RKO
Yeah, let's take a look at the world of tomorrow. ("Doctor Garven": Richard Egan)

The Spy Who Loved Me
1977   United Artists
Keeping the British end up, sir. ("James Bond": Roger Moore)

The Squaw Man
1931   MGM
Naturich. ("Capt. James Wynnegate/ Jim Carsten": Warner Baxter)

Stakeout
1987   Buena Vista
What a boner. ("Bill Reimers": Emilio Estevez)

Stalag 17
1953   Paramount
Maybe he just wanted to steal our wirecutters? You ever think of that? ("'Animal' Stosh": Robert Strauss)

Stallion Road
1947   Warner Brothers
Then I guess I'll have to learn how to read, for the both of us. ("Chico": Fernando Alvarado)

Stand and Deliver
1988   Warner Brothers
Castro, Monica, four. ("Molina": Carmen Argenziano)

Stand by Me
1986   Columbia
Yeah, my dad's weird. He gets like that when he's writing. ("Gordon's son": Chance Quinn)

Stanley & Iris
1990   MGM/UA

Iris, anything is possible. ("Stanley Cox": Robert De Niro)

Star 80
1983   Warner Brothers
I'll go shopping in a store and I'll see people going, "Hey, that's Dorothy Stratten," or, "Hey, can we have a picture of you, can we have an autograph?" Or even in the airport, you know, people rushing up to me to get my autograph or something. That's really exciting for me. ("Dorothy Stratten": Mariel Hemingway)

A Star Is Born
1937   United Artists
Hello, everybody. This is Mrs. Norman Maine. ("Esther Blodgett/Vicki Lester": Janet Gaynor)

A Star Is Born
1954   Warner Brothers
Hello, everybody. This is Mrs. Norman Maine. ("Esther Blodgett/Vicki Lester": Judy Garland)

A Star Is Born
1976   Warner Brothers
Ladies and gentlemen, Esther Hoffman Howard. (Announcer)

Star Trek: The Motion Picture
1979   Paramount
Out there. That-a-way. ("Capt. James T. Kirk": William Shatner)

Star Trek II: The Wrath of Khan
1982   Paramount
Young. I feel young. ("Kirk": William Shatner)

Star Trek III: The Search for Spock
1984   Paramount
Yes. ("Kirk": William Shatner)

Star Trek IV: The Voyage Home
1986   Paramount
All right, Sulu. Let's see what she's got. ("Kirk": William Shatner)

Star Trek V: The Final Frontier
1989   Paramount
You just gonna sit there and pluck that thing or are you gonna play something? ("Kirk": William Shatner)

Star Wars
1977   20th Century–Fox
He'll be all right. ("Luke Skywalker": Mark Hamill)

Starman
1984   Columbia
Good-bye. ("Jenny Hayden": Karen Allen)

Stars and Bars
1988   Columbia
Mister Dores! ("Duane": Will Patton)

State Department—File 649
1949   Four Continents
You are a fool to speak to me like that. ("Marshal Yun Usu": Richard Loo)

State Fair
1962   20th Century–Fox
Jerry, stop! ("Margie Frake": Pamela Tiffin)

Stay Hungry
1976   United Artists
Squirrels abound where Mary Tate

and I'll be living, so come spy on them and us. Your most loving nephew, Craig. ("Craig Blake": Jeff Bridges)

Staying Alive
1983   Paramount
Strut. ("Tony Manero": John Travolta)

Staying Together
1989   Hemdale
Yeah. ("Duncan McDermott": Sean Astin)

Stealing Heaven
1989   Film Dallas
My love, I'm here. I'm waiting. ("Abelard": Derek de Lint)

Steel Magnolias
1989   Tri-Star
Come on, Sammy, get your tail hoppin'. ("Louie Jones": Tom Hodges)

Stella
1990   Buena Vista
You got a minute, lady. ("Police Officer": Philip Akin)

Stella Dallas
1937   United Artists
All right, folks, you've seen enough. Move along, please. Come on, clear the sidewalk. (Police officer)

Step by Step
1946   RKO
My, my, you sure had some persuading to do to get him to the altar, didn't you? (Justice of the peace)

Step Lively
1944   RKO

That's all. ("Glen": Frank Sinatra/ "Christine": Gloria DeHaven/"Miller": George Murphy)

The Stepford Wives
1974   Columbia
Fine. Fine. ("Joanna": Katharine Ross)

Stewardess School
1986   Columbia
It's amazing. I knew he was going to say that. ("George Bunkle": Donald Most)

The Sting
1973   Universal
Nah. I'd only blow it. ("Johnny Hooker": Robert Redford)

Stir Crazy
1980   Columbia
Come on. ("Skip Donahue": Gene Wilder)

Stolen Hours
1963   United Artists
Good night, Peter. ("Laura Pember": Susan Hayward)

The Stone Killer
1973   Columbia
You remember that cartoon of an old Roman circus where all the lions are roaring and the page boy yells down the corridor, "You've got five minutes, Christians."? ("Detective Lou Torrey": Charles Bronson)

Stopover Tokyo
1957   20th Century-Fox
Koko, I love you. ("Mark Fannon": Robert Wagner)

Stormy Monday
1988 Atlantic
Come on, Brendan. Come inside, huh. ("Finney": Sting)

Stormy Weather
1943 20th Century–Fox
Everybody dance. (Cab Calloway as himself)

The Story of Alexander Graham Bell
1939 20th Century–Fox
When are you going to work on it, Mr. Bell? ("Mrs. Bell": Loretta Young)

The Story of Louis Pasteur
1936 Warner Brothers
You young men, doctors and scientists of the future, do not let yourselves be tainted by a barren skepticism nor discouraged by the sadness of certain hours that creep over nations. Do not become angry at your opponents for no scientific theory has ever been accepted without opposition. Live in the serene peace of libraries and laboratories. Say to yourselves first, "What have I done for my instruction?" and as you gradually advance, "What am I accomplishing?" until the time comes when you may have the immense happiness of thinking that you have contributed in some way to the welfare and progress of mankind. ("Louis Pasteur": Paul Muni)

The Story of Mankind
1957 Warner Brothers
Gentlemen. In the matter of the story of mankind, this high tribunal has weighed most carefully the good of man against his evil, and finds that man is as evil as he is good. His holiness has been equalled by his tyranny, his nobility by his lack of faith. And so the scales balance much too evenly for this high tribunal to determine whether to bring an end to mankind or to assure him eternal life. We therefore reserve judgement in order to allow mankind more time to set his house in order at the earliest possible date. Take heed and listen well. Time runs swiftly, and the fate of man is now laid at the doorstep of man himself. By the villains you encourage, by the heroes you create, you shall soon achieve eternal life or oblivion. Therefore, it is the decision of this high tribunal of outer space this court shall soon convene again to determine finally whether mankind shall continue or be destroyed by the super H bomb. This choice is entirely up to you. ("High Judge": Sir Cedric Hardwicke)

The Story of Vernon and Irene Castle
1939 RKO
Go tell Maggie. ("Irene Castle": Ginger Rogers)

The Story of Will Rogers
1950 Warner Brothers
How many times had I said good-bye to him. Yet somehow never before did we seem so close. I had the feeling our whole life together was being summed up in this moment of parting. I think Will must have felt it too, as though a premonition, because the plane banked and he came back over the field to wave one more good-bye. As if reluctant to end something that

I know now can never be ended. ("Mrs. Will Rogers": Jane Wyman)

Stowaway
1936 20th Century–Fox
Judge, you're simply 'stravagant. ("Ching-Ching, Daughter of Missionaries": Shirley Temple)

Stranded
1987 New Line
Oh, I feel tired. . . . ("Grace Clark": Maureen O'Sullivan)

Strange Cargo
1940 MGM
Good-bye, monsieur. ("Fisherman": Victor Varconi)

The Strange One
1957 Columbia
I'll be back! I'll get you guys! You can't do this to Jocko De Paris! I'll get you guys! I'll be back! I'll be back! ("Jocko De Paris": Ben Gazzara)

The Stranger
1946 RKO
Good night, Mary. Pleasant dreams. ("Wilson": Edward G. Robinson)

The Stranger Wore a Gun
1953 Columbia
Why, honey child, we'll fix them on the way, they'll heal in California. ("Josie Sullivan": Claire Trevor)

Strangers When We Meet
1960 Columbia
Good-bye, Maggie. ("Larry Coe": Kirk Douglas)

Strategic Air Command
1955 Paramount

That's our new B forty-seven wing flying the first training mission. We'll have four full new wings by the end of the year. ("Gen. Ennis C. Hawkes": Frank Lovejoy)

The Stratton Story
1949 MGM
Monty Stratton has not won just a ball game, he's won a greater victory as he goes on pitching, winning, leading a rich, full life and stands as an inspiration to all of us as living proof of what a man can do if he has the courage, determination, to refuse to admit defeat. (Narrator)

The Strawberry Blonde
1941 Warner Brothers
When I want to kiss my wife, I'll kiss her anytime, anyplace, anywhere. That's the kind of hairpin I am. ("Biff Grimes": James Cagney)

Street Justice
1989 Lorimar
I love you. ("Catherine Watson": Joanne Kerns)

A Streetcar Named Desire
1951 Warner Brothers
Hey, Stella! Hey, Stella! ("Stanley Kowalski": Marlon Brando)

Strictly Dynamite
1934 RKO
. . . They'd make a swell pair of bookends. ("Moxie Slaight": Jimmy Durante)

Strike Up the Band
1940 MGM
Ladies and gentlemen, well, I, I guess

this is it. I don't have to tell you how I feel. If I felt any better, gosh, I couldn't stand it. When something wonderful like this happens to anybody, I suppose you ought to thank somebody. They're not here but I know they're listening in. Mr. Judd, I was all wrong about you. You'll always be a swell guy with us because you said, "I'll buy the first ticket." And as for you, Willie, you little shortstop, even though you're in love with my girl, I, I want you to know that we're all thinking about you and we want you to hurry up and get out of bed because we all need you. And of all the people throughout the United States who might be listening to this program, there's only one thing I'd like to say, to the most important one of all, Mom. I don't know what I was thinking about when I said that some-day I'd make you a queen, because if you hadn't been a queen all along, I'd never be here now. Well, here it comes, Mom. ("Jimmy Connors": Mickey Rooney)

Stripes
1981   Columbia
One, two, seventeen. . . . (A soldier)

Stripped to Kill
1987   Concorde
My thigh is not fat. ("Cody": Kay Lenz)

The Stripper
1963   20th Century-Fox
Good luck to you, too. ("Kenny Baird": Richard Beymer)

The Stunt Man
1978   20th Century-Fox

Sam, rewrite the opening reel. Cross the little bastard in the first act. ("Eli Cross": Peter O'Toole)

The Subject Was Roses
1968   MGM
I don't know why I bother bringing good coffee into this house. If it isn't too weak it's too strong. If it isn't too strong, it's too cold. ("John Cleary": Jack Albertson)

Such Good Friends
1971   Paramount
No, mother. ("Julie Messinger": Dyan Cannon)

Sudden Impact
1983   Warner Brothers
Yeah, it's over. ("Harry Callahan": Clint Eastwood)

Suddenly
1954   United Artists
Oh, I don't know. I don't know about that. ("Sheriff Tod Shaw": Sterling Hayden)

Suddenly, Last Summer
1959   Columbia
She's here, doctor. Miss Catherine's here. ("Catherine Holly": Elizabeth Taylor)

Suez
1938   20th Century-Fox
And when the day comes, I want to stand beside you and see the ships go through the canal and know you built it for all the people in the world. ("Toni": Annabella)

The Sugarland Express
1974   Universal

He took my gun, but he wasn't going to use it. ("Officer Slide": Michael Sacks)

The Sullivans
1944   20th Century–Fox
Tom, our boys are afloat again. ("Mrs. Sullivan": Selena Royle)

Sullivan's Travels
1941   Paramount
I'll tell you something else. There's a lot to be said for making people laugh. Did you know that's all some people have? It isn't much, but it's better than nothing in this cockeyed caravan. Boy. ("John L. Sullivan": Joel McCrea)

Summer Heat
1987   Atlantic
Daddy, I know I won't stay in Tarboro my whole life. But right now my child needs her family. She needs a stable home. I'm gonna stay right here and I'm gonna ride it out, just the same as you, and Ruth, and our whole family. ("Roxanna 'Roxy' Walston": Lori Singer)

Summer of '42
1971   Warner Brothers
I was never to see her again. Nor was I ever to learn what became of her. We were different then. Kids were different. It took us longer to understand the things we felt. Life is made up of small comings and goings, and for everything we take with us there is something that we leave behind. In the summer of forty-two we raided the Coast Guard station four times, we saw five movies, we had nine days

of rain. Benjie broke his watch, Oscy gave up the harmonica, and in a very special way, I lost Hermie forever. ("Hermie": Gary Grimes)

A Summer Place
1959   Warner Brothers
In front of God and everybody this time? ("Molly Jorgenson": Sandra Dee)

Summertime
1955   United Artists
Jane! ("Renato di Rossi": Rossano Brazzi)

Summertree
1971   Warner Brothers
Rescue helicopters.... (TV announcer)

Sunday in New York
1963   MGM
And so they were married and went to Japan for their honeymoon, and had three lovely daughters, who grew up and were lectured by their father and of course me, their uncle, on the nice things that can happen to a girl if she remains virtuous, even on a rainy Sunday in New York. ("Adam Tyler": Cliff Robertson)

The Sundowners
1960   Warner Brothers
Twenty-five quid. Lucky for you we've got a sense of humor. ("Venneker": Peter Ustinov)

Sunset
1988   Tri-Star
Adios, amigo. ("Tom Mix": Bruce Willis)

Sunset Boulevard

1950   Paramount

I can't go on with this scene, I'm too happy. Mr. DeMille, do you mind if I say a few words? Thank you. I just want to tell you all how happy I am to be back in a studio making a picture again. You don't know how much I've missed all of you, and I promise you I'll never desert you again 'cause after Salome we'll make another picture and another picture. This is my life. It always will be. There's nothing else. Just us and the cameras and those wonderful people out there in the dark. All right, Mr. DeMille, I'm ready for my close-up. ("Norma Desmond": Gloria Swanson)

Sunset in Eldorado

1945   Republic

No, I'm continuing my tour, with a cowboy. ("Lucille Wiley": Dale Evans)

The Sunshine Boys

1975   MGM

Well, here's what he said. You remember Dunlap and Rosita? Well, he used to go around with Rosita. And Rosita wore a red velvet ribbon on her neck and she tied it very tight because she was skinny and she wanted her cheeks to puff up. But she tied it so tight it affected her hearing. She couldn't hear the music. ("Al Lewis": George Burns)

Superchick

1973   Crown

Hey, hold it. Boys, please. Take a number. ("Tara B. True": Joyce Jillson)

Superfly

1972   Warner Brothers

When you do my dirty laundry ain't gonna help you. And all them honky big partners you got ain't gonna be able to protect your ass, either, because in case you're thinking I'm trying to pull some of that old-time legal shit on you, Captain, I think you ought to know something. I hired the very best killers there are. White killers. White ones, baby, so you better take good care of me. Nothing, nothing better happen to one hair of my gorgeous head. Can you dig it? ("Youngblood Priest": Ron O'Neal)

Superman

1978   Warner Brothers

No, sir, don't thank me, warden. We're all part of the same team. Good night. ("Superman": Christopher Reeve)

Superman II

1980   Warner Brothers

Good afternoon, Mr. President. Sorry I've been away so long. I won't let you down again. ("Superman": Christopher Reeve)

Superman III

1983   Warner Brothers

Si, grazie. ("Pisa Vendor": John Bluthal)

Superman IV:
The Quest for Peace

1987   Cannon

No, Luthor, it's as it always was, on the brink, with good fighting evil. See you in twenty. ("Superman": Christopher Reeve)

The Supernaturals

1987   Republic Ent. Intl.

OK, soldiers, let's haul ass out of here. ("Sgt. Leona Hawkins": Michelle Nichols)

Surrender
1987   Warner Brothers
At least he left us tied up exactly the way we asked him. ("Sean Stein": Michael Caine)

The Surrogate
1984   Cinepix
What stranger? This is Paris. It's a very friendly town. ("Frank Waite": Art Hindle)

Survival Game
1987   Trans-World
I'm fine. ("Michael Hawkins": Mike Norris)

The Survivors
1983   Columbia
Not really. ("Sonny Paluso": Walter Matthau)

Susan Lenox, Her Fall and Rise
1931   MGM
I'll make you believe in me. ("Susan Lenox": Greta Garbo)

Susan Slade
1961   Warner Brothers
I love you, Hoyt. I love you. ("Susan Slade": Connie Stevens)

Susan Slept Here
1954   RKO
The dangerous age. Will you be satisfied to stay home and take care of a broken-down man of sixty? No, you'll want to go out and live. And me, I'll be just around the corner from social security. ("Mark, Screen Writer": Dick Powell)

Susanna Pass
1949   Republic
But worth it, Doc. Work done by hatcheries like this doesn't just mean restocking lakes and streams. It means the sportsman and the youth of America will have a chance to get away from crowded cities and their troubles, go fishing, and enjoy the privileges our forefathers had. So good luck to you, Doc. (Roy Rogers as himself)

Suspect
1987   Tri-Star
Leave the door open. Go. ("Kathleen Riley": Cher)

The Suspect
1944   Universal
Scotland Yard. ("Huxley": Stanley C. Ridges)

Suspicion
1941   RKO
My darling. ("Lina McLaidlaw": Joan Fontaine)

Svengali
1931   Warner Brothers
Avanti, signori. ("Svengali": John Barrymore)

The Swan
1956   MGM
Take me in, Albert. ("Princess Alexandra": Grace Kelly)

Sweet Bird of Youth
1962   MGM

You? You can go straight to hell. ("Aunt Nonnie": Mildred Dunnock)

Sweet Dreams
1985 Tri-Star
I know it. I know it. ("Charlie": Ed Harris)

Sweet Hearts Dance
1988 Tri-Star
Wiley, you want me to go back and get your bathing suit, sweetheart? ("Sandra Boon": Susan Sarandon)

Sweet Lies
1989 Island
Oh, I'm afraid they will. ("Peter Nicholl": Treat Williams)

Sweet Lorraine
1987 Angelika
No matter what was wrong, she always looked beautiful. ("Lillian Garber": Maureen Stapleton)

Sweet November
1968 Warner Brothers
I think December will be a lovely month, Gordon. You'll see. A lovely month. ("Sara Deever": Sandy Dennis)

Sweet Revenge
1987 Concorde
Mommy! ("Jaimie Grey": Ruth Arras)

Swing Time
1936 RKO
Yes. I guess so. ("Penelope Carrol": Ginger Rogers)

The Swinger
1966 Paramount

Ric! Ric! ("Kelly Olsson": Ann-Margret)

Sylvester
1985 Columbia
Life's too short. ("Foster": Richard Farnsworth)

T. R. Baskin
1971 Paramount
Good-bye. ("T. R. Baskin": Candice Bergen)

Table for Five
1983 Warner Brothers
I missed you too. I missed you, lots. ("Mitchell": Richard Crenna)

Tail of the Tiger
1984 Roadshow
Yeah. ("Orville Ryan": Grant Navin)

Take the High Ground
1953 MGM
That is infantry. But you poor, miserable young people, you will never make it. My name is Sergeant Ryan. Pick up your bags. Left face. Forward double time. Hup two three four. Hup two three four. Hup two three four. Hup two three four. Hup two three four. ("Sgt. Thorne Ryan": Richard Widmark)

Take This Job and Shove It
1981 Avco Embassy
Screw 'em. ("Frank Macklin": Robert Hays)

Taking Off
1971 Universal
I really don't know if I could, uh, under the circumstances, get my, uh, rocks off. ("Jamie": David Gittler)

A Tale of Two Cities
1935   MGM
It's a far, far better thing I do than I have ever done. It's a far, far better rest I go to than I have ever known. ("Sidney Carton": Ronald Colman)

A Talent for Loving
1969   Paramount
Blessing. ("General Molina": Topol)

Tales from the Crypt
1972   Cinerama
And now, who's next? Perhaps you. ("The Crypt Keeper": Sir Ralph Richardson)

Tales from the Darkside: The Movie
1990   Paramount
I just love happy endings. ("Timmy": Matthew Lawrence)

Tales of Manhattan
1942   20th Century–Fox
So that's what they mean when they say the Lord moves in mysterious ways. ("Luke": Paul Robeson)

Talk Radio
1988   Universal
Barry and I have worked together for over seven years, and whenever you'd threaten him over the air, man, he'd stick it right back in your face. It was like his dick was flapping in the wind and he'd like to see if he could get an erection. The guy had a, he had a little dick, but he liked to flap it out there. And they cut it off and now he's dead. I don't know if you understand that analogy, but it's the clearest one I can make. (Radio caller)

Tall in the Saddle
1944   RKO
Hey, Rock! Rock, where are ya? ("Dave": George "Gabby" Hayes)

The Tall T
1957   Columbia
Come on, now, it's gonna be a nice day. ("Pat Brennan": Randolph Scott)

The Taming of the Shrew
1929 United Artists
Drink! ("Petruchio": Douglas Fairbanks)

Tammy and the Bachelor
1957   Universal
Well, I, I told him you and I had some unfinished business. ("Peter Brent": Leslie Nielsen)

Tammy and the Doctor
1963   Universal
It's a medical experiment. I drank some of your river water. ("Dr. Mark Cheswick": Peter Fonda)

Tammy Tell Me True
1961   Universal
Uh-oh, Tom. I am a woman fully growed. ("Tammy Tyree": Sandra Dee)

Tank
1984   Universal
You done real good, old girl. ("Zack": James Garner)

Tap
1989   Tri-Star
It's still a little weak. ("Little Mo": Sammy Davis, Jr.)

Target
1985 Warner Brothers
Come here, son, come here. ("Walter
Lloyd": Gene Hackman)

Tarzan and His Mate
1934 MGM
No, dear, always is just beginning for
you and me. ("Jane Parker": Maureen
O'Sullivan)

Tarzan and the Trappers
1958 RKO
You can see it was good. ("Boy":
Rickie Sorenson)

Tarzan Finds a Son
1939 MGM
Yes, darling, everything's all right
now. ("Jane": Maureen O'Sullivan)

Tarzan the Ape Man
1932 MGM
Good-bye. You'll be coming back,
Harry. I can see a huge safari with
you at the head bearing ivory down to
the coast. Only this time there'll be no
danger because we'll be there to protect you, every step of the way. ("Jane
Parker": Maureen O'Sullivan)

Tarzan the Ape Man
1959 MGM
Wait, please wait. ("Jane Parker":
Joanna Barnes)

Tarzan the Ape Man
1981 MGM/UA
Mr. Holt, believe it. ("Jane": Bo
Derek)

Tarzan's Desert Mystery
1943 RKO

Oh, no, not with me, you don't.
("Sheik": Lloyd Corrigan)

Taste the Blood of Dracula
1970 Warner Brothers
Please run, run! Do as I say! ("Paul
Paxton": Anthony Corlan)

Tattoo
1980 20th Century–Fox
No, oh, no! ("Maddy": Maud Adams)

The Tattooed Stranger
1950 RKO
You know, you're smart enough for a
college boy. What you need is a
steadying influence. Get him to tell
you about the tattooed wife. ("Lieutenant Corrigan": Walter Kinsella)

Taxi
1931 Warner Brothers
Well, it's pretty hard to explain.
They're feathering their love nest all
over again. ("Ruby": Leila Bennett)

Tea and Sympathy
1956 MGM
These are terrible things to write to
you, Tom, about guilt and right and
wrong. But you are old enough now to
know that when you drop a pebble in
the water there are ever-widening
circles of ripples. There are always
consequences. Anyway, Tom, I have
often wondered if I didn't show a lack
of faith in you, in your ability to meet
a crisis by yourself, and come through
it alone. They say about dreadful experiences if they don't kill us they
make us strong. I was just afraid that
that one would kill you. Dear Tom, I
was so pleased to read that you are
married. Have a good life, a full life,

and understanding life. Write good stories, true stories. About one thing you were correct, the wife did always keep her affection for the boy, somewhere in her heart. ("Laura Reynolds": Deborah Kerr)

The Teahouse of the August Moon
1956   MGM
Little story now concluded. But history of world unfinished. Lovely ladies, kind gentlemen, go home to ponder. What was true at beginning remains true. Pain make man think, thought make man wise, and wisdom make life endurable. So, may August moon bring gentle sleep. Sayonara. ("Sakini": Marlon Brando)

Telefon
1977   MGM
Make those telephone calls. ("Barbara": Lee Remick)

The Telephone
1988   New World
Yes, I'll hold. ("Vashti Blue": Whoopi Goldberg)

Tell Me That You Love Me, Junie Moon
1969   Paramount
I know your type, but you're going to like me, a lot, if it takes a lifetime, and don't you forget it. ("Mario": James Coco)

Tell Them Willie Boy Is Here
1969   Universal
Tell them we're all out of souvenirs. ("Christopher Cooper": Robert Redford)

10
1979   Warner Brothers
I show him mine, he don't show me his. Come on, Rapunzel. From now on we do it in the dark. ("Neighbor": Don Calfa)

The Ten Commandments
1956   Paramount
Go, proclaim liberty throughout all the lands and to all the inhabitants thereof. ("Moses": Charlton Heston)

Ten Little Indians
1966   Warner Brothers
This. ("Hugh Lombard": Hugh O'Brian)

Ten Little Indians
1975   Avco Embassy
When we get out of here, I'm gonna teach you how to shoot straight. ("Captain Lombard": Frank Stallone)

Ten Tall Men
1951   Columbia
My mother's. I know she'd have wanted you to have it. ("Sgt. Mike Kincaid": Burt Lancaster)

10 to Midnight
1983   Cannon
No, we won't. ("Les Kesler": Charles Bronson)

The Tenant
1976   Paramount
Simone, Simone, you do recognize me, don't you? It's me, Stella, your friend Stella. Don't you recognize me? ("Stella": Isabelle Adjani)

The Tender Trap
1955   MGM

Uh, that is, I mean, uh. I'll pick you up. We could go to the license bureau and get married and then have a baby and have another baby in the country and, oh, Julie. ("Charlie Y. Reader": Frank Sinatra)

Tension
1950 MGM
No, that would have been a lot of work, wouldn't it? ("Lt. Collier Bonnabel": Barry Sullivan)

Tequila Sunrise
1988 Warner Brothers
Yeah, well, they're probably talking about me right now. ("Lt. Nick Frescia": Kurt Russell)

Term of Trial
1962 Warner Brothers
I am, am I? ("Graham Weir": Laurence Olivier)

Terminal Entry
1988 Intercontinental
You're damn right. ("Styles": Yaphet Kotto)

The Terminator
1984 Orion
I know. ("Sarah Connor": Linda Hamilton)

Terms of Endearment
1983 Paramount
Oh, I think it is. Come on, I'll show you the internationally infamous, uh, Breedlove crawl. It's a little stroke I picked up in space. ("Garrett Breedlove": Jack Nicholson)

Terror House
1942 Pathe

They did. That's why I let them go. This is the path that goes across. ("Stephen Deremid": James Mason)

The Terror of the Tongs
1960 Columbia
May my ancestors look kindly upon me. ("Chung King": Christopher Lee)

The Terror Within
1989 Concorde
Come on, Butch. ("Linda": Terri Treas)

Tess
1979 Columbia
I am ready. ("Tess": Nastassia Kinski)

Test Pilot
1938 MGM
I'll betcha they don't make it, I don't know why I'm not up there in front of 'em. A man spends his whole life getting somewhere and where's he end up? Nowhere, just where he started. ("Jim Lane": Clark Gable)

Texas
1941 Columbia
Oh, Danny. ("Tod Ramsey": Glenn Ford)

The Texas Rangers
1952 Columbia
Turn around, son. ("Johnny Carver": George Montgomery)

The Texican
1966 Columbia
So do I. ("Jess Carlin": Audie Murphy)

Thank God It's Friday
1978 Columbia
There. ("Bobby Speed": Ray Vitte)

That Certain Feeling
1956   Paramount
Needs work. ("Francis X. Dignan": Bob Hope)

That Certain Woman
1937   Warner Brothers
You're coming over? Oh. ("Mary Donnell": Bette Davis)

That Hagen Girl
1947   Warner Brothers
The family? Oh, glory. ("Kathleen Davis": Shirley Temple)

That Hamilton Woman
1941   United Artists
There is no then. There is no after. ("Lady Emma Hart Hamilton": Vivien Leigh)

That Touch of Mink
1962   Universal
Take a look. ("Roger": Gig Young)

That Was Then...This Is Now
1985 Paramount
Lighten up, dude. ("Byron Douglas": Craig Sheffer)

That's Life
1986   Columbia
I know what I'm talking about. It works. My God, we're going on our second honeymoon. I don't want you to get sick on me. ("Harvey Fairchild": Jack Lemmon)

That's Right—You're Wrong
1939   RKO
So long, everybody. ("Kay": Kay Kyser)

They All Kissed the Bride
1942   Columbia
Make that indefinitely. ("Margaret J. Drew": Joan Crawford)

They Call Me Mister Tibbs!
1970   United Artists
A case is never solved until the judge. ("Virgil Tibbs": Sidney Poitier)

They Came to Cordura
1959   Columbia
Stop! Come back! Chawk, Trubee, Renziehausen! All of you stop! You'll be court-martialled! You'll hang, you fools! You fools! ("Lt. William Fowler": Tab Hunter)

They Gave Him a Gun
1937   MGM
Yeah, you made a soldier out of him. You gave him a gun and told him how to be a hero. Why don't you pin a medal on him now, Sergeant Meadowlark, he was your star pupil. ("Fred": Spencer Tracy)

They Made Me a Criminal
1939   Warner Brothers
Then come on. ("Johnny Bradfield/ Jack Dorney": John Garfield)

They Met in Argentina
1941   RKO
Hey, Mac, watch me in the fourth. (A horse)

They Rode West
1954   Columbia
Ah, you're a great man, doctor. You're a great man. ("Sgt. Creever": Roy Roberts)

They Still Call Me Bruce
1987 Shapiro
Inspector Bruce. ("Polly": Bethany Wright)

They Were Expendable
1945 MGM
Check. ("Gardner": Marshall Thompson/"Cross": Cameron Mitchell)

They Won't Believe Me
1947 RKO
We the jury in the above entitled action find the defendant, Lawrence Ballentine, not guilty. ("Court Clerk": Milton Parsons)

Thief
1981 United Artists
No, I'm OK. ("Leo": Robert Prosky)

The Thief of Bagdad
1940 United Artists
Some fun, an adventure at last. ("Abu": Sabu)

The Thin Man
1934 MGM
Oh, yeah? ("Nick Charles": William Powell)

The Thing
1951 RKO
And now before I give you the details of the battle, I bring you a warning. Every one of you listening to my voice, tell the world. Tell this to everybody, wherever they are. Watch the skies, everywhere, keep looking. Keep watching the skies. ("Ned 'Scotty' Scott": Douglas Spencer)

Things Are Tough All Over
1982 Columbia
Hey, man, I bet you thought we'd had it, huh? Hey, well, so did we. But as things turned out all we had to do was go back and make love to these girls twenty-four hours a day. Hey, but at least we had a job, you know, 'cause, hey, things are tough all over. (Richard "Cheech" Marin, as himself and "Mr. Slyman")

Things Change
1988 Columbia
The car comes on the corner at four p.m. I shot the son of a bitch three times in the heart. (Don Ameche)

The Third Man
1949 British Lion
I haven't got a sensible name, Calloway. ("Holly Martins": Joseph Cotten)

13 Ghosts
1960 Columbia
Real soon, I hope. ("Buck Zorba": Charles Herbert)

-30-
1959 Warner Brothers
Well, who asked you to? ("Sam Gatlin": Jack Webb)

The 39 Steps
1935 Gaumont
Thank you, thank you. I'm glad it's off my mind, at last. ("Mr. Memory": Wylie Watson)

Thirty Seconds Over Tokyo
1944 MGM
I had to be, if I was going to get such a good-looking fellow. ("Ellen Jones Lawson": Phyllis Thaxter)

36 Hours
1964   MGM
Good-bye. ("Anna Hedler": Eva Marie Saint)

This Is Spinal Tap
1984   Embassy
Well, I don't know. What are the hours? ("Nigel Tufnel": Christopher Guest)

This Island Earth
1955   Universal
Thank God it's still here. ("Cal Meacham": Rex Reason)

This Land Is Mine
1943   RKO
Article Six. The law is the expression of the will of the people. All citizens have the right to assist personally, or through their elected representatives, in its formation. It ought to be the same for all whether it protects or whether it punishes. All citizens being equal in the eyes of the law have equal rights to all dignities, places and public positions according to their capacity and without any other distinction than those of their virtues and talents. ("Louise Martin": Maureen O'Hara)

Thoroughbreds Don't Cry
1937   MGM
You bet we are. ("Roger Calverton": Ronald Sinclair)

Thoroughly Modern Millie
1967   Universal
Like a squirrel storing the nuts of life. ("Millie Dillmount": Julie Andrews)

Those Magnificent Men in Their Flying Machines
1965   20th Century–Fox
May I have your attention please. We regret to announce that the departure of all planes from London to Paris has been delayed again owing to bad weather. Busses are waiting outside to take you back to your hotel. Will you all come this way please. Will you all follow me. ("Airline Hostess": Millicent Martin)

Three for the Road
1987   Vista
Ow. ("Blanche": Sally Kellerman)

Three Fugitives
1989   Buena Vista
Maybe I better stay with you guys a little longer. ("Daniel Lucas": Nick Nolte)

Three Godfathers
1948   MGM
I'd be proud for you to take your pen in hand, Miss Latham. ("Robert Marmaduke Hightower": John Wayne)

Three Kinds of Heat
1987   Cannon
Cromwell! ("Kirkland": Jack Headley)

Three Men and a Baby
1987   Buena Vista
Yes! ("Michael": Steve Guttenberg)

Three Men and a Little Lady
1990   Buena Vista
You may now kiss the bride, again. ("Vicar Hewitt": Jonathan Lynn)

The Three Musketeers
1948   MGM

Dismissed. ("King Louis XIII": Frank Morgan)

Three O'Clock High
1987   Universal
Looks like it's gonna be one of those days. ("Jerry Mitchell": Casey Siemaszko)

Three on a Match
1932   Warner Brothers
And my own dear mama, wherever she is, God bless her and keep her safe from harm. Amen. ("Junior": Buster Phelps)

Three Steps North
1951   United Artists
Come on. ("Frank Keeler": Lloyd Bridges)

The Three Stooges Go Around the World in a Daze
1963   Columbia
No, no, it's on the both of us. Come on, what's the matter with you guys? (Moe Howard, as himself)

Three Stripes in the Sun
1955   Columbia
Come. ("Yuko": Mitsuko Kimura)

3:10 to Yuma
1957   Columbia
Well, my job's finished when I get you there. ("Dan Evans": Van Heflin)

Three the Hard Way
1974   Allied Artists
Well, let's go. ("Jimmy Lait": Jim Brown)

The 3 Worlds of Gullliver
1959   Columbia

Thank you. Thank you, sir. ("Dr. Lemuel Gulliver": Kerwin Matthews)

Threshold
1983   20th Century-Fox
Ready to go on bypass? ("Dr. Thomas Vrain": Donald Sutherland)

The Thrill of It All
1963   Universal
Hooray for Mommy! Hooray for Daddy! ("Maggie Boyer": Kym Narath/ "Andy Boyer": Brian Nash)

Throw Momma from the Train
1987   Orion
Keep going a little further, Owen, maybe somebody will harpoon you. ("Larry Donner": Billy Crystal)

Thunder Alley
1967   American International
That's it, race fans, a great day of racing. You've seen the greatest, both with cars and drivers. Turning into victory lane, Tommy Callahan, the winner. And here comes Johnny Reb carrying the traditional victory flag. And here is Tommy Callahan, the winner of the Southern five hundred. ("Announcer": Sandy Reed)

Thunder in the East
1951   Paramount
Dr. Paling! Dr. Paling! Dr. Paling! ("Singh": Charles Boyer)

Thunder Pass
1954   Lippert
That kind of scalping ain't going to hurt even a little bit. ("Injun": Andy Devine)

Thunderbolt and Lightfoot
1974   United Artists
You all right, kid? What's the –? ("John 'Thunderbolt' Doherty": Clint Eastwood)

Thundering Hoofs
1941   RKO
Fountain pen. Sure is. ("Whopper": Les "Lasses" White)

A Ticket to Tomahawk
1950   20th Century–Fox
'Bye. ("Johnny Behind-the-Deuces": Dan Dailey)

A Ticklish Affair
1963   MGM
Good-bye, Harrigan. ("Grover Martin": Peter Robbins)

A Tiger's Tale
1988   Atlantic
Come on over here! Come on! ("Rose Butts": Ann-Margret)

Tight Spot
1955   Columbia
At present, gangbuster. ("Sherry Conley": Ginger Rogers)

Till the Clouds Roll By
1946   MGM
Like her? I love her. I'd rather hear her sing one of my songs than anyone else in the world. ("Jerome Kern": Robert Walker)

Tillie and Gus
1933   Paramount
No. Don't forget Lady Godiva put everything she had on a horse. ("Augustus Winterbotton": W. C. Fields)

Time After Time
1980   Warner Brothers
Just don't expect miracles. I'm changing my name to Susan B. Anthony. Let's go. ("Amy Robbins": Mary Steenburgen)

Time Bandits
1981   Embassy
Mom? Dad? ("Kevin": Craig Warnock)

The Time Machine
1960   MGM
One cannot choose but wonder. You see, he has all the time in the world. ("David Filby": Alan Young)

A Time of Destiny
1988   Columbia
This is my husband. Please accept us. ("Josie Larraneta": Melissa Leo)

The Time of Your Life
1948   United Artists
Enough is enough. ("Nick": William Bendix)

Time Trackers
1989   Concorde
And R. J. would always find her love. ("R. J. Craig": Kathleen Beller)

Tin Men
1987   Buena Vista
What have I got? You told me you had heads. ("Bill 'BB' Babowsky": Richard Dreyfuss)

To Be or Not to Be
1942   United Artists
To be or not to be. ("Joseph Tura": Jack Benny)

To Catch a Thief
1955   Paramount
So this is where you live. Oh, Mother will love it up here. ("Frances Stevens": Grace Kelly)

To Have and Have Not
1945   Warner Brothers
What do you think? ("Marie Browning": Lauren Bacall)

To Live and Die in L.A.
1985   MGM/UA
You're working for me now. ("John Vukovich": John Pankow)

Tom, Dick and Harry
1940   RKO
What? ("Dick Hamilton": Alan Marshall)

Tom Horn
1979   Warner Brothers
Sam, I've never seen such a pasty-faced bunch of sheriffs in my life. ("Tom Horn": Steve McQueen)

Tom Sawyer
1973   United Artists
'Bye, Tom. 'Bye. ("Aunt Polly": Celeste Holm)

Tommy
1975   Columbia
Stop! ("Tommy Walker": Roger Daltrey)

Tony Rome
1967   20th Century-Fox
If you ever see Tony Rome, give him my love. ("Ann Archer": Jill St. John)

Too Late Blues
1961   Paramount

Well, it's just a little too late to be crying the blues now, isn't it? Now I'll tell you what you do. You take your little pink cotton candy dreams and you get them out of here and I mean out of here. And on your way out, my friend, you take a look around you and you take a look at this place. And you realize when you take your little look that this is everything we got in the world. This is everything we got. For which we say many thanks. Now I want to play number six, I want to play it now. Let's go. Number six. Play it. ("Shelly": Bill Stafford)

Too Many Girls
1940   RKO
Run, Clint, run! ("Connie Casey": Lucille Ball)

Too Much
1987   Cannon
I love you, TM, you really are too much. ("Susie": Bridgette Anderson)

Too Much, Too Soon
1958   Warner Brothers
Do that. ("[Link] Lincoln Forrester": Martin Milner)

Tootsie
1962   Columbia
What are you going to use it for? ("Julie Nichols": Jessica Lange)

Top Gun
1986   Paramount
I don't know, but, uh, it's looking good this time. ("Pete Mitchell 'Maverick'": Tom Cruise)

Top Hat
1935   RKO
Well, well, well. Mr. Beddini, what are you doing in this young lady's room? ("Jerry Travers": Fred Astaire)

Top Secret Affair
1956 Warner Brothers
Not here, Miss Peale. Don't you know the old saying, generals die in bed. ("Maj. Gen. Melville Goodwin": Kirk Douglas)

Torch Song Trilogy
1988   New Line
Mama! ("Arnold Beckoff": Harvey Fierstein)

Torchlight
1984   Film Ventures
Yeah, I know. ("Jack Gregory": Steve Railsback)

Torn Curtain
1966   Universal
Michael. ("Sarah Sherman": Julie Andrews)

Tortilla Flat
1942   MGM
That's right. ("Jose Maria Corcoran": John Qualen)

Total Recall
1990   Carolco
Well, then, kiss me quick before you wake up. ("Melina": Rachel Ticotin)

Touch of Evil
1958   Universal
Adios. ("Tanya": Marlene Dietrich)

A Touch of Larceny
1959   Paramount
Unreliable, untrustworthy, wicked, but I love you. ("Virginia Killain": Vera Miles)

Touched by Love
1980   Columbia
Karen. Karen. Karen. ("Lena Canada": Deborah Raffin)

Tough Guys Don't Dance
1987   Cannon
Carry me over the threshold, you dummy. ("Madeleine": Isabella Rossellini)

Tovarich
1937   Warner Brothers
Oh, I forgot. I am putting these bottles out for the milkman. The Russian saints won't do it for me. ("Grand Duchess Tatiana Petrovna": Claudette Colbert)

The Towering Inferno
1974   20th Century–Fox
You know where to reach me. So long, architect. ("Fire Chief Michael O'Halloran": Steve McQueen)

A Town Like Alice
1957   Lopert
Joe. ("Jean Paget": Virginia McKenna)

The Toy
1983   Columbia
Mr. Brown, please! ("Honey Russell": Linda McCann)

Toy Tiger
1956   Universal

Could be. ("Timmie Harkinson": Tim Hovey)

Trading Hearts
1988   Cineworld
Autograph. ("Yvonne Rhonda Nottingham": Jenny Lewis)

Trading Places
1983   Paramount
Feeling good, Louis. ("Billy Ray Valentine": Eddie Murphy)

The Trap
1967   Continental
They'll sell well in San Francisco. Go, clean the house. ("Jean LaBete": Oliver Reed)

Traveling North
1988   Queensland
To Frank. ("Frances": Julia Blake)

Traveling Saleswoman
1950   Columbia
Pretty baby. ("Mabel King": Joan Davis)

Travels with My Aunt
1972   MGM
All right, all right, toss the coin into the air, Mr. Wordsworth, and let it fall where it will. ("Aunt Augusta": Maggie Smith)

Treasure Island
1934   MGM
Certain we will. ("Jim Hawkins": Jackie Cooper)

Treasure Island
1950   Buena Vista
I could almost find it in my heart to hope he makes it. ("Jim Hawkins": Bobby Driscoll)

Treasure Island
1972   National General
Pieces of eight. Pieces of eight. Pieces of eight. Pieces of eight. Pieces of eight. (A parrot)

The Treasure of Pancho Villa
1955   RKO
You've tasted everything, you buzzard. But if you'd ever tasted Juan Castro, you'd have tasted a man. ("Tom Bryan": Rory Calhoun)

The Treasure of the Sierra Madre
1948   Warner Brothers
Same to you. ("Curtin": Tim Holt)

A Tree Grows in Brooklyn
1945   20th Century–Fox
Oh, cut the mush. ("Neely Nolan": Ted Donaldson)

Trenchcoat
1983   Buena Vista
All right, you big gorilla. ("Mickey Raymond": Margot Kidder)

Trigger, Jr.
1950   Republic
Well, Trigger, let's show him that you're still boss. (Roy Rogers, as himself)

The Trip to Bountiful
1985   Island
Good-bye, Bountiful. Good-bye. ("Mrs. Watts": Geraldine Page)

Tripoli
1950   Paramount

Aye, aye, Sergeant. City is secured. (Signalman)

Trog
1970   Warner Brothers
Doctor. Doctor Brockton. Now that the trog that died has been destroyed, have you anything to say? ("Reporter": Maurice Good)

The Trojan Women
1971   Cinerama
Up, up from the ground, trembling body, old weak legs. You must carry me on to the new day of slavery. ("Hecuba": Katharine Hepburn)

Troop Beverly Hills
1989   Columbia
Attention, K-Mart shoppers, blue light special, Aisle thirteen, cookies. ("Velda Plendor": Betty Thomas)

Trouble in Paradise
1932   Paramount
Gaston! ("Lily": Miriam Hopkins)

The Trouble with Angels
1966   Columbia
If she does, I quit. ("Mother Superior": Rosalind Russell)

The Trouble with Harry
1955   Paramount
A double bed. ("Capt. Albert Wiles": Edmund Gwenn)

True Believer
1989   Columbia
I mean the very heart. ("Eddie Dodd": James Woods)

True Grit
1969   Paramount

Well, come see a fat old man sometime. ("Reuben J. 'Rooster' Cogburn": John Wayne)

True Stories
1986   Warner Brothers
Well, I really enjoyed forgetting. When I first come to a place, I notice all the little details. I notice the way the sky looks, the color of white paper, the way people walk, doorknobs, everything. They I get used to the place and I don't notice those things anymore. So only by forgetting can I see the place again as it really is. ("Narrator": David Byrne)

Tucker: The Man and His Dream
1988   Paramount
Here we go. ("Jimmy Sakuyama": Mako)

Tugboat Annie
1933   MGM
Who put that in there? ("Terry Brennan": Wallace Beery)

Tunes of Glory
1960   United Artists
Left, right, left, right, left, right, left. Left, right, left, right, left, right, left. (A soldier)

The Tunnel of Love
1958   MGM
Listen, honey, let's put this house on the market and move back in the city. The country's no place to bring up kids. Our baby's going to be born in Manhattan in a normal, healthy atmosphere. And this time I hope it looks like you. ("Augie Poole": Richard Widmark)

Turtle Diary
1986 Goldwyn
Cheerio. ("William": Ben Kingsley)

The Tuttles of Tahiti
1942 RKO
Oh, but I wouldn't, Jonas. I'm a Tuttle now. ("Tamara Taio": Peggy Drake)

12 Angry Men
1957 United Artists
So long. ("Juror No. 8": Henry Fonda)

The Twelve Chairs
1970 UMC
Epilepsy, my friends, epilepsy! The same disease that struck down our beloved Dostoevsky! Give! Give! Give, from the bottom of your hearts. ("Ostap Bender": Frank Langella)

12 to the Moon
1960 Columbia
Prepare for landing. ("Captain John Anderson": Ken Clark)

Twentieth Century
1934 Columbia
You can't do this to me! ("Lily Garland": Carole Lombard)

The 25th Hour
1967 MGM
Come on, you can do better than that, a big happy smile. ("Photographer": Paul Maxwell)

20 Million Miles to Earth
1957 Columbia
Why is it always, always so costly for man to move from the present to the future? ("Dr. Judson Uhl": John Zaremba)

20,000 Leagues under the Sea
1954 Buena Vista
There is hope for the future. And when the world is ready for a new, better life, all this will someday come to pass, in God's good time. (Narrator)

Twice Dead
1989 Concorde
Now you're talking. ("Scott": Tom Breznahan)

Twilight for the Gods
1958 Universal
What's a couple of years. ("Capt. David Bell": Rock Hudson)

Twilight Zone: The Movie
1983 Warner Brothers
There is a fifth dimension beyond that which is known to man. It is the middle ground between life and shadow, between science and superstition, and it lies between the pit of man's fears and the summit of his knowledge. This is the dimension of imagination that is an area which we call the twilight zone. ("Narrator": Burgess Meredith)

Twilight's Last Gleaming
1977 Allied Artists
Will you keep your word? Will you tell the people? ("President Stevens": Charles Durning)

Twins
1988 Universal
I just can't get over how alike they are. ("Mary Ann Benedict": Bonnie Bartlett)

Twist Around the Clock
1961   Columbia
Finale. ("Mitch Mason": John Cronin)

Two-Faced Woman
1941   MGM
I'm not Larry, I'm his twin brother. Oh, Karin, Katherine. ("Larry Blake": Melvyn Douglas)

Two for the Road
1966   20th Century–Fox
Bastard. ("Joanna Wallace": Audrey Hepburn)

The Two Jakes
1990   Paramount
It never goes away. ("Jake Gittes": Jack Nicholson)

Two Loves
1961   MGM
Well, because it's so smug. ("Anna Vorontosov": Shirley MacLaine)

Two Moon Junction
1988   Lorimar
I'm sorry, sir, I didn't mean to inconvenience you. It's just that I was in the neighborhood, I needed a nice, hot shower. Sure is nice-smelling soap. ("April": Sherilyn Fenn)

The Two Mrs. Carrolls
1947   Warner Brothers
Just a moment. Before we go would you gentlemen like a drink? A glass of milk, perhaps? ("Geoffrey Carroll": Humphrey Bogart)

Two Mules for Sister Sara
1969   Universal
Come on. ("Hogan": Clint Eastwood)

Two of a Kind
1983   20th Century–Fox
Sure has. ("Debbie": Olivia Newton-John)

Two Smart People
1946   MGM
'Board. (Conductor)

2001: A Space Odyssey
1968   MGM
Good day, gentlemen. This is a prerecorded briefing, made prior to your departure, and which for security reasons of the highest importance, has been known on board during the mission only by your H-A-L nine thousand computer. Now that you are in Jupiter's space, and the entire crew is revived, it can be told to you. Eighteen months ago, the first evidence of intelligent life off the earth was discovered. It was buried forty feet below the lunar surface near the crater Tycho. Except for a single, very powerful radio emission aimed at Jupiter, the four-million-year-old black monolith has remained completely inert, its origin and purpose still a total mystery. ("Dr. Heywood Floyd": William Sylvester)

Two Years Before the Mast
1946   Paramount
The only law a sailor's ever known is the personal decision of his captain. If a sailor objects, he's sentenced to starvation, flogging or even death. Gentlemen, they'll keep it that way as long as the government will let them whether sailors die or not, that decision is up to you. If you believe that we've told the truth, that the things

we did were justified, we beg you to make just laws to protect the lives of the men who serve our country on the seas. Thank you very much. ("Charles Stewart": Alan Ladd)

UHF
1989   Orion
I knew she was gonna say that. ("George Newman": Al Yankovic)

The Ugly Dachshund
1965   Buena Vista
Honey, females always make the difference. ("Fran Garrison": Suzanne Pleshette)

The Ultimate Warrior
1975   Warner Brothers
We're gonna go together, together. ("Carrot": William Smith)

The Uncanny
1977   Rank
There you are. ("Frank Richards": Ray Milland)

Uncertain Glory
1944   Warner Brothers
He was a Frenchman. ("Marcel Bonet": Paul Lukas)

Unchained
1955   Warner Brothers
Nobody's going over that fence. ("Bill Howard": Todd Duncan)

Uncle Buck
1989   Universal
That's funny, Chanice, that's really good. You see what I put up with? And don't drive fast. I'm not fixing any more tickets for you. ("Buck Russell": John Candy)

Unconquered
1947   Paramount
And close that door. ("Captain Simeon Ecuyer": Victor Varconi)

Under Cover
1987   Cannon
'Bye, Shef. ("Tanille Laroux": Jennifer Jason Leigh)

Under Fire
1983   Orion
I'd do it again. ("Russell Price": Nick Nolte)

Under Ten Flags
1960   Paramount
Well, if I were her captain, I don't think I'd wish myself better end than that. ("Adm. Russell": Charles Laughton)

Under the Gun
1989   Marquis
Well? ("Mike Braxton": Sam Jones)

Under the Rainbow
1981   Warner Brothers
Aw, he's fine. ("Bruce Thorpe": Chevy Chase)

Under the Volcano
1985   20th Century-Fox
Why didn't you pray to die, huh? ("Geoffrey Firmin": Albert Finney)

Under the Yum Yum Tree
1963   Columbia
There we are, careful now. ("Hogan": Jack Lemmon)

Undercover Man
1949   Columbia

Come on, break it up, break it up, come on, come on. Come on, buddy, this doesn't concern you. (A policeman)

Undertow
1949   Universal
Come on, let's go. ("Chuck Reckling": Bruce Bennett)

The Underwater City
1962   Columbia
Amphibious City is only the beginning. In the future we will see other undersea colonies, great cities on the sea bottom. In truth, the great, the rich, bountiful ocean depths, cradle of all life, the world of innerspace, may provide a future home and a safe haven for mankind. (Narrator)

Underwater Warrior
1958   MGM
Angel hair. ("Comdr. David Forest": Dan Dailey)

Unfaithfully Yours
1983   20th Century–Fox
We can go if you want to but I'm fine, really. They're nice people, very nice people. I'll have a cup of coffee and I'll be raring to go. . . . ("Claude Eastman": Dudley Moore)

The Unforgiven
1960   United Artists
Andy. Andy. Andy. ("Rachel Zachary": Audrey Hepburn)

The Unholy
1988   Vestron
Take me out of here. ("Father Michael": Ben Cross)

Unholy Garden
1931   United Artists
I'm sorry, I, I met a dame. ("Barrington Hunt": Ronald Colman)

Unholy Three
1930   MGM
I'll send you a postal card. ("Echo": Lon Chaney)

Union Depot
1932   Warner Brothers
Gentleman for a day. Come on, let's get going, huh. ("Miller": Douglas Fairbanks, Jr.)

The Unsinkable Molly Brown
1964   MGM
Thank you. ("Molly Brown": Debbie Reynolds)

Until September
1984   MGM/UA
Mo! Mo! Wait for me! Wait for me! ("Xavier de la Perouse": Thierry Lhermitte)

The Untouchables
1987   Paramount
I think I'll have a drink. ("Eliot Ness": Kevin Costner)

Up the Creek
1984   Orion
Well, let's find out. ("Bob McGraw": Tim Matheson)

Uptown Saturday Night
1974   Warner Brothers
Yes. I got my, my red dress and my high-heel sneakers at home waiting, baby. ("Sarah Jackson": Rosalind Cash)

Urban Cowboy
1980   Paramount
Damn. ("Bud": John Travolta)

Used Cars
1980   Columbia
Uh, yes, ma'am, uh, it's being used on a lot of cars these days. It's a rust preventive. It adds life to the body. You know. . . . ("Rudy Russo": Kurt Russell)

The Valachi Papers
1972   Columbia
That's got to be the one thing I do, Joe. Make sure you live long after Genevese's dead and gone. ("FBI Agent Ryan": Gerald O'Loughlin)

Valdez Is Coming
1971 United Artists
Or paid the one hundred dollars. ("Valdez": Burt Lancaster)

The Valley of Decision
1945   MGM
Just a minute, Mac. I'll take the reins. ("Paul Scott": Gregory Peck)

Valley of the Dolls
1967   20th Century–Fox
Perhaps someday, Lyon, I don't know. Good-bye. ("Anne Welles": Barbara Parkins)

Valley of the Kings
1954   MGM
And the future, the future. ("Ann Mercedes": Eleanor Parker)

Valmont
1989   Orion
My angel. My sweet angel. ("Madame de Rosemonde": Fabia Drake)

Vanessa, Her Love Story
1935   MGM
Bless my soul. ("Judith Paris": May Robson)

Vendetta
1986   Concorde
You have the rest of your life to think about that. ("Miss Dice": Roberta Collins)

Vengeance Valley
1951 MGM
I'd like to tell her myself. ("Owen Daybright": Burt Lancaster)

Vera Cruz
1953   United Artists
That was Ace's mistake. ("Joe Erin": Burt Lancaster)

Verboten
1959   Columbia
Franz! ("Helga Schiller": Susan Cummings)

The Verdict
1982   20th Century–Fox
Yeah, OK. ("Frank Galvin": Paul Newman)

Vertigo
1958   Paramount
God have mercy. ("Nun": Sara Taft)

Vibes
1988   Columbia
No. Oh, my God, it's Harry. ("Sylvia Pickel": Cyndi Lauper)

Vice Versa
1988   Columbia
And you said yes. Sure, I told him.

He's almost as thrilled about it as I am. ("Marshall Seymour": Judge Reinhold)

Victor/Victoria
1982   MGM/UA
I might as well. They're the last roses I'll ever see. ("Toddy": Robert Preston)

Vigil in the Night
1940   RKO
Come, my Dr. Prescott. There's work for us to do. ("Anne Lee": Carole Lombard)

The Vikings
1958   United Artists
Prepare a funeral for a Viking. ("Eric": Tony Curtis)

Village of the Damned
1960   MGM
A brick wall, a brick wall, I must think of a brick wall. A brick wall, a brick wall, I must think of a brick wall. A brick wall, a brick wall, I must think of a brick wall. It's almost half past eight. A brick wall. Only a few seconds more. Brick wall. Brick wall. Brick wall. A brick wall. ("Gordon Zellaby": George Sanders)

The Violent Men
1955   Columbia
Now, your father once told me he'd get my ranch one way or another. ("John Parrish": Glenn Ford)

Violets Are Blue
1986   Columbia
You and I. ("Jessie Sawyer": Sissy Spacek)

Virginia
1940   Paramount
I made up my mind a long time ago. You're my kind of people, Stonewall, and I'm home. ("Charlotte Dunterry": Madeleine Carroll)

The Virginian
1946   Paramount
Oh, darling, you're safe. It wasn't you. ("Molly Wood": Barbara Britton)

The Visit
1964   20th Century–Fox
The visit is over. ("Karla Zachanassian": Ingrid Bergman)

Visit to a Small Planet
1960   Paramount
Help! Mr. Delton! ("Kreton": Jerry Lewis)

Vital Signs
1990   20th Century–Fox
The oil. Suzanne, check the oil. ("Michael Chatham": Adrian Pasdar)

Viva Zapata
1952   20th Century–Fox
Yes, he's in the mountains. (A villager)

Vivacious Lady
1938   RKO
Look out! Walter! ("Frances Brent [Francey]": Ginger Rogers)

Volunteers
1985   Tri-Star
Laurence! Laurence! (Islanders)

WUSA
1970   Paramount

Not me. I'm a survivor. Ain't that great? ("Rheinhardt": Paul Newman)

W. W. and the Dixie Dancekings
1975 20th Century–Fox
I'll bet you think that's the end of W. W. Well, it ain't. 'Cause W. W.'s always on the job. ("W. W. Bright": Burt Reynolds)

The Wackiest Ship in the Army
1960 Columbia
Well, I can let the man talk, can't I? ("Lt. Rip Crandall": Jack Lemmon)

Wagon Team
1952 Columbia
Yeah. And it wouldn't surprise me to see you tried to grab all the credit. ("U.S. Marshal Taplan": Gordon Jones)

Wagonmaster
1950 RKO
Well, I'll be dog-gonned. I'll be dog-gonned. ("Elder Wiggs": Ward Bond)

The Wagons Roll at Night
1941 Warner Brothers
I, I wonder if they could use a smart promoter where I'm going. ("Nick Coster": Humphrey Bogart)

Wait 'Til the Sun Shines, Nellie
1952 20th Century–Fox
No. Yes. Nothing makes a man feel better than a good, clean shave. Come on, Nellie, we've got to start this parade. ("Bel Halper": David Wayne)

Wait Until Dark
1967 Warner Brothers
Oh, Sammy. ("Susy Hendrix": Audrey Hepburn)

Wake Island
1942 Paramount
These Marines fought a great fight. They wrote history. But this is not the end. There are other leathernecks, other fighting Americans, a hundred and forty milllion of them, whose blood and sweat and fury will exact a just and terrible vengeance. (Narrator)

A Walk in the Spring Rain
1969 Columbia
Good-bye, Will. ("Libby Meredith": Ingrid Bergman)

Walk in the Sun
1946 20th Century–Fox
Dear Frances. We just blew a bridge and took a farmhouse. It was so easy, terribly easy. ("Windy": John Ireland)

Walk Like a Dragon
1960 Paramount
I need you, Kim Sung. I swear by my ancestors that I will make you happy. ("Chen Lu": James Shigeta)

Walk Like a Man
1987 MGM/UA
Forever and ever and ever and see you later. ("Bobo Shand": Howie Mandel)

Walk on the Wild Side
1962 Columbia
Dove, I. ("Hallie": Capucine)

Walk Softly, Stranger
1950 RKO
Just do one thing, belong to me. ("Chris Hale": Joseph Cotten)

Walk the Proud Land
1956   Universal
I am Mister. I capture all my emenies
[*sic*]. ("Tono": Eugene Mazzola)

Wall Street
1987   20th Century–Fox
All right. ("Bud Fox": Charlie Sheen)

Waltz of the Toreadors
1962   Continental
Yes, it doesn't mean anything, but it
makes one feel less lonely....
("General Fitzjohn": Peter Sellers)

The Wanderers
1979   Orion
Yeah, I know. I know. I know.
("Joey": John Friedrich)

Wanted: Dead or Alive
1987   New World
Leave him alone. Leave him the fuck
alone. ("Philmore Walker": Robert
Guillaume)

War and Peace
1956   Paramount
You're like this house. You suffer, you
show your wounds, but you stand.
("Natasha Rostova": Audrey Hepburn)

The War Lover
1962   Columbia
That's what he always wanted. Darling, I'm so glad you're here.
("Daphne": Shirley Anne Field)

The War of the Roses
1989   20th Century–Fox
Hi, what are you doing? I'm comin'

home. Love you. 'Bye. ("Gavin
D'Amato": Danny DeVito)

The War of the Worlds
1953   Paramount
The Martians had no resistance to the
bacteria in our atmosphere to which
we have long since become immune.
Once they had breathed our air,
germs which no longer affect us
began to kill them. The end came
swiftly. All over the world their
machines began to stop and fall.
After all that men could do had failed,
the Martians were destroyed and
humanity saved by the littlest things
which God in his wisdom had put upon
this earth. ("The Narrator": Sir
Cedric Hardwicke)

The War Wagon
1967   Universal
That's your problem, pardner. ("Taw
Jackson": John Wayne)

Wargames
1983   MGM/UA
Yes, sir. ("Colonel Conley": Joe
Dorsey)

Warkill
1968   Universal
Yes. Yes, he was a brave man. Let's
just leave it at that. And now whether
you like it or not, you poor, I suppose
you'll be a legend. ("Phil Sutton": Tom
Drake)

Warlock
1959   20th Century–Fox
Yeah. ("Clay Blaisdell": Henry
Fonda)

Water
1986   Rank

And if she doesn't, Sir Malcolm, Dolores certainly will. ("Baxter": Michael Caine)

Waterloo Bridge
1940 MGM
I loved you. I've never loved anyone else. I never shall. That's the truth, Roy. I never shall. ("Myra Lester": Vivien Leigh)

Watusi
1959 MGM
You know, the drums carry a long distance. I hope one day they'll tell me you have a fine son. ("Rick": David Farrar)

Wavelength
1983 New World
Bobby was right. For the Air Force it was back to business as usual, and the whole thing would go down in the books as just another unconfirmed UFO sighting. But for the rest of us, well, we all spend a lot of time these days looking up at the night sky. Bobby's afraid we'll never see them again, but I'm not so sure. Like I said, I have a sense about some things. ("Iris Longacre": Cherie Currie)

Waxwork
1988 Vestron
This is our only chance. ("Mark": Zach Gallingan)

Way Out West
1937 MGM
Fish and chips. ("Ollie": Oliver Hardy)

The Way We Were
1973 Columbia

Write your congressman today. ("Katie Morosky": Barbra Streisand)

We Were Strangers
1949 Columbia
No, Guillermo, they only think they killed him. He's out there in the streets. The people are singing on his breath. Oh, Tony, whenever I hear people singing I'll hear your voice, whenever I see joy in their faces, I'll see you. You'll be in their legs when they dance. You'll be in their eyes when they give thanks to God. ("China Valdes": Jennifer Jones)

Weeds
1987 DEG
I saw a prison near Plymouth Rock. It was overgrown with weeds, ragweed and thistles, milkweed and fetch. They sprang from every crack. Someday their roots will pry the walls apart. I won't be around, but I saw them last summer and they were in bloom. They were springing up from the wall with all the strength they were given to tell the world they were there. And bees came and drank from them. Just like any garden flower, they had nectar to give, too. ("Lee Umstetter": Nick Nolte)

Weekend at Bernie's
1989 20th Century–Fox
What did she say? ("Larry Wilson": Andrew McCarthy/"Richard Parker": Jonathan Silverman)

We're in the Money
1935 Warner Brothers
Aunt Emma can be the bridesmaid. ("C. Richard Courtney": Ross Alexander)

We're No Angels
1954   Paramount
Well, things don't work out right,
we'll do it all over again next year.
("Joseph": Humphrey Bogart)

We're No Angels
1989   Paramount
All in good time. All in good time.
("Ned/Fr. Reilly": Robert De Niro)

The Werewolf
1956   Columbia
Yeah, he'll stay. Now we can go home.
("Jack Haines": Don Megowan)

West of the Divide
1934   Monogram
Lecture? He needs a good spanking.
("Ted Hayden": John Wayne)

West Side Story
1961 United Artists
Don't you touch him! ("Maria":
Natalie Wood)

Western Union
1941 20th Century-Fox
It's a long way from Salt Lake City to
Boot Hill in Elkville, but I think he
can hear it. ("Edward Creighton":
Dean Jagger)

The Westerner
1940   United Artists
What'd I tell you. They're coming
back, wagons by the score. It's the
promised land. Jane Ellen, someday
Texas is going to be the biggest and
the finest. ("Cole Harden": Gary
Cooper)

Westward the Women
1951   MGM

Nice and smooth. It's a beautiful face,
and I love it. ("Fifi Danon": Denise
Darcel)

What a Way to Go
1963   20th Century-Fox
My wonderful, wonderful failure.
("Louisa": Shirley MacLaine)

What Ever Happened to Baby Jane?
1962   Warner Brothers
Look at her now. (Spectator at beach)

What Every Woman Knows
1934   MGM
That's right, John. ("Maggie Wylie":
Helen Hayes)

What, No Beer?
1933   MGM
Oh. It's your turn next, folks. It won't
be long now. Hotza. ("Jimmy Potts":
Jimmy Durante)

What Price Hollywood
1932   RKO
Lonny. ("Mary Evans": Constance
Bennett)

What's New, Pussycat?
1965   United Artists
Perhaps I haven't lost a son. Maybe
I've gained another patient. ("Dr.
Fritz Fassbender": Peter Sellers)

What's the Matter with Helen?
1971 United Artists
My partner is not quite finished with
our recital yet. ("Helen Hill": Shelley
Winters)

What's Up, Doc?
1972   Warner Brothers

Th-th-th-that's all, folks. (Voice of Porky Pig)

When Harry Met Sally
1989 Columbia
Right. ("Harry Burns": Billy Crystal)

Where Angels Go, Trouble Follows
1968 Columbia
Well, we forded the rivers and crossed the mountains and fought off the Indians. But we made it to the rally all right, and it was worth everything we went through to get there. It opened our eyes and our hearts and our minds. But what's more important, we got involved. Not just in caring because we've always cared, but in doing. Though Sister George and I haven't resolved all of our differences there is a good, stiff breeze blowing through St. Francis. And you'll see we have changed some of our habits. ("Mother Superior Simplicia": Rosalind Russell)

Where Eagles Dare
1969 MGM
I'll try, Lieutenant. ("John Smith": Richard Burton)

Where Is Parsifal?
1984 Terence Young
Thank you. ("Parsifal Katzenellenbogen": Tony Curtis)

Where the Boys Are
1960 MGM
Uh-huh. ("Merritt Andrews": Dolores Hart)

Where the Buffalo Roam
1980 Universal
If they're out there I'm gonna find them and I'm gonna gnaw on their skulls because it still hasn't gotten weird enough for me. ("Hunter S. Thompson": Bill Murray)

Where the Heart Is
1990 Buena Vista
Well, nobody can do better than that. ("Jean": Joanna Cassidy)

Where the Lilies Bloom
1974 United Artists
Oh, this is a fair place to spend eternity. The air smells like honeysuckle. The wind in the pine trees makes a joysome sound. Sometimes in the wind I feel something say my name, telling me to come to some far-off place: Mary come. Mary, come. Once I'm through raising Romey and Ima Dean, I think I'll go. ("Mary Call": Julie Gholson)

Which Way Is Up?
1977 Universal
And here's the keys to your house and goddam company car. You know where you can park it, right? Now if you don't like that, you better shoot me in my ass right now 'cause that's the last part you're ever gonna see of me, motherfucker. ("Leroy Jones": Richard Pryor)

The Whipped
1950 United Artists
You'll never get a better chance. ("Munsey": Michael O'Shea)

Whipsaw
1936 MGM

You don't have to ask it, Ross. Yes. ("Vivian Palmer": Myrna Loy)

Whirlpool
1950   20th Century–Fox
Hello, Lieutenant Colton speaking. Send an ambulance to fourteen hundred Canyon Drive. To pick up a body. ("Lt. Colton": Charles Bickford)

Whistle Down the Wind
1961 Rank
Yes. Yes, you missed him this time, but he'll be coming again. ("Kathy Bostock": Hayley Mills)

Whistling in Brooklyn
1943 MGM
Well, now we don't have to go to Niagara Falls. ("Wally Benton": Red Skelton)

Whistling in Dixie
1942 MGM
Every shooting man knows he must keep his powder dry. See, it's absolutely harmless. ("Wally Benton": Red Skelton)

White Cargo
1942 MGM
Don't ever use that word to me. ("Worthing": Richard Ainley)

White Feather
1955   20th Century–Fox
As I told you in the beginning, this is a true story. We were married in the Methodist church in Council Bluffs. Broken Hand lived to see his grandson enter the military academy at West Point. ("Josh Tanner": Robert Wagner)

White Heat
1949 Warner Brothers
He finally got to the top of the world, and it blew right up in his face. ("Hank Fallon/Vic Pardo": Edmond O'Brien)

White Hunter, Black Heart
1990 Warner Brothers
Action. ("John Wilson": Clint Eastwood)

White Nights
1985 Columbia
Thanks, Nick, thanks. ("Greenwood": Gregory Hines)

Who Framed Roger Rabbit
1988 Buena Vista
OK, move along. There's nothing else to see. Th-th-th-that's all, folks. Hm, I like the sound of that. Th-th-th-that's all, folks. ("Porky Pig": Mel Blanc voice)

Who Is Harry Kellerman and Why Is He Saying Those Terrible Things About Me?
1971 National General
Yeah, Doc, baby. ("Georgie Soloway": Dustin Hoffman)

Who Is Killing the Great Chefs of Europe?
1978 Warner Brothers
I knew that divorce was too good to last. ("Max": Robert Morley)

Wholly Moses!
1980 Columbia
Mohammed, stop it. ("Harvey/Herschel": Dudley Moore)

The Whoopee Boys
1986   Paramount
Well, the boys were very apt pupils.
("Colonel Phelps": Denholm Elliott)

Who's Afraid of Virginia Woolf?
1966   Warner Brothers
I am, George, I am. ("Martha": Elizabeth Taylor)

Who's Harry Crumb?
1989   Tri-Star
Yeah, I'm gonna need it. Looks like this one could get a little rough. ("Harry Crumb": John Candy)

Who's Minding the Store?
1963   Paramount
Mush! Mush! Wait for me! Mush! Mush! Wait for me! Mush! ("Norman": Jerry Lewis)

Who's That Girl
1987   Warner Brothers
Shut up and kiss me. ("Nikki Finn": Madonna)

Whose Life Is It Anyway?
1981 MGM/UA
OK. OK. ("Ken Harrison": Richard Dreyfuss)

Why Would I Lie
1980   MGM/UA
George with a J. ("Jeorge": Gabriel Swann)

Wicked Stepmother
1989   MGM/UA
Oh, this is a dream, it's gotta be a dream. Does this mean there's going to be a sequel? Oh, my God. ("Lt. MacIntosh": Tom Bosley)

The Wild and the Innocent
1959   Universal
Didn't you hear what I said? I said stop looking at me like that. ("Yancey": Audie Murphy)

Wild at Heart
1990   Goldwyn
Sailor! ("Lula": Laura Dern)

The Wild Bunch
1969   Warner Brothers
Well, me and the boys here, we got some work to do. You wanna come along? It ain't like it used to be, but, uh, it'll do. ("Sykes": Edmond O'Brien)

The Wild Geese
1978   Allied Artists
Let's talk about your father. ("Col. Allen Faulkner": Richard Burton)

Wild in the Country
1961 20th Century–Fox
All aboard! (Conductor)

The Wild Life
1984   Universal
Yeah. ("Jim Conrad": Ilan Mitchell-Smith)

The Wild One
1954   Columbia
Some coffee. ("Johnny": Marlon Brando)

The Wild Pair
1987   Trans World Entertainment
I guess it's me and you. ("Benny Avalon": Bubba Smith)

Wildcats
1986   Warner Brothers

Not at my house. ("Molly": Goldie Hawn)

Will Penny
1967   Paramount
'Bye, Will. 'Bye. ("Horace Greeley Allen": Jon Francis)

Willow
1988   MGM/UA
Good to see ya. ("Willow": Warwick Davis)

Windy City
1984   Warner Brothers
Come on. Here, buddy. Come here. Hey. ("Danny": John Shea)

The Wings of Eagles
1957   MGM
So long. ("Frank W. 'Spig' Wead": John Wayne)

Winning
1969   Universal
Now, if you think we can make it we can make it. ("Frank": Paul Newman)

Winter People
1989   Columbia
Lord, bless this clock, keep it accurate. Thank you for sending us a man who believed he could make such a thing and in the making of it, could inspire and unite us. Thank you for suggesting to him that he could make my daughter happy. One is as silly as the other, Lord, neither one of them does anything the regular way, so help them, Lord. These two need more help than most to find in each other a future to cherish. ("William Wright": Lloyd Bridges)

Wisdom
1986   20th Century–Fox
You know, America is a funny place. We can fabricate just about anything we want now, even heroes. America tried to make a hero out of John Wisdom and found out that it was wrong. Shit, I could have told them that. ("John Wisdom": Emilio Estevez)

Wise Blood
1979   New Line
Mister Motes. ("Landlady": Mary Nell Santacroce)

Wise Guys
1986   MGM/UA
I'm in the mood for a cannoli. ("Moe": Joe Piscopo)

Wish You Were Here
1987   Atlantic
Yes, it's mine. All mine. ("Lynda": Emily Lloyd)

The Witches
1990   Warner Brothers
Don't forget Bruno. ("Luke": Jasen Fisher)

Witches of Eastwick
1987   Warner Brothers
Aw, ladies, come on. ("Daryl Van Horne": Jack Nicholson)

Without a Clue
1988   Orion
Right you are, Watson. And so, without further ado, I hereby declare this case closed. ("Sherlock Holmes": Michael Caine)

Witness
1985 Paramount
You be careful out among them, English. ("Eli Lapp": Jan Rubes)

Witness for the Prosecution
1957 United Artists
Sir Wilfrid. You've forgotten your brandy. ("Miss Plimsoll": Elsa Lanchester)

The Wiz
1978 Universal
Home. ("Dorothy": Diana Ross)

The Wizard of Oz
1939 MGM
Oh, but anyway, Toto, we're home. Home. And this is my room. And you're all here. And I'm not going to leave here ever, ever again, because I love you all. And, oh, Auntie Em, there's no place like home. ("Dorothy": Judy Garland)

The Wolf Man
1940 Universal
Larry! ("Gwen Conliffe": Evelyn Ankers)

Woman Chases Man
1937 United Artists
We're going to carve a new majestic empire out of the wilderness. ("Kenneth Nolan": Joel McCrea)

The Woman in Red
1984 Orion
What's that girl doing? What is she doing, taking more pictures? Oh, no, give me a break. She is cute, though. Look at those legs. Hey, come on now, stop it, none of that stuff. I made

a mistake, I learned my lesson, and I will never do it again. ("Theodore Pierce": Gene Wilder)

Woman of the Year
1942 MGM
I've just launched Gerald. ("Sam Craig": Spencer Tracy)

Woman They Almost Lynched
1952 Republic
Whoopee! Bartender, give me a drink! ("Mayor Delilah Courtney": Nina Varela)

A Woman's Secret
1949 RKO
Once around Central Park, driver, very slowly. ("Marian Washburn": Maureen O'Hara)

A Woman's Vengeance
1948 Unviersal
All right, I'll hold on. ("Dr. Libbard": Sir Cedric Hardwicke)

Woman's World
1954 20th Century–Fox
Thank you. ("Gifford": Clifton Webb)

The Women
1939 MGM
No pride at all. That's a luxury a woman in love can't afford. ("Mary Haines": Norma Shearer)

Won Ton Ton, the Dog Who Saved Hollywood
1976 Paramount
No, just an ordinary dog, and, and, my friend. ("Elsie Del Ruth": Madeline Kahn)

The Wonderful World of the Brothers Grimm
1962   MGM
Once upon a time, there were two brothers. ("Wilhelm Grimm": Laurence Harvey)

Working Girl
1988   20th Century–Fox
Cyn? Guess where I am. ("Tess McGill": Melanie Griffith)

The World According to Garp
1982   Warner Brothers
I'm flying. Ta-ranta-ranta-ra. ("T. S. Garp": Robin Williams)

A World Apart
1988   Atlantic
Solomon Martinson was one of us. What he suffered we all suffer. We do not mourn him, we honor him and we say that the only true tribute to him is to pick up the spear from where it has fallen. Solomon is just one, one man, and when we defy them, when we resist in ourselves, when we resist in our hundreds, when we resist in our thousands, in our millions, then victory is certain. . . . ("Priest": Jude Akuwidike)

The World of Suzie Wong
1960   Paramount
That long. ("Robert Lomax": William Holden)

The World's Greatest Athlete
1973   Buena Vista
Kid, wait for me! My name's Archer! I'm a coach! I want to talk to you! ("Coach Sam Archer": John Amos)

The World's Greatest Lover
1977   20th Century–Fox
Oh, boy, look at those gams. Whatcha doing tonight, honey? Maybe we could meet later for a little snack. ("Rudy Valentine": Gene Wilder)

The Wrecking Crew
1968   Columbia
Hey, do you think we can have our little talk now? ("Freya Carlson": Sharon Tate)

Written on the Wind
1956   Universal
Yes. My brother always drank too much. He was sad, the saddest of us all. He needed so much, and had so little. ("Marylee Hadley": Dorothy Malone)

The Wrong Guys
1988   New World
Gentlemen, let's salute Den seven, Pack eighteen, nineteen sixty-one. ("Scoutmaster": Jimmy Weldon)

Wuthering Heights
1939   United Artists
No, not dead, Dr. Kenneth. Not alone. He's with her. They've only just begun to live. Good-bye, Heathcliff. Good-bye, my wild, sweet Cathy. ("Ellen Dean": Flora Robson)

Xanadu
1980   Universal
I mean I'd just like to talk to you. ("Sonny Malone": Michael Beck)

The Yakuza
1975   Warner Brothers
Japan Air Lines Flight nine six six for

Seoul is now boarding at Gate thirteen. (Announcer)

A Yank at Eton
1942 MGM
Yes, you really do. I know what Roger meant about Eton and the great things that have stood for a thousand years, the traditions that belong to both our countries. I've learned some of them here. I guess you'll learn some more in America. Only remind me to get rid of this before I show up at Notre Dame, will you? ("Timothy Dennis": Mickey Rooney)

A Yank at Oxford
1938 MGM
So you can't take it, huh, England? ("Lee Sheridan": Robert Taylor)

A Yank on the Burma Road
1942 MGM
And it's gonna stay open. Start those trucks through. We're not stopping at Chungking. We're headed for Tokyo, Yokohama and points east. Let's go. ("Joe Tracey": Barry Nelson)

Yankee Doodle Dandy
1942 Warner Brothers
Well, I don't hear anything. (Marching soldier)

The Year of Living Dangerously
1982 MGM/UA
You bring that here. (Customs inspector)

The Year of the Dragon
1985 MGM/UA
I'm really proud of you. ("Tracy Tzu": Ariane)

The Yearling
1946 MGM
'Night, Ma. ("Jody Baxter": Claude Jarman, Jr.)

Yellow Sky
1948 20th Century–Fox
I paid for it. ("Stretch": Gregory Peck)

Yolanda and the Thief
1945 MGM
But I don't understand, it's impossible. But it is rather sweet. ("Yolanda": Lucille Bremer)

You and Me
1938 Paramount
Well, he's got a right to know what's goin' on, ain't he? ("Gimpy": Warren Hymer)

You Came Along
1945 Paramount
Roger. ("Ivy Hotchkiss": Lizabeth Scott)

You Can't Cheat an Honest Man
1939 Universal
It's a great race, folks. They're all heading for the state line. Whipsnade's in front, and Vicky and Bergen are neck and neck. Glad I'm safe up here. (Mortimer Snerd, as himself)

You Can't Hurry Love
1988 Vestron
Kiss her. ("Skip Dooley": Scott McGinnis)

You Can't Take It with You
1938 Columbia

I hope you like it, Mr. Kirby. ("Rheba": Lillian Yarbo)

You Can't Win 'Em All
1970 Columbia
Do me a favor. Will you shut up and peel. ("Adam Dyer": Tony Curtis)

You Light Up My Life
1977 Columbia
Ah, listen. Come on. Come on. Now you get your stuff together, and cut out, huh. ("Si Robinson": Joe Silver)

You Never Can Tell
1951 Universal
Good-bye, Goldie. ("Rex Shepherd": Dick Powell)

You Were Never Lovelier
1942 Columbia
Darling, that's all I wanted to know. ("Robert Davis": Fred Astaire)

You'll Find Out
1940 RKO
Hold it, fellas. I knew there was something I wanted to tell you. Ladies and gentlemen of the motion picture audience, we've had a lot of fun making our picture and we certainly hope you've enjoyed it. But there's one thing I want to get clear in your minds. Remember Boris Karloff, Peter Lorre, Bela Lugosi? Well, they aren't really murderers at all. In fact, they are nice fellas and good friends of mine. You know things like this don't actually happen. It's, uh, all in fun. And so we'll be on the air as usual next Wednesday night. And until then we'll be thinking of you. So long, everybody. ("Kay": Kay Kyser)

Young Bess
1953 MGM
Your majesty. ("Mr. Parry": Cecil Kellaway)

Young Billy Young
1969 United Artists
Somebody came to town. ("Billy Young": Robert Walker, Jr.)

The Young Doctors
1961 United Artists
And I'm staying. ("Dr. David Coleman": Ben Gazzara)

Young Einstein
1988 Warner Brothers
Well, I could tell you my latest theory. ("Albert Einstein": Yahoo Serious)

Young Frankenstein
1974 20th Century–Fox
No, oh, I don't believe, oh! Ah! Oh! Oh! ("Inga": Teri Garr)

Young Fury
1965 Paramount
Same to you, boy. ("Clint McCoy": Rory Calhoun)

The Young Lions
1958 20th Century–Fox
Hey! (Taxi driver)

Young Mr. Lincoln
1939 20th Century–Fox
No, I think I might go on a piece. Maybe to the top of that hill. ("Abraham Lincoln": Henry Fonda)

The Young Philadelphians
1959 Warner Brothers
Well, I'm a chili girl my – I'd like a

hamburger. ("Joan Dickinson": Barbara Rush)

The Young Savages
1961 United Artists
A lot of people killed your son, Mrs. Escalante. ("Hank Bell": Burt Lancaster)

Young Sherlock Holmes
1985 Paramount
As I watched Holmes settle into his seat, a sudden feeling came over me, that I would most certainly be seeing him again. So ended my first adventure with Mr. Sherlock Holmes. As I watched his carriage disappear into the distance I realized that I had forgotten to thank him. He had taken a weak, frightened boy and made him into a courageous, strong man. My heart soared, I was filled with confidence. I was ready for whatever mystery or danger lay ahead. I was ready to take on the greatest and most exciting adventure of them all. And I knew it was bound to involve Sherlock Holmes. ("Voice of Older Watson": Michael Horndern)

Young Tom Edison
1940 MGM
A while back he was Sam Edison's son, and now I'm Tom Edison's father. And I like it. ("Samuel Edison": George Bancroft)

Young Winston
1972 Columbia
It was an end and a beginning. My darling mother continued on her headlong, headstrong, but always gallant and courageous way, whilst seven years later Clementine Hozier and I were married and lived happily ever afterwards. ("Sir Winston Churchill's voice": Simon Ward)

Your Cheatin' Heart
1964 MGM
He was comin' here by automobile to sing for you tonight. The doctor said his heart just stopped. So we won't be seeing Hank again, least not in this world. He was my friend. He was your friend. He was one of you, a poor boy who, who never forgot you. He was on this earth twenty-nine years. Now he's gone home. ("Shorty Younger": Red Buttons)

You're Never Too Young
1955 Paramount
No! No! No! ("Bob Miles": Dean Martin)

You're Only Young Once
1938 MGM
Well, honest, Pop, man to man. I was just showing Polly what I'm not going to do anymore. ("Andy Hardy": Mickey Rooney)

You're Telling Me
1934 Paramount
This will be the first real drink I've had in months. ("Sam Bisbee": W. C. Fields)

Zebra in the Kitchen
1965 MGM
Well, Harry, come on, welcome to the family. ("Branch Hawksbill": Andy Devine)

Zelig
1983 Orion

"Wanting only to be liked, he distorted himself beyond measure," wrote Scott Fitzgerald. One wonders what would have happened if right at the outset he'd had the courage to speak his mind and not pretend. Near the end it was not after all the approbation of many but the love of one woman that changed his life. ("The Narrator": Patrick Horgan)

Zelly and Me
1988   Columbia
Whatever happens, I am with you and you are with me. ("Phoebe": Alexandra Johnes)

Ziegfeld Follies
1944   MGM
Like the one we've been rehearsing for two weeks? (Gene Kelly, as himself)

Ziegfeld Girl
1941   MGM
We're gonna raise ducks and grandkids, little, young, fuzzy ones. ("Sheila Regan": Lana Turner)

Zorba the Greek
1964   20th Century–Fox
The sad time, the sad time was the best. Nothing left. ("Basil": Alan Bates)

Zorro, the Gay Blade
1981 20th Century–Fox
The best music. You gotta be joking. I spent a week in Boston once, and I don't think I heard a decent mariachi player in the city. ("Don Diego Vega": George Hamilton)

"The End"

McFarland Classics